MILES TO GO

MIT Press Series in Transportation Studies
Marvin L. Manheim, editor
Center for Transportation Studies, MIT

MILES TO GO:
EUROPEAN AND AMERICAN
TRANSPORTATION
POLICIES

James A. Dunn, Jr.

The MIT Press
Cambridge, Massachusetts, and London, England

© 1981 by
The Massachusetts Institute of Technology

This book was set in Univers by Grafacon, Inc. and printed and
bound in the United States of America.

Library of Congress Cataloging in Publication Data

Dunn, James A   1943–
  Miles to go.

  (MIT Press series in transportation studies; 6)
  Includes bibliographical references and index.
  1. Transportation and state—United States.
  2. Transportation and state—Europe.   I. Title.
  II. Series.
  HE206.2.D86   380.5'094   80-25523
  ISBN 0-262-04062-X

To my mother and father

CONTENTS

SERIES FOREWORD

The field of transportation has emerged as a recognized profession only since the last ten years, although transportation issues have been important throughout history. Today more and more government agencies, universities, researchers, consultants, and private industry groups are becoming truly multimodal in their orientations, and specialists of many different disciplines and professions are working on multidisciplinary approaches to complex transportation issues.

The central role of transportation in our world today and its recent professional status have led The MIT Press and the MIT Center for Transportation Studies to establish The MIT Press Series in Transportation Studies. The series will present works representing the broad spectrum of transportation concerns. Some volumes will report significant new research, while others will give analyses of specific policy, planning, or management issues. Still others will show the interaction between research and policy. Contributions will be drawn from the worldwide transportation community.

In recent years policy makers and interested private citizens, as well as transportation professionals, increasingly have found it very valuable to learn from the experiences of other countries. This book, the sixth in the series, will contribute significantly to this multinational perspective by its comparative analysis of transportation policies in the United States and several European countries.

Marvin L. Manheim

PREFACE

It is easy to criticize U.S. transportation policy by holding that policy up to an ideal model of what it ought to be. By any set of abstract standards—efficiency, equity, environmental impact—performance necessarily falls far short of the goal. One of the credibility problems of many recent critical studies of transportation policy is that they tend toward this kind of inadvertant perfectionism. They base their policy judgments on an implicit comparison of the real world situation with a utopian construct of transport perfection. This is virtually inevitable when the focus of analysis is on a single nation. Judgment implies comparison, and, when a single system is being judged, there is the tendency to use an abstract ideal as the standard for comparison and judgment. There is nothing inherently wrong with this method. It is useful in sensitizing the reader to the faults and problems in the existing situation that need to be corrected, in showing how things could be so much better if they were arranged differently. But often this type of policy criticism leaves itself open to the charge of being unrealistic and theoretical, not anchored in the real world of power and influence where it is very difficult to arrange things differently. The readers may feel that they are being offered a choice between policy prescriptions that are either hopelessly utopian or mere marginal tinkering, with little information as to how to achieve feasible changes in real world situations.

Perhaps, by comparing American transportation problems and policies with those of other nations, it will be possible to avoid these problems. Cross-national comparisons can help take the utopian element out of our judgments, while still giving us the possibility of showing how things could be done differently. Moreover they can give us some means of estimating the chances for different policy reforms by enabling us to identify the political, economic, and cultural factors that permitted other nations to adopt policies different from our own. Perhaps the most important benefit of such a cross-national approach is the opportunity to see how other nations have used very different sets of values and assumptions when deciding on policies in transportation. By viewing America's problems from these different perspectives, it can help us to see ourselves as others see us, which is always a useful, if sometimes humbling, experience.

In a comparative study of this sort an author is dependent upon the aid and advice of many organizations and individuals, and I wish to acknowledge that assistance here. A research fellowship from the Alexander von Humboldt Foundation of Bonn, West Germany, and a sabbatical leave from the University of Missouri at Kansas City enabled me to spend a year in Europe doing research for the book. I am especially grateful to Gerd Steierwald, director of the Institut für Strassen-und Verkehrwesen at the University of Stuttgart and to Fritz Voigt, director of the Institut für Industrie-und Verkehrspolitik at the University of Bonn for making the facilities of their institutes available to me. Many other people at these two institutes also contributed greatly to this study, among them Manfred Brenner, Manfred Zachcial, Stefan Rommerskirschen, and Hans-Heinz Kreuter. I also gratefully acknowledge the assistance of the following organizations that provided me with access to material I needed in preparing this book: Bundesministerium für Verkehr, Société National des Chemins de Fer Français, Régie Autonome des Transports Parisiens, London Transport Executive, Greater London Council Transport Department, Department of the Environment, and London Motorway Action Group. In the United States Alan Altshuler of MIT read the entire manuscript and improved it greatly with his comments. James P. Womack read chapters 8 and 9 and made many helpful comments. I also would like to thank my parents, to whom this book is dedicated, not only for a lifetime of support and encouragement but also for providing me with an office in their home where much of the final part of the book was written. Finally, I want to express publicly my gratitude to my wife, Bernadette. Without her support, inspiration, and plain hard work, caring for three children in Europe and America, this book would not have been possible.

MILES TO GO

1
PROBLEMS, POLICIES, AND PARADIGMS IN TRANSPORTATION POLICY

TRANSPORTATION AS A PUBLIC PROBLEM

Transportation, like taxes, is an inescapable aspect of the human condition. Primitive canoes, ox carts, and eighteen-wheel semitrailers are all essential implements in the societies that depend on them for mobility. It can be said that the more extensive and intricate the transportation network, the more economically developed and technically advanced the society. By this standard the United States stands at the pinnacle of human achievement, having developed an unparalleled capacity to move people and goods over local, regional, national, international, and even interplanetary distances. It is difficult to overestimate the importance of transportation in shaping our physical and social environments. No one can look closely at this magnificent system, in which Americans spend nearly $200 billion for direct purchases of transportation services and equipment and not be awed.[1]

Yet despite the achievements of the transportation system, there is today a growing malaise among specialist and layman over the increasingly evident flaws and intolerable costs of the system. Transportation is becoming a public problem in a way that it never was before. In the past public policy on transportation amounted to little more than encouraging the greatest possible growth of all modes so that Americans could travel on the biggest, fastest, newest conveyance going their way. Public policies for the several transport modes tended to be isolated from each other. The making of these policies also tended to be relatively isolated from the scrutiny of the general public. It was a game for insiders and specialists, and people were willing to leave it that way as long as they were not greatly inconvenienced in their traveling. All this is now changing. The very success of past efforts to foster transportation growth has created new problems in the relationship between society and transport systems that are of broad public concern. The present national anxiety over energy and environment has brought to the fore issues concerning the planning, coordination, and utilization of transportation systems in which questions of general principles and the public interest are clearer and more intense than ever before.[2]

The new public concern over transportation policy begins with the debate over what is wrong and continues on to what is to be done. The old ways used to decide policy questions are no longer suited to present

problems and future needs. There is a sense of urgency about the need
to find new ways of formulating policy questions, new ways of deciding
issues and goals to guide policy. With the prevailing concern for limiting
energy consumption, many critics, opinion molders, policy makers, and
would-be policy makers are saying that we can no longer afford the luxury of unbridled transportation growth. We may have to trade in our
first-class accommodations for something more modest. Historically it
was America's good fortune to be able to avoid facing the difficult problem of deciding politically how to distribute economic benefits and burdens. Americans have been able to concentrate on expanding the size of
the pie, rather than worrying about how to divide it. As a result they tend
to be culturally and intellectually less prepared than other nations to face
an era that threatens to impose limits upon material growth. While this is
true in many areas of the American lifestyle, nowhere is it more pressing
than in transportation. Energy shortages, ecological problems, urban
difficulties all point to the need for a transportation system that puts conservation of resources, harmony with the environment, and less social
disruption above the incessant pressure for growth that has characterized the system. But how can the changes be brought about fairly and
feasibly? Inevitably a thorough reappraisal of the assumptions underlying past policies must be undertaken. We need a new perspective on
the past, new directions for the present, and new options for the future. It
is not so much that we lack specific proposals for dealing with any given
problem. Rather we lack a new overall framework by which our problems can be reformulated and made more amenable to solution by our
political and economic processes.

MARKET PLANNING AND PARADIGMS OF
PUBLIC CHOICE

The frameworks by which public problems are formulated and decided
are what Charles W. Anderson has called paradigms of public choice.
Anderson describes these paradigms and their functions in this manner:

A paradigm of public choice specifies the grounds that are appropriate
for making claims within a given political order. It tells us about the kinds
of arguments that are apt to appear acceptable to political actors in arriv-
ing at policy conclusions. It defines the boundaries of the plausible, the
range of reasons that will be taken as legitimate in political argument
and public choice. . . . Its function is to provide criteria for selection of
definitive public commitments from among rival claims and possibilities
and to justify decisions on behalf of the community.[3]

Most discussions of policy issues are carried on within the terms of a prevailing paradigm of public choice. Policy makers must have some set of
principles that enables them to choose among a set of options and then
legitimize this choice to themselves and also to individuals and community organizations most likely to be affected by the decision. This is
not to say that the paradigm determines each and every choice. All para-

digms must be applied by human beings with varying intelligence, preferences, and interests. But it is likely that substantial differences in paradigms will result in at least some alternatives in public choice.

Charles E. Lindblom and Aaron Wildavsky recently described two antithetical types of paradigms of public choice, one based on authority and planning and the other on markets and exchange.[4] In the first model, Lindblom's intellectually guided society, which Wildavsky calls intellectual cogitation, it is assumed there is an underlying harmony of men's needs that can be known to the guiding elite. The elite studies the problem, diagnoses the difficulty, and draws up plans to remedy the situation. The elite possesses the authority to see that its plan is carried out. If the chosen plan does not make everyone in the society happy, causing grumbling and even some opposition, the dissatisfaction is assumed to be selfish and short-sighted and thus is rather easily disposed of by the elite, which plans and rules in the long-term best interests of the whole society. In the second model, the market or social interaction model, it is assumed that a harmony of men's needs is not only undiscoverable but nonexistent: an elite cannot and should not be entrusted with discovering and designing policies in the public interest. Different processes of social interaction are set up so that everyone has a chance to express a preference. Public decisions depend on the outcomes of such interaction processes, with market exchange being the leading interaction process.

Clearly all real societies have paradigms of public choice that contain some degree of mixture of these two types. Communist countries permit a certain amount of market exchange. Capitalist countries have some authoritative planning practices. But all capitalist countries make a crucial distinction between public and private domains, especially in areas relating to economic production and exchange. As a result policy conflicts tend to become conflicts between private rights and collective coercion. Governments in liberal democracies override private rights only in certain circumstances, for reasons that generally must be consonant with the prevailing paradigm. Eliot J. Feldman notes that "an embracing perspective for comparative public policy, then, may be the distinction between public and private and the forces, conditions, and consequences of choice in favor of public action."[5]

In general the U.S. policy paradigm concerning the authoritative planning component has been weak by tradition and design. Transportation, however, is an area that demands a high degree of planning. Investors need assurance of stability and an adequate return on their money. As transport systems become ever more extensive and impinge on more and more aspects of society, it is necessary for the public authorities at a minimum to organize and maintain a market for transportation services. The manner in which this is done is by no means predetermined by technology and geography. Power and ideas are equally as important. Market mechanisms and their outcomes are the products of a social

Problems, Policies, and Paradigms in Transportation Policy

and political process. But the American propensity for relying on the invisible hand of the market in transportation can be seen to be increasingly problematic.

The conventional wisdom embodied in the prevailing American paradigm has emphasized the negative aspects of authority: government intrusion in market exchange processes tends to distort or slow down economic growth. It assumes that too much reliance on authority interferes with market solutions to problems. However, this paradigm pays scant attention to the obverse possibility: too much reliance on markets can interfere with authority solutions to problems.

Recent events have forcefully brought such a possibility to our attention. Policy analysts now recognize that market solutions once thought perfectly satisfactory often create new and serious problems not easily remedied by conventional market mechanisms. The unrestricted growth of the automobile, for example, solved one kind of mobility problem, only to create others that leave public authorities struggling with additional problems of air quality, public transportation, and energy conservation. The very success of the market in fostering auto ownership impedes attempts to use authority to solve these problems.

Thus among policy analysts a new concern is rising for the impact of past solutions on future problems and the tendency of short-term market remedies to generate long-term problems of authority and planning. As Theodore Lowi has pointed out, "The impacts for which political scientists can claim some analytic expertise are impacts back on the political system rather than forward toward elements of the social process. . . . For example: what will policy alternative X do to the capacity of the government to change later to policy alternative Y if X fails?"[6] This concern is important, indeed crucial, to a reformulation of the American paradigm of public choice in transportation. In the area of transportation, comparisons between the U.S. paradigm and its consequences and the paradigms of other nations can make a valuable contribution.

We will proceed to compare systematically and critically the American transportation policy paradigm with those of selected European countries. To keep the study within manageable bounds, the number of transportation topics and countries covered are necessarily limited. The topics—highways, railroads, urban mass transit, the automobile—are closely interrelated and are currently undergoing public policy debate in the United States. The countries selected for each comparison were chosen because they seemed to provide the best and most instructive contrast to U.S. policy and hence help to highlight the benefits and drawbacks of each paradigm. The final issue focuses on the great question of what to do about the motor car. Some changes are suggested that might and eventually will have to be made in this realm of American public choice.

I
RAILROADS

INTRODUCTION TO PART I

Rail transportation spans two eras of technology and policy making. The apogee of nineteenth-century transport technology, railroads had a virtual monopoly on the overland movement of passengers and freight. There was little difficulty attracting capital for rail investments in areas where demand for rail services was likely to be high. In the age of rail dominance policy debate centered on whether private rail entrepreneurs could be regulated and thus prevented from abusing their monopoly power. This question was crucial and was ultimately decided by the governments of the nations concerned. The contemporary rail problem is quite different. It is concerned with how to deal with railroads in an era of decline, how to adapt a nineteenth-century mode of transportation to twentieth-century social and economic conditions. The options open to modern policy makers are to a great extent limited by the choices made in the past. While in most of the world's industrial democracies rail systems have long since been brought under public ownership, in the United States the railroads are still predominantly privately owned. The preference for private ownership has been firmly established in the U.S. paradigm of public choice. Many policy makers defend private ownership and stress the drawbacks and difficulties of the public ownership systems chosen by other nations. Recently Secretary of Transportation Brock Adams released a statement opposing public ownership of U.S. railroads on the grounds that foreign experience has shown it to be too costly. His statement maintained:

In 1975, the Japanese National Railways needed $875 million in subsidies, representing 14.7% of its total revenue. The German Federal Railways needed $3.4 billion in subsidies, or 44.5% of revenue. The subsidy received by British Railways was $1.6 billion, nearly 60% of total revenue. A comparable subsidy level for the American railroads would exceed $10 billion a year. [1]

The argument for public ownership, drawing on other nations' experiences, is essentially that articulated by Senator Vance Hartke (Dem., Ind.) at hearings on the U.S. Department of Transportation (DOT) recommendations for restructuring the northeast rail net:

The country is also faced with an extreme crisis . . . in the field of energy. . . . We are a nation that has some reserve oil. Two nations that have no reserve oil whatsoever are Japan and Germany. Both of them are completely reliant upon importation of energy. . . . The rails are an efficient utilization of energy in the field of transportation. When we talk about efficient, healthy, modern, effective use of rail transportation, these two countries, Japan and Germany, are always pointed to as examples. I think it is high time for the DOT . . . to recognize . . . the transportation system is contributing to the energy crisis and contributing to the balance of payments difficulty. At the same time, we have the same old doctrine from the Transportation Department of gradualism, which has been a miserable failure in the last 15 years in the railroad industry, and they are still advocating more of the same. [2]

The arguments advanced by these two spokesmen disagree over which political-economic decision mode—market or authority—is better able to formulate, legitimize, and achieve the new rail policy goals required by present and future conditions. Of course neither side maintains that the present U.S. rail system responds only to market cues. The government obviously has an important role in shaping the rail system. The debate is specifically over whether the authority the federal government exercises should support private ownership as a first priority, even if it means sacrificing other goals such as energy conservation, or whether these other goals should come first, even at the cost of losing private ownership of some or all of the railroads.

If other nations' experiences are to be useful in clarifying the U.S. debate, we must go beyond merely pointing out the money lost by publicly owned railroads or the potential energy savings of greater reliance on trains. We must determine if other countries make use of a different paradigm that results in significantly better railroad performance than in the United States. In addition we must show how this type of paradigm could be adapted for use in the special conditions of the United States that may not exist abroad. In chapters 2 and 3 we will focus on the policy paradigms of France and America and examine how they have affected the development and performance of their rail systems. There are several reasons why France is a particularly appropriate choice for a comparison with the United States. From the very beginning the French paradigm of public choice put more stress on the needs of the nation, as defined by the authorities and the obligation of the state to coordinate and control the activities of private rail entrepreneurs. Laissez faire was always tempered with a strong dose of dirigisme. Yet France was one of the last European countries to nationalize her rail system. Many other countries created publicly owned rail systems in the nineteenth century because domestic capitalists were incapable of building the kind of rail system the country needed for national defense and economic development. Like the United States, France let private capital carry much of the burden of financing the rail system. But in contrast to the laissez faire stance of the United States, the French government established a policy framework that guided private rail companies in directions of national interest. It resorted to outright public ownership only on an ad hoc, piecemeal basis where private capital could not be attracted. The government gradually acquired direct responsibility for an ever larger share of the rail system until the 1930s depression when the pressure of financial collapse of the remaining private rail companies moved the French government to acquire control of the entire rail industry. Since then, the French national railways have had perhaps the most successful operating record of any large national rail system in Europe. Thus the French experience offers insight into the perennial U.S. debate about public-

versus-private ownership by highlighting the importance of the different policies pursued before the rail system became completely publicly owned. As the U.S. government moves gradually toward ever more responsibility for planning and operating the rail system, it can learn valuable lessons from the French path of piecemeal public ownership.[3]

Railroads

2
FRANCE: TECHNOCRATIC PLANNING AND THE MARKET

THE FRENCH RAILROADS AND THE STATE

The railroads of France were shaped from the start by a paradigm that permitted the French state to play a much stronger role in railroad development than the American federal government had. The public interest in railroads was something far more serious than just ensuring fair rates to the farmer. It was clear that rail transport would revolutionize the economy of the nation, and the state could not be indifferent to such a process. Private capital would have a significant role, but one properly and formally subordinate to the interests of the state, whose plan for the rail system would be in the best interests of the nation as a whole.[1]

Rail planning was put under the jurisdiction of the Corps des Ingénieurs des Ponts et Chaussées, the principal civil engineering division of the ministry of public works. These highly trained specialists were the technocrats of their day, imbued with the spirit of planning large-scale projects for the public good. The economic historian Charles P. Kindleberger stresses the importance of this technocratic ethos in French economic development in both the public and private sectors:

The Corps des ponts et chaussées was in many respects the forerunner of the post-World War II Commissariat au plan. . . . The famous *Étoile* design for the railroads, which tied the country to a center at Paris, came from Le Grand—the Louis Armand . . . of his day—at Ponts et Chaussées in 1830. . . . Such was the prestige of the graduatesof the École des Ponts et Chaussées that they took precedence at state functions over colonels in the army.[2]

These early technocrats planned the routes the rail lines would take, supervised the technical details of construction, set safety standards, and approved the charters that granted concessions to private companies to operate given stretches of line. These charters governed the relations between the company and the state. At first, they were issued for extremely short durations, but this caused difficulties in attracting capital from the notoriously cautious French investors. By 1842 the state charters were granting concessions for ninety-nine years. Included in each charter was a clause that transferred to the state the ownership of the railroad and all its assets at the end of that period. The charters assigned a given territory to each company and conferred a monopoly of rail transport within that territory. The sectors assigned to the private companies radiated outward from Paris like spokes from the hub of a wheel, with the exception of the territory of the southern company, located at the extreme southwest of France from Bordeaux to Toulouse and the Spanish frontier. By 1859 the number of rail companies chartered by the government had been reduced from thirty-three in 1849 to six. Thus quite early in rail history the French government solved the problems of overbuilding and rail consolidation that continue to plague the U.S. rail system to this very day.

The state was also active in supplying financial assistance to the private rail companies it chartered. This assistance took many forms: direct start-up and other grants, treasury loans, loan guarantees, and even guarantees on the dividends of the stocks and bonds issued by the railroads to the public. Throughout the entire history of private railroading in France the state was involved with "an endless procession of public appropriations and guarantees which for a century plagued the national treasury whenever insufficient revenues . . . threatened to unbalance the budgets of the rail companies."[3]

In the late nineteenth century national defense considerations impelled the French government to go even further in the direction of underwriting the cost of the rail network. The French defeat by the Prussians in 1870 was at least in part attributable to Prussia's superior rail system, which had been able to deliver troops and supplies to the front more rapidly than the French railroads. Military necessity thus required the government to prevent any part of the rail system from remaining underdeveloped and hence a bottleneck to mobilization and deployment. In 1878 the state took over the operation of 2,600 km of unprofitable branch lines it considered too strategically important to allow the companies to close down. At the time of the takeover the minister of public works assured parliament that the move was purely provisional and temporary and not the prelude to a general takeover of the railroads. Nonetheless, the state decided to organize these lines into a state network and expand the length of the state network whenever the national defense or the public convenience required it. In 1909 the state acquired the debt-ridden western lines in an annuity agreement. This added a further 6,000 km to the state network. During World War I all the railroads, public and private, were run directly by the army. At the war's end the five private networks were returned to their management. The state retained control of its own system, of course, but had now annexed the rail system in the recaptured provinces of Alsace-Lorraine, which out of deference to local sentiment it did not fuse with its own system but operated as a separate seventh network.

Thus by the 1930s, despite the large private ownership component in the French rail industry, the state was operating directly a substantial portion of the rail system. The state possessed more than one-third of the track in France and just below one-third of the rolling stock and other capital equipment. More important still was the fact that this piecemeal acquisition of financially troubled rail properties gave the public authorities, as the minister of finance pointed out in 1908, "a decisive experience in a public industrial and financial organism which could be improved on and perfected . . . and whose performance could demonstrate whether or not it could render the services which [the public] had a right to expect."[4] Thus, when the issue of incorporating the country's remaining privately owned railroads arose, the government and the rail companies could discuss in pragmatic, factual terms how state-owned railways functioned, rather than debate on purely ideological grounds.

Many factors were involved in the financial collapse of the private railroads in the 1930s. The first and most obvious was the impact of the worldwide depression. But there were some contributing factors specific to the rail sector. One was the rise of competition from the motor freight industry. The full effect of trucking competition was not felt until well into the 1920s. The truckers initially operated with the advantage of being much less encumbered by government regulation because they were never perceived as a monopoly like the railroads.[5] Another factor in the private railroads' financial demise was that as regulated monopolies they were never permitted to raise their fares fast enough to cover rising costs. The ministry of public works had the right to approve or deny any request for a rate increase, and the ministry's decision then had to be ratified by the parliament. Between 1918 and 1928 freight rates were allowed to rise by 370 percent and passenger rates by 240 percent.[6] This allowed the railroad companies enough revenue to produce a substantial operating profit, a profit before the fixed or capital costs were deducted. But the repayment of these capital costs was the final factor in the private companies downfall.

Two types of capital charges were incurred. The first was the annual debt charges, principal and interest on money the private companies borrowed from various sources. The state was the railroads' largest creditor and also guaranteed a large proportion of the loans the railroads had received from private sources. The second type of capital charge was the interest, dividends, bonuses, and other payments the companies paid out to their stockholders. A peculiarity of French rail financing was that payment of interest and dividends on stocks and bonds was a legal, contractual obligation of the companies and was not contingent upon the earnings of the companies. Even though these payments had been guaranteed by the state, their amount, above the fixed, legal minimum, was determined by the officers of the rail companies, who were always generous with their distribution with a view toward keeping up the value of the stock on the Paris bourse. In 1929 and 1930 one company declared a combined dividend and bonus of 105 Fr on shares with a par value of 400 Fr—a payment of more than 26 percent. Doukas writes,

The dividends might be reasonably defensible had the operations of the companies been showing even a limited net income. But . . . operations for the entire rail industry were extremely bad. . . . The operators of the private roads simply knew how to protect their vested interests at all times; business fluctuations might affect capital stock profits of ordinary enterprises; theirs remained outside such economic and financial cycles. . . . One may well be justified in indicting the stock ownership for fiddling with dividend coupons while the public treasury burned.[7]

Right through the worst years of the great depression the officials of the private railroads managed to wring the last centime of profit out of their companies, most of it at the expense of the French taxpayer. This is symptomatic of the whole relationship of the French railroads and the state in the first hundred years. Despite what might appear to American observers to be a substantial statist infringement on the rights of capital and free enterprise, the state's *dirigisme* was basically very benevolent. It took most of the risk out of investing in the railroads and guaranteed a high rate of return to investors, in return for limiting the companies' ability to engage in wasteful overbuilding, uneconomic competition, and unbridled speculation. France was not as rich as America and so could not afford the unplanned proliferation of rail lines in which America indulged. The French state had both the incentive and the inclination to step in and assure a rational and orderly development for the benefit of the nation as a whole. But given the strength of the bourgeois interests in the various French regimes between the 1820s and the 1930s, it is not surprising that state *dirigisme* was exercised with due regard, some might even say excessive regard, for the profit of private investors.

Thus a latent dialectical tension was always present in the French policy paradigm applied to railroads. Technocratic *dirigiste* tendencies within the bureaucracy had to contend with the liberal French private enterprise perspectives present in the larger society. In times of economic crisis or national emergency the technocratic tendencies were strengthened, and the state expanded its involvement in managing and financing of the railroads. In relatively untroubled prosperous times the liberal tendencies came to the fore, and the state would try to make more room for private profit in the rail sector.

POLITICS AND PUBLIC OWNERSHIP

The economic collapse of the private railroads did not dictate their nationalization, however. True, it was out of the question to permit the companies simply to stop service. Some way had to be found to enable them to continue operation, and massive public aid to the rail industry appeared to be the only answer. This could have taken the form of another reorganization of the capital structure of the companies, with the treasury being the lender of last resort. But this option was ruled out by developments in the political system, namely, the coming to power of the Popular Front coalition of left-wing parties.

The Popular Front was an electoral alliance of the three major parties of the French left, the radicals, the socialists, and the communists.[8] They agreed on a common program and took advantage of the French election law that permitted parties that formed electoral alliances to win more seats than parties that stood alone. In the legislative elections in the spring of 1936 the Popular Front was able to win 65 percent of the seats in parliament with only 57 percent of the popular vote. The socialists were the largest party in the coalition with 147 seats, and their leader, Léon Blum, became prime minister. The radicals had won 109 seats, and they shared the remaining ministerial posts. The communists, who had won 72 seats, chose not to accept any cabinet posts but agreed to support Blum's government in the chamber of deputies. The summer of 1936 was the summer of France's New Deal. The workers, jubilant over the left's victory, peacefully occupied the factories. They demanded the forty-hour week, substantial pay raises, paid vacations, the right to collective bargaining, and many other social advances they had sought for years. The Popular Front government brought representatives of the workers and owners together and saw to it that most of the workers' demands were met. It also brought the Bank of France under firm government control and began to nationalize the armaments industry.

Interestingly enough, during that summer of 1936, when the tide of support for the Popular Front was at flood, no progress was made on the question of public ownership of the railroads. Nationalization had long been one of the Socialist party's main goals. But Blum felt he had to move carefully and avoid frightening the bourgeoisie too greatly, especially since many of this class were represented among the Radical deputies and senators who supported his government. Blum soon had to announce a pause in the pace of his social reform program, and his cabinet came under attack from the left because of its refusal to intervene in Spain against Franco's fascist-supported rebellion. A year after coming to power, Blum's Popular Front government was falling apart. The senate refused to pass a crucial bill giving the government emergency powers to deal with the worsening economic situation. Blum resigned as premier.

Then a brief flicker of hope was revived. A government still calling itself the Popular Front was formed in June, 1937, with the opportunistic Radical politician Camille Chautemps as premier and Blum as vice-premier. The balance of power had clearly shifted to the right. The senate voted Chautemps the powers it had withheld from Blum, and he used them to resume the pre-Popular Front policies of deflation, tax increases, and cuts in public spending, in short, retrenchment. But the Chautemps government also managed to push through a plan for reorganizing the railroads that was tantamount to nationalizing them. It did so under the special powers granted it to issue decree-laws that did not need the approval of parliament. Under this special powers law the ministry of public works was authorized to sign an agreement with the management of the railroads for their unification. This agreement was then ratified by a decree-law issued by the government on August 31, 1937, ironically the same day that the government's special powers expired. Thus it was in no sense a radical, Marxist regime that extended public ownership to all of France's railroads. It was not even the Popular Front at its height, but rather a sagging and disspirited shadow of itself, a government that was slipping inexorably to the right. The details of the negotiations with the management of the private railroads were left to the ministry of public works, supervised by the treasury, to work out to the satisfaction of all parties. The final plan did not even have to receive a ratifying vote of parliament. It was much more a victory for technocracy than for socialism. This of course was largely what made the nationalization politically acceptable to both the railroad management and the property-owning classes of the nation. It contributed mightily to the calm mood with which the public accepted the nationalization, and it smoothed over many obstacles in the negotiations between the technocrats on the government side and the managers on the side of the private companies.

In formal legal terms the French railroads retain a great amount of private interest and ownership. The French national railways were created by merging the seven existing networks (five private and two public) into a single new operating unit, the Société Nationale des Chemins de Fer Français (SNCF). This new unit was given the legal designation of a mixed economy company (*société d'économie mixte*).[9] The private rail companies were required to turn over all their assets, liabilities, and franchises to the SNCF. In return they received 49 percent of the stock in the new company. These shares had a par value fixed by agreement between the private companies and the government and were entitled to a guaranteed rate of 6 percent interest payable semiannually until the end of 1982. At the beginning of 1983 the private companies will be considered to have been paid in full for their assets, and ownership of all shares in the SNCF will revert to the state. The compensation given to the private shareholders was not based on any considerations of original cost of their assets, reproduction value, going concern value, liquidation value, or any of the other notions that lawyers, economists, and financiers in this country struggle with in the course of rail mergers and reorganizations. It was fixed by an agreement between the government and the companies in which both parties agreed that the state's ownership of 51 percent of the stock in the new company was justified as representing the value of the two publicly owned rail networks plus the various loans, subsidies, and other payments the state had made to the private companies over the years.

Naturally ownership of 51 percent of the new company's stock gave the state control of the SNCF's board of management (*le conseil d'administration*) as well as its executive committee (*le comité de direction*). The state named the chief executive officer of the company and exercised general policy supervision (*tutelle*) through the ministry of public works. The ministry had to approve any request for rate increases, but, if it turned down a request, the state was obligated to make up the lost revenue. The state was also obligated to balance the company's budget and pay for any deficit that occurred. The railroad workers were transferred to the SNCF at the same level of wages, seniority, and pension rights that they had with their old companies. This did not provoke much difficulty since the railway unions had won equal wages and pensions from the companies earlier in the century. The workers were also given the right to have four representatives on the twenty-member board of management.

A companion bill to the nationalization decree-law of August 31, 1937, was passed on the same day. This provided for the coordination of rail transport with other modes through a new agency, the superior transport council (*conseil supérieur des transports*). This new council was given jurisdiction over all matters relating to transport, including entry into or elimination of service, coordination of schedules, and standardization of equipment, but its principal job was to control the competition from trucks that was hurting the railroads. The council was composed of representatives from the various modes of transport, users of transport, government representatives, and labor unions. The council immediately issued several regulations restricting long-distance trucking: their timetables and routes were certified only after they had been examined and found not to constitute a competitive threat to the railroad. Moreover long-distance motor freight rates for items weighing more than 100 kilos (220 lb) could not, under any circumstances, be lower than comparable railroad rates.[10]

The creation of the SNCF and the superior transport council revealed once again the basic elements of the French paradigm of public choice, to a large extent still operative in the transport sphere: the market mechanism alone cannot be trusted to produce the transportation services the nation needs. The state must not only plan and control rail operations but also provide the necessary operating capital. In addition the state will shape a transport regulatory structure that will protect the railroads, now more than ever clothed with an aura of the public interest. Competition in and of itself is not seen as desirable. Private trucking firms interested only in profit cannot be allowed to harm unduly the national railways. Coordination of modes to benefit from their unique and complementary characteristics is much preferred to competition. This coordination can only be carried out by the state, working closely with appointed representatives of the transport-producing and consuming sectors.

RECONSTRUCTION AND REFORM

The operation of the SNCF had just begun to show some improvements when France was plunged into World War II. This had disastrous consequences for rail operations, as has been vividly documented by General De Gaulle in his description of the destruction that faced the French government on the morrow of the liberation.[11] While reconstruction crews had to face a sorrowful litany of disabled ports, dismantled factories, dislocated power systems, and downed bridges, the most extensive damage had been done to the railroads, which had been bombed by the allied air forces for two years. Practically every line north of the Seine had been put out of action. Trains leaving from Paris could not reach Lyon, Bordeaux, Nantes, Lille, or Marseille. The retreating Germans had taken whatever rolling stock they could back across the Rhine with them and sabotaged the rest. Over 7,000 locomotives, 16,000 passenger cars, and 315,000 freight cars had been destroyed or stolen; 960 railroad stations had been flattened, 2,600 bridges were downed, and over 5,000 km of rail lines needed to be rebuilt from the roadbed on up. Whole regions of the country in the northwest and Normandy were without any rail service whatsoever.

Reconstruction of the railroads and the general economic infrastructure was greatly helped by the institution of national planning. Of course some form of planning was dictated by the circumstances. But the French had a tradition of producing competent technocrats who were perfectly suited to carrying out the tasks of guiding postwar reconstruction. The technocrats in the Commissariat Général du Plan under Jean Monnet got along quite well with the technocrats at the SNCF under Louis Armand. Many had been technically trained as engineers and had gone to the same group of *grandes écoles.* They spoke the same language.[12] Not surprisingly the SNCF along with energy, cement, steel, and agricultural machinery were identified as the keys to recovery and given top priority in the first national plan that went into effect in 1947.[13]

Despite the urgency of reconstruction and the temptation to plan for the greatest possible short-run gains, France's planners made some important decisions with the long term in mind. Probably the most important of these decisions concerned electrification of the main line segments of the French rail system. Under private ownership only a small number of lines near important hydroelectric power sources in the Alps or Pyrenees had been electrified. But after World War II the entire power industry of France became nationalized. The planners were eager to foster cooperation between the two giant publicly owned enterprises, the SNCF and Eléctricité de France, and encouraged the railway to plan the electrification of its principal lines. This was a costly, and to some critics an unnecessary procedure. Diesel traction would be substantially cheaper in the short run as a replacement for the old steam locomotives. Nevertheless the electrification was decided on and proceeded step by step from the second through the fifth plans. Today approximately 80 percent of the rail traffic in France is moved under electric power.[14] Thus the obstinacy and supposed economic irrationality of the rail planners in the period when petroleum energy was abundant now gives France and its technocratic planners an important option in an age of growing uncertainty over imported supplies of petroleum energy. Electricity can be provided from domestic sources through expanded hydroelectric production, including tidal generation, solar collection, and nuclear power.

The reconstruction and modernization of the French railways were outstanding technical successes. From that perspective the SNCF is one of the most admired state-run systems in the world. The British observer and admirer of France, John Ardagh, wrote: "France's state railways provide an example of the technocratic system at its best: they show just how efficient the French can be, when everything is rationally directed by one state body and nothing is left to the vagaries of private collaboration. Thanks to this, France's trains are reputed as amongst the most modern, swift, and comfortable in the world."[15] In the actual transport of passengers and freight the SNCF must also be judged successful. In the two and one-half decades that followed World War II, while America's privately owned railroads were abandoning passenger service as fast as they could, the SNCF was making every effort to increase its passenger business. This was especially true of the long-distance trains on the country's main lines, trains that could take advantage of France's favorable geographic location as a crossroads of European traffic. Some omnibus local trains were taken out of service and replaced by bus transport operated by the SNCF or local authorities, but long-distance trains and commuter rail trains in the Paris region continued to receive high priority. Table 2.1 shows that between 1950 and 1976 the number of passenger-kilometers produced by the SNCF very nearly doubled. This stands in stunning contrast to the passenger transport performance of American railroads whose passenger-miles total dropped from 31.7 billion in 1950 to only 10.7 billion in 1970.[16]

Table 2.1 Passenger traffic on French railways (1950–1976)

Year	Number of passengers (millions)	Passenger-kilometers (billions)
1950	545	26.4
1955	509	27.8
1960	570	32.0
1965	620	38.3
1970	613	41.0
1975	658	50.7
1976	676	51.6

Sources: *Annuaire statistique de la France. Resumé retrospectif,* 1961 and 1966; INSEE, *Les Transports en France* 1971–1972, pp. 35–36; SNCF, *Rapport du conseil d'administration sur l'exercice 1976* (Paris: SNCF, June 6, 1977), p. 69.

Freight traffic also continued to increase, as shown in table 2.2. The growth in freight rail transport was not as superior to American rail performance as that of passenger traffic because U.S. railroads specialized in freight transport, and enjoyed a number of important geographical and economic advantages such as longer hauls, a larger GNP, and more traffic in bulk commodities. French rail's share of the total freight transport market compares very favorably with other European nations, and growth of output was accompanied by increasing productivity. The number of employees declined by 41 percent, from 470,000 in 1949 to 276,000 in 1975. Expressed in terms of kilometer units of transport per man-hour of work, this meant a rise in the productivity index from 50 to 231 over the same period.[17]

The SNCF's performance was all the more impressive for having come in a period when rail transport enterprises all over the world were losing ground to competing transport modes. Even in France rail faced a severe challenge from its competitors. In passenger travel the growth of private automobile ownership meant that private transport choices distinctly favored the automobile. Taking 1959 as the base year, French spending on automobiles rose from 100 to 222 in 1966, but spending on collective means of transport rose only to 123.[18] The automobile reduced rail's share of the passenger market from a quasi monopoly before the war to only 11.7 percent in 1972 (see table 2.3).

In goods transport the SNCF faced a similar challenge. Not only was rail freight being hurt by structural shifts in the French economy such as the switch from coal carried by rail to oil shipped by pipeline, but some of the restrictions that had been imposed on competitive trucking were being lifted also. In 1961 the coordination of rail and road decree-law which forbade trucking to compete directly with rail was suppressed.[19] This enabled motor freight to cream off much of the most profitable high-value traffic, while still leaving the railroad with the obligation to

Table 2.2 Freight traffic on French railways (1950–1976)

Year	Number of tons (millions)	Number of ton-kilometers (billions)
1950	152	38.9
1955	192	46.9
1960	227	56.9
1965	239	64.6
1970	250	70.4
1975	219	64.0
1976	227	68.5

Sources: *Annuaire statistique de la France, Resumé retrospectif* (1961 and 1966); SNCF, *Rapport du conseil d'administration sur l'exercice 1976* (Paris: SNCF, June 6, 1977), p. 70.

Table 2.3 Modal split of intercity passenger travel in France (1972)

Mode	Total travel (billions of vehicle km)	Percent of total travel
Private auto	316.0	83.0
Bus service	17.6	4.6
Rail service	44.7	11.7
Airline service	2.2	0.6

Source: Réné Parès, *Le Chemin de fer en France* (Paris: La Documentation Française, Notes et études documentaires 4121–4122, 1974), p. 43.

haul anything that customers brought to it. By 1971 the number of ton-kilometers of road transport produced surpassed rail's total for the first time. In that year short- and long-distance road transport produced 68.2 billion ton-kilometers goods transport compared to rail's 66.2 billion ton-kilometers.[20]

The growth in the challenge from road transport was accompanied by an increase in the annual subsidy that the state had to pay to balance the enterprise's accounts. This balancing subsidy (*subvention d'équilibre*) was politically tolerable as long as it remained relatively modest. But when it—and similar subsidies to other nationalized industries—began to enlarge substantially, this practice created discontent even among the technocrats and financial managers of the French public sector. In 1966 the government appointed a special panel to review the relations between the state and public enterprises and recommend steps to increase productivity that would at the same time reduce the need for subsidies. The report of this group, the Nora report, was suffused with a neoliberalism that saw greater management freedom for public enterprises as the solution to most of the difficulties.[21] Times had changed, said the report. It is no longer a question of depression and lack of resources. In the present period of prosperity the theme of competition must replace that of

Table 2.4 Modal split of freight transport in France (1959–1974)

Mode	Percent of total traffic		
	1959	1970	1974
Rail	66	47.0	41
Road (over 50 km)	24	35.0	42
Waterway	10	8.5	7
Pipe line	—	9.5	10
Total	100	100	100

Source: Commissariat Général du Plan, *Rapport de la commission transports et communications* (Paris: La Documentation Française, 1976), p. 88.

production. For this to happen the relationship between the state and the public enterprises must be reconstituted on a new basis. The old style of unilateral action by the public powers must be replaced by the more flexible and subtle relationship of a contract. This contract between the state and public enterprise would spell out the rights and duties of the enterprise. If the state wishes to oblige the enterprise to do something against sound business principles, it must compensate the enterprise for any losses in income or profit. If, for example, the state wants to forbid the railroad from raising its ticket prices or closing down a little-used branch line because these actions would contribute to inflation or deprive a town of rail links with the outside, then the state must pay the enterprise for the cost of producing these public services. But generally the state should leave the enterprise alone and let its management operate with a view toward fulfilling contracted-for tasks in the most efficient manner possible. This was not a return to the principle of the old liberalism, laissez faire. Rather it discarded the notion that the state should do everything itself (*faire par lui-même*). The operative principle of this new relation between the state and public enterprise thus would be *faire faire,* to cause to be done.[22] The state should have the enterprise do what the state wanted done, and the terms of the contract should be acceptable to both parties.

The management of the SNCF eagerly embraced this new contractual philosophy. It resented the appearence of incompetence that the rising deficits were presenting to the general public and gladly offered to reduce its annual deficits if the state would grant it greater commercial freedom and compensate it for any uneconomic services required to operate in the name of the public interest. It did not believe that French policy-making and planning circles would ever permit the kind of drastic cutbacks in rail service that had taken place in Britain.[23] In July 1969 an exchange of letters between the SNCF and the minister of transport spelled out in general terms what the government would expect of the railways. In January 1971 a new codicil was added to the agreement of 1937, the basic charter of the SNCF. Finally in December the government issued a decree modifying the railway's *cahier des charges,* the specifications of its powers and duties. These several documents constitute the legal basis of the reform of public policy toward the SNCF.

The basic transport policy principles that the reform set out were rather simple, although of course their execution was quite complex. In the contracted exchange the state gave the SNCF more autonomy and managerial discretion and in addition would:

• compensate the railway for the costs of providing public welfare services such as special low fares for students and the handicapped, continuing unprofitable branch lines, special freight rates for depressed areas such as Britanny;

- pay part of the cost of maintaining the railroad infrastructure such as track and bridges so that rail service would be on a more equal competitive footing with road transport;

- pay the difference between the costs of the special rail pension fund and the general social security plan;

- pay the difference between the costs of the special rail health care plan and the general public health care plan;

- pay the cost of grade-crossing guards and equipment out of the roads budget;

- continue to limit directly the amount of road transport competition by restricting the number of long-haul trucking licenses granted by the state.

The SNCF in turn agreed to eliminate its budgetary deficit, hence the need for any state subsidies by

- closing down deficit-producing branch lines or replacing them with bus service;

- reducing the number of employees by some 10 percent from 300,000 to 270,000;

- making a greater effort to adopt modern methods of management and marketing such as regional decentralization, more auto-couchette trains, and car rentals in railroad stations.[24]

To a layman or a skeptic it must have seemed that the SNCF reform was being done with bookkeeping. The public revenues were still to be paid out to the railway. Only instead of being part of a general *subvention d'équilibre* they were now carried as payments for services rendered or as part of the process of equalizing advantages between rail and road transport. But even with the reform progress toward eliminating

Table 2.5 Public rail subsidies in France (1962–1975)

Year	Total subsidies[a] (millions of francs)
1962	2,382
1968	5,698
1970	5,432
1972	6,135
1974	7,887
1975	9,768

Sources: Les Comptes de la nation pour l'année, *Encyclopaedia universalis* 11 (Paris, 1971), p. 581. La SNCF en 1975, *Les Echos* (June 21, 1977), p. 11.
[a]Includes compensation for public service charges, payments to equalize the conditions of competition between modes, state infrastructural investment, payments to offset artificially low fares.

the railway's budget deficit was slow. By 1973 it was already clear that only a miracle could eliminate the need for continuing the *subvention d'équilibre* beyond the projected 1974 cutoff date (see table 2.5). In 1973 the SNCF and the transport ministry entered into negotiations for a new agreement that would extend the transitional continuation of the *subvention d'équilibre*. But then the neoliberal concern with balancing the budget of the enterprise was overtaken by more urgent events.

ENERGY, EUROPE, AND THE FUTURE OF RAIL PLANNING

The policy outlook for the railroad changed with dramatic suddeness in the winter of 1973 to 1974. The Arab oil embargo and subsequent fivefold increase in the price of petroleum highlighted how dangerously vulnerable the nations of Europe were in the supply of imported oil. France imports virtually 100 percent of the oil she consumes, and in the postwar period the imports had increased rapidly. Oil was used to produce 39 percent of France's energy in 1959; by 1973 oil accounted for 73 percent of the nation's energy.[25] Oil consumed in the transport sector represented 17 percent of the total oil consumed.[26] Given the need to conserve energy and the enormously increased costs of imported petroleum, the financial deficit of the SNCF suddenly appeared in a different perspective. A few billion francs for the railroads were more defensible than they had been only a year previously. What counted in the energy crisis was that the rail system offered a means of assuring national mobility when motor fuel was in short supply. Rail was also seen as a long-term alternative to the increasing reliance on petroleum-powered cars and trucks. If the amount of oil consumed by the transport sector could be reduced by heavier use of the rails, this could reduce dependence on foreign oil suppliers, improve the French balance of payments, and fight air pollution in the bargain. The political leaders of the French government were anxious to demonstrate they had responses to the energy crisis in hand that were more than just stopgap emergency measures. The technocrats who ran the SNCF were eager to redeem politically their earlier expensive decisions on electrification and to offset the public impact of the company's failure to eliminate its budget deficit in the agreed upon time. It was natural then that, when the prime minister announced his long-term energy program in the spring of 1974, the railroads would have an important role in the plan. The prime minister said that the state would substantially increase the amount of money it would make available to the SNCF for investments in new energy-saving infrastructures.[27] Primarily this meant that the rail company was now being given the go-ahead to construct an important new rail line between Paris and the southeast. This would be an entirely new, high-speed rail line that would cut travel time between Paris and Lyon substantially. The new line would be used exclusively for passenger trains and would thus free up the existing line, the most heavily traveled route in France, to be used entirely for freight service. For a while the railway was once again the darling of the state and the hope of the nation.

The research and publicity services of the SNCF were quick to capitalize on the changed energy situation. They counterattacked vigorously against the inroads that trucking had been making into rail's freight business.[28] A campaign was mounted, documenting the difference in energy consumption between rail and road haulage. According to the SNCF some simple calculations that any physics undergraduate could make would demonstrate rail's inherent energy efficiency. In transport energy is needed to overcome inertia, friction, wind resistance, and gravity. It takes five times less energy to move a vehicle on steel rails than to move a vehicle of the same weight on rubber tires and concrete. Friction resistance is much weaker. Wind resistance is related to the size of the frontal area and a fifteen-car train does not have much more frontal area than a single truck. The grades of the rail lines are much less steep than the grades of highways. The energy counterattack was so successful that even spokesmen for the trucking industry were obliged to concede the validity of the railroad's energy claims. They admitted that the long-distance heavy trucks of France (*poids lourds*) consume three and one-half times the energy of the SNCF's freight operations, while actually producing fewer ton-kilometers of freight transport. As far as passenger travel is concerned, it would take four times as much energy to produce the same number of "seat-kilometers" using private autos as it would using an electric fifteen-car train.[29] The national railways could point to the most energy efficient record of all of French transport modes. They were moving more passengers and freight with far less energy than in the past. Since 1960 total energy consumption by French railroads declined more than 50 percent, and the amount of energy per unit of transport declined by some 65 percent (see table 2.6).

The energy crisis gave the technocrats in the ministry of transport the extra stimulus needed to beat back the first wave of neoliberalism and

Table 2.6 Energy consumption by French railways (1960–1975)

Year	Total energy consumption[a]	Energy consumption per unit of transport[b]
1960	5,362	61.1
1965	4,296	41.7
1970	2,782	24.9
1975	2,462	21.4

Source: SNCF, *Rapports sur l'exercice 1975* (Paris: SNCF, 1976), p. 63.
[a]Millions of coal ton equivalents.
[b]Coal ton equivalent per million unit kilometers.

the accompanying pressure from road interests which would have resulted in the continuing steady decline of the national railways. They were determined not only to increase public investment in expanding the capacity of the energy-saving rail system but also to follow a program of steadily raising the costs of rail's principal competitor, the energy-intensive trucking industry. This was to be done in stages to avoid any undue inflationary impact on prices or undesired dislocation of production or unemployment. The ministries of finance and transport agreed on a series of increases in the already high taxes on gasoline. In addition there were increases in the special truck transport, axle tax (*la taxe à l'essieu*), with a view to making the trucks pay a greater share of the costs of providing the roads they use. There was also talk of stiffer controls on the hours and working conditions of truck drivers which would limit the overtime of drivers and require hiring more drivers, thus raising the wage costs in the trucking industry.[30] Overall the ministry of transport envisaged a slowing down of the trucking industry growth rate, which prior to the energy crisis had been growing at a rate between 8 and 9 percent per year. These restraining measures were planned to slow trucking growth to around 4 percent per year.[31]

It is not surprising that the government policy planners should grant the French national railways a major role in this move to make France more energy efficient and independent. Stepping up investment in rail capacity and increasing rail's share of the transport market can easily be seen as positive, constructive actions, limiting as well pollution and high-way congestion. Such policy measures taken in aid of a public enterprise are much easier to sell to the general public (although not to the truckers of course) than harsher methods such as higher taxes on gasoline and higher prices for electricity. Because the SNCF was able to weather the worst storms of the automotive decades by actually maintaining its passenger and freight traffic, it is in condition to make a real contribution toward achieving national policy goals rather than just serve as a symbolic gesture.

As the worldwide repercussions of the energy crisis demonstrated, national governments are having to cope with problems increasingly international in scope. In the European Economic Community of course common institutions were created for the very purpose of harmonizing national policies in many different sectors including transportation. The European commission in Brussels and its secretariat are mostly staffed with technocrats. One would expect that the transport sector would be among the easiest for these European technocrats or Eurocrats to integrate. But this has not been the case.[32] Road transport and the relation between road, rail, and waterways have been especially thorny. This is in large part due to the economic importance and political influence of the motor freight interests in some of the countries such as the Netherlands and Italy where a much larger proportion of total freight transport is handled by truck than in nations such as France and Germany. Progress in integrating the total transport sector has therefore been disappointingly slow. It took nine years before the first transport accords envisioned by the Treaty of Rome could be reached and another nine years before they could be significantly extended.[33] Translating agreements in principle into specific commission regulations has presented many difficulties to the Eurocrats.

When the technical aspects of the rail sector alone are considered, the picture is much brighter. International cooperation among European rail systems goes back to the early days of railroading when the problems of standardizing gauges and signals had to be solved by agreement. In more recent times the national railroads of Europe have given consumers tangible evidence of the benefits of transnational cooperation through such innovations as the Trans Europe Express trains, the Eurail pass, and the auto-couchette trains that speed vacationers and their automobiles from the misty north to the sunny south without clogging the highways. Technocratic competence and self-confidence have probably been best displayed in the future growth planning of the west European rail system. Working within the framework of the International Railway Union and the Conference of European Transport Ministers, French rail planners and their colleagues from the other European nations have devised an elaborate, expensive, and far-sighted master plan for keeping railways in the forefront of the European transport system.[34] The plan calls for the individual nations to coordinate their future infrastructural investments to produce a modern, high-capacity, high-speed European rail grid that will overlay the existing national rail networks. This grid of *grandes magistrales européennes* will utilize the latest rail technology and traction, including magnetic suspension. Its trains will attain speeds between 125 and 200 miles per hour, which will make them competitive with airplanes for trips of up to 400 to 500 miles and much less energy consuming. The two principal north–south axes of the Europe grid will be

• Manchester–Marseille, via London, the Parisian basin, Lyon, and the Rhone valley, (a corridor with some 50 million inhabitants);

• Randstad, Holland–Genova, via the Ruhr, the Rhine-Main complex, Basel and the Swiss plateau, the Saint Gothard pass and Milan (another corridor with 50 million inhabitants).

These north–south axes will be traversed by five major east–west axes:

• Channel Ports–Belgium–Hamburg,

• Paris–Lorraine–Stuttgart–Munich

• Lyon–Swiss plateau,

• Lyon–Po valley,

• Barcelona–Marseille–Genova–Verona.[35]

Yet the traditional technocratic planning tendency reinforced by events and forces coming outside of France does not mean that French planning is rigid, mired in orthodoxy, or not subject to controversy. On the contrary, debate among planners remains lively. The neoliberal outlook was returned to the center of the policy debate in 1978 with the publication of the Guillaumat report by a special commission charged with redefining the policy orientations of land transport.[36] This new report echoed and extended the line of reasoning of the Nora report of a decade earlier. It was an affirmation of faith in the salutary effects of competition and a declaration that the state should not attempt to preserve outdated, uneconomic practices or enterprises simply because they were part of a state-owned concern. The report stated that in general there was no reason to subsidize a transport undertaking such as the SNCF. Rather it should be given the freedom to manage its commercial affairs and be self-supporting. If in specific instances the state desired to preserve some service the SNCF management wished to abandon because it was unprofitable, then the state would pay a specific sum for this service. The notion of public service would be replaced by that of the contract for service as the guiding principle of the national railways. Specifically the Guillaumat report recommended a draconian shrinking of the French rail net by about one-third of its length and the closing down of between 3,000 and 4,500 small and underutilized railway stations. Passenger traffic thus displaced was to be shifted to railway-operated buses or dropped altogether. The state sought to encourage the railway company to spend its resources where there is the greatest prospect of future growth of ridership, on the *grandes lignes* and the commuter lines serving Paris. In the domain of freight traffic the state preferred to act as a referee enforcing the rules of competition between rail and truck transportation. The conditions of competition would be made as equal as possible, now, while continuing to give more commercial freedom to the management of the SNCF, also suppressing the Malthusian regulation of trucking and permitting it to compete for any traffic it can get regardless of whether it takes freight from the railroad or not.

The recommendations contained in the Guillaumat report form the basis for a new contract signed in February 1979 between the SNCF and the French government.[37] Scheduled to last four years, it like its predecessor plans the elimination of the SNCF's deficit by the end of 1982. The terminal date is significant. At the end of 1982 the SNCF's original 1938 charter as a mixed enterprise runs out. Whether the experiment is judged a success or a failure, one thing is clear: the French rail system is likely to undergo another searching examination as the expiration date of its charter approaches.

Thus a review of the development of the French paradigm of public choice in railroad transportation suggests that it has been characterized by a constructive tension between *dirigisme* and laissez faire, between the planning and market paradigms. From the beginning the capitalists' involvement in the rail sector was organized and guided by the state to achieve the maximum national benefits for each unit of rail investment. The state did not permit private enterprise to build costly parallel lines over lucrative routes while ignoring less profitable ones; each company got a monopoly of transport in its assigned area. In periods of depression, when private rail investment lagged, public funds were used to ensure the maintenance of high levels of service in the rail system. The transition from private to public ownership was a gradual one that did not cause much disruption in the operations of the rail system. Even in the 1950s and 1960s, when rail seemed to have entered into a long-term decline vis-à-vis its rising competition on the roads, public investments in the rail system were maintained at high levels. The energy crisis of the 1970s is seen by traditional rail technocrats as a vindication of this policy. They have not hesitated to capitalize on the situation to win support among the press, people, and political figures. The SNCF is not simply a helpless tool in the hands of the government. As two French scholars recently observed, "The SNCF . . . is a nationalized enterprise which nevertheless acts as an autonomous agent toward the state. This autonomy is partly the result of bureaucratic dysfunctions, but it is also the consequence of a situation of interdependence and exchange among groups for whom the SNCF represents a significant stake."[38]

Recent neoliberal attempts to introduce more competition in the land transport market represent something quite different from a return to nineteenth-century laissez faire. The new competitive approach is being sponsored by political leaders, Barre and Giscard foremost among them, who are themselves technocrats by training and temperament. Their strategy in transport, as in the economy in general, tries to take advantage of both the *dirigisme* and laissez faire approaches by planning for competition. It is a forward-looking planning that resolutely refuses to preserve the old preautomobile railway network in which every small town and village had its station with half a dozen arrivals and departures daily. It seeks instead to maximize the social return on capital invested in rail transportation by planning investments in areas that promise the greatest growth in ridership: the Paris region's new growth and Europe's new transnational travel needs. By concentrating rail investments in these selected areas, French rail planners seek to preserve a national rail system that will not be merely a nostalgic relic of the past but an essential and increasingly important component of the land transport system well into the twenty-first century.[39]

3
THE UNITED STATES: THE
POLITICAL ECONOMY OF
PRIVATE OWNERSHIP

PRIVATE OWNERSHIP AND PUBLIC REGULATION

Speculative and uncoordinated development of railroads lasted only a few early years in France. In the United States it persisted throughout the entire nineteenth century and well into the twentieth. Railroads became the first really big businesses in this country, and the excesses of the robber barons who directed the industry in its formative years did much to create the negative image of big business in general and railroad companies in particular that generations of public relations consultants have been trying to erase. The shades of Vanderbilt, Gould, Harriman, and Hill, among others, hover over the industry like ghosts in a graveyard.[1] American railroad companies received their charters from the states, whose legislatures were either predisposed or persuaded to be very generous in dispensing such charters and the privileges they entailed. Unlike French rail charters there were no time limitations or recapture provisions imposed on U.S. rail companies. Nor was there any central direction in the planning of routes to avoid wasteful duplication of facilities. In fact duplication was encouraged in the belief that the resulting competition would lower prices and bring about better service. The federal rail policy view was to promote as much rail construction as possible, especially in the west to open up and bind the nation together. Washington fostered this goal mainly by grants of federal land along rail rights of way. By 1871, when land grants were ended, 130 million acres— an area nearly as large as all of France—had been deeded over to the rail companies. In return they agreed not only to raise money and build the railroads but also to carry federal property and the U.S. mail at reduced rates.[2]

One consequence of this type of laissez faire promotional policy was the very rapid construction of the world's largest rail network. This may have fulfilled the hopes of some of the more far-sighted policy makers, since it helped make possible the exploitation of the wealth of the continent. In many cases, however, policy makers were simply responding to pressures and enticements from railroad developers hoping to make money. The American rail system was shaped to a far greater degree by rampant capitalism and widespread political corruption than the French system. In consequence there was a great overbuilding of lines, terminals, and other facilities that saddled the U.S. rail system with a costly burden of excess capacity which has remained a problem to the present day. By the 1880s this overbuilding along with fierce rate wars that flared now and again between rail companies led to growing dissatisfaction with railroad practices among the industry's customers, the shippers of agricultural and manufactured goods. Exhorbitant rates, rebates to large shippers, discrimination against short-haul traffic, pooling schemes, and other abuses angered important elements of the business community that depended on rail transportation. The traditional protection of competition in a free market did not seem to be working as it was supposed to. Farmers, merchants, manufacturers, and others caught in the inequities of rail practices turned to public authorities for redress. The U.S. Supreme Court ruled that state regulation of interstate commerce was unconstitutional, so efforts for public action focused on Congress. In 1887, at a time when the French government was already operating its own state rail network alongside five private ones, the U. S. federal government took its first hesitant steps toward extending its authority over the railroads. This came not in the form of public ownership, but in the guise of the Interstate Commerce Commission (ICC), the first of the federal regulatory agencies, established by the Interstate Commerce Act. The modicum of power Congress granted to the ICC was soon whittled down by the railroads. They appealed sixteen of the commission's rulings to the Supreme Court during the 1890s and won fifteen of them. It took the Elkins Act of 1903, the Hepburn Act of 1906, and the Mann-Elkins Act of 1910 before the ICC could begin to do more than just collect and publish statistics.[3]

Scholars are still in disagreement over which interests were most important in pushing for these actions and for what purposes. Many traditional histories see the railroad regulation movement as a product of a rural rebellion led by the grangers. Others give more emphasis to the role played by manufacturers. Gabriel Kolko offers a left-wing view in *Railroads and Regulations, 1877–1916*.[4] He maintains that the rail companies themselves wanted federal regulation to stabilize the industry and deter rate wars. Albro Martin's thesis in *Enterprise Denied: The Origins of the Decline of American Railroads 1887–1917* is that the railroads did not dominate the ICC. Progressive politicians and shippers allied to impose the palsied hand of the commission on the railroads and thus begin the financial decline of the industry.[5] Regardless of the view one takes of this period one thing is clear: the thrust of public policy was not aimed at replacing private ownership or even eliminating private domination of basic decision making in the rail industry. It sought only to remedy those defects in the market for rail transportation services that impinged on the rights and interests of the railroads' customers. These customers, representing a substantial segment of the nation's business community, provided the political base that helped push for and legitimize the limited extension of federal authority over the railroads the ICC constituted.

American entry into World War I brought on a crisis that provides an instructive interlude in the developing relationship between the industry and public authorities. When war was declared in April 1917, the railroads attempted to preclude government control by creating their own Railroads' War Board to coordinate rail transport for the war effort. This private, purely advisory body depended on the voluntary cooperation of the individual railroads. By the end of 1917 the board had failed miserably; freight car shortages were snarling production, traffic to east coast ports was backed up for weeks, coal shortages loomed, and the war effort was threatened. President Wilson, acting under wartime emergency authority, took possession of the country's railroads and named Treasury Secretary William G. McAdoo the Director General of the Railroads. McAdoo's railroad administration ran the lines well enough to make a significant improvement in mobilizing the country's resources. But in the process it frightened the rail industry with visions of permanent nationalization, or at best a private industry much more strictly controlled than before the war. The rail industry mounted a campaign to discredit the railroad administration, charging it with losing vast sums of the taxpayers' money, running down the rail properties, and coddling the rail unions for political purposes. After the armistice their campaign moved into high gear, and events conspired to ensure its success. Susan Armitage, who has studied the events closely, sums up the factors that led to the denationalization of the American railroads and the failure to impose stricter regulation of the once again private industry:

President Wilson's preoccupation with foreign affairs and William G. McAdoo's resignation removed from the executive branch the personalities forceful enough to impose a solution of railway problems on Congress. In addition American railway executives were vociferous in their opposition to continued government control. The result was that the American government or more precisely, the executive branch of government, adopted a "hands-off" policy after the war, abandoning the railway problem to Congress . . . and the Transportation Act (of 1920) was an admission that for political reasons the Congress would not compel the railways to do what they would not do voluntarily.[6]

The Transportation Act of 1920 was the first attempt by the federal government to articulate anything resembling a national transportation policy. In the railroads sector it aimed at (1) establishing a reasonable basis for railroad rates, (2) ensuring the necessary degree of harmony between the rail companies and employees' unions, and (3) promoting consolidation of the hundreds of rail companies into a manageable number of large lines. The most tangible consequence of the rate provisions was a rise of some 25 to 35 percent in rail rates. The other two goals were not even close to being achieved. As Armitage writes, the rail companies, "setting their faces against change, . . . destroyed the provisions of the Transportation Act—the amalgamation and labor clauses—which would have been of greatest benefit to the railway system."[7]

Thus by 1920 the legal framework that would regulate the rail industry for the next fifty years was well established. The goal of public policy was to create an administrative process that would function as an ersatz market. Regulation was to be a substitute for competition. When and where the nature of the rail industry prevented free market competition from determining prices, the ICC would act to ensure just and reasonable rates. It had the power to set maximum rates and approve requests for abandonment of service and mergers between railroad companies. Moreover it was not just charged with protecting the shippers from being gouged by the railroads. According to the terms of the transportation act it was also obligated to see that the railroad companies had high enough rates to ensure a fair return on the aggregate value of their rail properties. To this end the commission was given the power to set minimum as well as maximum rates. At long last, but much too late, it was given the power to approve the construction of new rail lines. Some economists describe this arrangement as a publicly sanctioned cartel that allocates traffic between its members by fixing prices rather than issuing quotas.[8] In hindsight it seems an inefficient cartel, because it lacked the power to bring about cost-lowering rationalizations on the production side and did not fully cover or control the growing body of producers of a substitutable transportation service, the truckers, barge operators, and pipeline companies.

During the great depression of the 1930s many American railroads were as hard hit by the economic slump as their European counterparts. By the late 1930s, 38 of the 147 class I railroads in the country were in bankruptcy or receivership. These roads represented some 31 percent of the nation's total rail mileage and 24 percent of its total rail capital investment. It was a grim picture; compared to the halcyon days of the twenties, profits had plunged by more than 75 percent. Yet unlike the situation in France the rail industry as a whole—as distinct from individual roads—continued to show a small profit (1.62 percent on capital in 1938), thanks in large part to the $738 million it had been loaned by the Reconstruction Finance Corporation.[9] The profitable rail companies, and even those that hoped someday to become profitable again, were not going to be panicked or pushed into any scheme for national consolidation, let alone for public ownership. Joseph B. Eastman, named by President Roosevelt as Federal Coordinator of Transportation, unsuccessfully attempted to get the rail companies to reduce costs by sharing terminal facilities and pooling equipment. Both management and labor rejected this plan.[10] Labor also failed to support Senator Burton K. Wheeler's bill authorizing the federal government to acquire "any common or contract carrier of property or passengers for hire by any means of transportation," partly because of fear of job losses and partly because the bill went too far and would have authorized public ownership of trucking, barges, buses, shipping, and other modes of transport as well as railroads.

During the Second World War U.S. railroads were not taken over by the government but merely coordinated by the Office of Defense Transportation. Consequently their profits rose to 6.5 percent on capital during the first full year of American participation in the war and stayed at about that level until 1945. When the war ended, there was no capital crisis (as in Britain) and no need for any public decision on returning the roads to their private owners. The rail industry was optimistic about its postwar prospects, but too optimistic as it turned out. Throughout the 1950s and 1960s the rail share of the transport sector shrank steadily. When business was booming in the general economy the railroads managed to scrape by, but in recessions their accounts were plunged into a sea of red ink. In the postwar years the rail sector consistently showed much lower net earnings than every other transport industry. In 1969, for example, the average rate of return on capital for all manufacturing industries was 11.5 percent, in the trucking industry it was 9.8 percent, while the railroads earned only 2.6 percent. The earnings crisis worsened during the recession in the next two years. Earnings for all manufacturing slipped to 9.3 and 9.2 percent, but those for rail plummeted to 0.4 percent and to 0 percent in 1970 and 1971.[11]

ECONOMIC CHANGE, POLICY PARALYSIS, AND THE DECLINE OF THE U. S. RAILROAD INDUSTRY

How had the once mighty railroad industry fallen so low? Each element involved with the industry had its own favorite scapegoat. It was, said some, the fault of sluggish, short-sighted management. No, said others, it was selfish, featherbedding unions. It was outdated technology, unfair competition from trucks, the heavy hand of government regulation, and so forth. Everything but communist conspiracy was mentioned as a cause of the railroad problem. In truth it was a very complex situation that stemmed from many diverse causes. Most observers agreed on the overarching importance of two broad factors, though. First, changes in the pattern of economic growth were adversely affecting the railroads' share of the transport market. Second, the existing public regulatory policies were inadequate to cope with the effects of this and other adverse trends. Let us consider each of these points in more detail.

Basic changes in the American industrial economy since the 1920s, and especially since 1945, have reduced the aggregate demand for rail services and deprived the rail industry of the opportunity to benefit proportionally from the GNP growth. As the economy has matured into the postindustrial stage, the greatest amount of economic growth has taken place in sectors stressing services or producing high technology, high value but light-weight goods. These two types of economic growth do not require rail transportation services to nearly the degree that the older coal-, iron-, and steel-based economic growth did. Between 1947 and 1972 the GNP grew at an annual average rate of 3.2 percent, but total intercity freight traffic, exclusive of oil pipeline movements, grew only an average of 2.2 percent per year. In that same period rail freight revenue ton-miles increased 30 percent, while the overall GNP increased 170 percent.[12] In addition changing technology has cut into the demand for rail transport even in its traditional areas of strength. The demand for coal, for example, stagnated and declined because utility companies switched to oil-fired generators. Coal shipments declined still further because of advances in the technology of long-distance transmission of high voltage electricity which encouraged construction of generating plants at mine mouth.

Geographical shifts in the population and industry have affected parts of the rail industry very seriously. As people and manufacturing firms migrated from the northeast and north central states to the south and west, and as population flowed from rural areas to the cities and suburbs, the old profitable patterns of rail traffic were disrupted. It was no longer possible to achieve the balanced two-way movement of commodities in which agricultural products from the south and west flowed to the industrial cities of the northeast and the same boxcars returned carrying manufactured goods back to the farmers. Freight cars returned empty because industry had relocated. Freight shipments declined by one-third in the eastern district between 1929 and 1976.[13]

In the face of these already immobilizing trends the railroads have had to respond to increasing competition from other modes. In 1939 rail could still claim to be dominant in freight transportation (62.3 percent of the total freight ton-miles) and in intercity for-hire passenger transportation (66.7 percent of for-hire revenue passenger miles). By 1976 rail's share of the passenger market had dwindled to only 5.3 percent, and its share of the freight market was down to only 35.3 percent of the total ton-miles (see table 3.1). If its freight share is measured by total revenue tons instead of ton-miles, the picture is even bleaker: rail moves only 29.3 percent of the traffic.[14] Rail's competitors have been experiencing spectacular growth while rail stagnates. The number of nongovernment-owned trucks grew from some 4.6 million in 1940 to nearly 25 million in 1975.[15] Pipelines have stripped the railroads of practically all their traffic in crude oil and petroleum products. A resurgent inland water transportation industry has become a strong competitor for the bulk commodity traffic that railroads have concentrated on. The airlines, the bus companies and of course the ubiquitous private automobile took so many passengers away that the rail companies were glad to turn over their passenger service to Amtrack.

All these competitors (except pipelines) have benefited from substan-

Table 3.1 Modal share of U.S. freight market (1939–1976)

| Year | Percent of private and for-hire freight ton-miles | | | |
	Rail	Road	Water	Pipeline
1939	62.3	9.7	17.7	10.3
1949	58.3	13.8	15.3	12.6
1959	45.3	21.7	15.3	17.7
1969	40.8	21.3	16.0	21.7[a]
1976	36.7	22.6	16.3	24.2[a]

Sources: Transportation Association of America, *Transportation Facts and Trends,* 13th ed., p. 8, and Association of American Railroads, *Railroad Facts,* 1977 ed., p. 36.
[a]Air freight is 0.2 percent of ton-miles.

tial public investments in physical facilities which have had the effect of subsidizing their growth to a greater or lesser extent. For example, between 1945 and 1975 some $10.7 billion in federal funds had been invested in improvements to internal navigation, such as the straightening and deepening of rivers, building canals, dams, and locks.[16] For the most part this has been a free gift to the barge industry, a product of pork barrel politics in Congress. Water carriers pay taxes of course, but only those taxes that any business is expected to pay; they pay no special user taxes on fees (except on the St. Lawrence Seaway) that underwrite the costs of public works from which they benefit. Trucks, on the other hand, do pay substantial user taxes in the form of the federal and state fuel taxes. The question of whether trucks pay their fair share of highway costs is hotly debated and hard to determine with any degree of scientific precision. The trucking industry claims that its vehicles pay 38 percent of all user taxes collected, while trucks constitute only 17 percent of the total national motor vehicle fleet.[17] However, many highway officials maintain that trucks are responsible for up to 95 percent of the damage done to road surfaces and bridges because damage increases exponentially with axle weight.[18] The railroads calculate that between

Table 3.2 Modal share of U.S. for-hire passenger market (1939–1976)

| Year | Percent of inter-city passenger miles | | | |
	Rail	Road	Air	Water
1939	66.7	26.8	2.3	4.2
1949	36.0	24.0	7.8	1.4
1959	29.7	27.1	40.5	2.7
1970	7.3	16.9	73.1	2.7
1976	5.3	13.1	79.5	2.1

Source: Transportation Association of America, *Transportation Facts and Trends,* 13th ed., p. 18.

1921 and 1976 federal, state, and local governments invested some $459.6 billion in roads and streets, which was a significant factor in the growth of the trucking industry.[19] In particular the railroads claim that the interstate highway system, funded by taxes from gasoline consumed mainly on local roads and streets, constitutes a subsidy to the large, long-distance tractor trailers that most directly compete with the railroads.[20] Even if it were to be conceded that trucks pay their fair share of highway costs, the user tax system still gives trucking firms a big advantage over the railroads. It makes expenses for their right of way a variable cost, one that rises and falls with the amount of fuel they consume. These costs are easily cut back when demand for freight transport declines during a recession. In contrast, the railroads' costs for maintenance of way include large amounts for repayment of principal and interest charges which must be paid regardless of the state of business.

The issue of subsidies to competing modes is just one facet of the second overarching factor in rail's decline, the inability of the traditional regulatory process to cope with long-term changes in the state of the transportation environment. The defects of the public regulatory process have been the subject of much criticism over the years.[21] For the purposes of this analysis two major components of that criticism will be summarized here. The first set of complaints come from the rail industry itself and reflect what is wrong with the regulatory process from the rail industry's point of view. The second critique may be viewed as what is wrong with regulation from the point of view of the general public. The railroad's criticism is very simple: regulation costs the railroads too much money. This point was made by the president of the Association of American Railroads when he told the House Subcommittee on Transportation and Commerce in 1975:

In substantial degree the depressed earnings experienced by the rail industry over many years are directly attributable to government action or inaction. . . . We estimate that the resulting annual cost to the industry is on the order of $2 ½ billion. About $1 billion of this comes from burdens imposed upon the railroads by government. The other $1.5 billion is the effect of government subsidation of modes of transportation with which the railroads compete.[22]

The costs imposed on the railroads by government include the income denied them by refusal of permission to raise rates ($500 million annually), losing branch line operations they are not permitted to abandon ($130 million per year), property taxes paid on right of way ($200 million), and grade-crossing costs ($173 million). Another $1.5 billion of income must be forsworn because of the necessity to keep rates low to compete with subsidized barge and truck traffic. Thus, say the railroads, regulation is a major contributor to the railroads' earnings difficulties and its attendant problems of deferred maintenance and declining service quality.[23]

From a public interest point of view regulation can be criticized as

The United States: The Political Economy of Private Ownership

being a very imperfect substitute for true market competition. Regulation may have been cumbersome but necessary seventy years ago when rail was the only realistic mode of inland transport available in many areas of the country. In today's transport system, where a number of different modes compete for traffic, it makes little sense to have 100 percent of rail traffic regulated, while less than 50 percent of trucking is subject to regulation, and only 10 percent of barge traffic is under the authority of the ICC.[24] This simply inhibits the real competition that should be taking place between the modes by weakening rail's ability to compete. Even within the rail sector regulation has unnecessarily suppressed competition in the name of preserving it. When the ICC refuses a rate reduction request or disallows a merger "in order to preserve competition," what it often really does is protect inefficient competitors from more efficient ones. This is precisely the wrong policy direction to take. It requires the duplication of facilities, poorer utilization of equipment, higher unit costs. Thus the public ends up paying more for rail services because the ICC protects competitors, not competition.

The traditional regulatory framework not only fails to protect true competition in many cases but also is ineffective in stimulating true cooperation among railroad companies. There are no truly national railroads in the United States. The industry developed on regional lines and remains balkanized geographically today. Consequently more than 50 percent of the traffic moves over more than one railroad. An efficient national rail system requires cooperation, not competition; the regulatory framework has put rail companies in the ambiguous position of being competitors and joint venturers simultaneously. When one company receives a freight car from another, its only incentive is to move that car to its destination as cheaply as possible. There is no premium for getting it there quickly, or even on time. If the cargo is damaged, the originating railroad must pay the costs, not the line on which the damage might have occurred. To cut costs, the railroads try to increase output per employee by running longer trains. This entails having loaded freight cars standing idle for long periods waiting to be made up into trains. The nature of rail technology is such that the longer the train, the more likely its cargo is to be damaged during coupling and uncoupling and the more likely the train is to derail. This lowers the timeliness and safety of rail service and makes it less able to compete in today's transport market.[25]

If the traditional regulatory framework's ability to foster competition and encourage cooperation has been disappointing, its ability to bring about rail consolidation and achieve intermodal coordination has been virtually nil. This is a function of both its style and substance. The ICC's judicial style of operation—case-by-case consideration of rate increases, mergers, service abandonments, and such—is not only slow and inefficient but also basically reactive and unsuited to the development of a projective planning capability. Basically the ICC was not supposed to plan a national rail system. But on those occassions when Congress did ask it to draw up a scheme for consolidating the railroads, such as in the Transportation Act of 1920, it failed to give the ICC any authority to enforce the plan, and the railroads ignored it. Inability to coordinate rail transport with competing modes threatened the industry with disaster. The ICC was given authority to regulate a portion of the trucking industry by the Motor Carrier Act of 1935. However, the hauling of agricultural produce and trucks carrying the goods for a single firm were exempted, with the effect that less than half of interstate trucking is subject to regulation. About 90 percent of the barge industry was exempted from regulation by the terms of the Transportation Act of 1940. Of course the ICC had no authority to determine the level of subsidies to the barge industry or the amount of money spent on highways. That was a privilege the Congress reserved to itself.

The potent combination of these factors of regulatory rigidity, adverse economic trends, and increased competition from other modes reduced railroad revenues to dangerously low levels. The revenue generated by rail operations was not sufficient to meet the capital requirements of the industry, and low earnings limited its ability to finance capital expenditures by selling stock. Table 3.3 shows that the rail earnings crisis was much more serious in the eastern district than in the southern or western districts.[26] Eastern railroads were built earlier, with denser networks of branch lines, shorter hauls, and more reliance on manufactured goods and passengers for revenue. They were the most vulnerable to the adverse trends in the transport market. In the early 1970s eight eastern railroads were on or over the brink of bankruptcy. They included the newly merged Penn-Central, and together these eight roads totaled 26,790 miles of line, somewhat more than 50 percent of all the rail mileage in the region.[27] By contrast, there were a number of railroads in the south and west that were doing quite well. The Norfolk and Western,

Table 3.3 Return on capital for U.S. railroads (1939–1977)

Year	United States	Eastern district	Southern district	Western district
1929	5.30	6.03	4.27	4.85
1939	2.56	3.14	2.77	1.85
1960	2.13	1.55	2.97	2.40
1970	1.73	deficit	4.50	3.02
1977	1.26	deficit	5.23	3.73

Source: Association of American Railroads, *Yearbook of Railroad Facts,* 1978 ed., p. 20.

The United States: The Political Economy of Private Ownership

Southern Railway, Missouri Pacific, Union Pacific, and Chesapeake and Ohio enjoy a rate of return of 6 to 8 percent.[28] Most rail companies even in the west did not have such favorable earnings, however.

Such regional differences, coupled with differences in profitability and future prospects, had for a long time prevented the companies from adopting a unified position on what public policy could do to improve the rail industry's performance. The managements, trustees, and creditors of the bankrupt eastern railroads desperately needed an infusion of cash just to continue operations. To get such funds, they were more than willing to accept government subsidies and even to submit to an unprecedented degree of government direction in reorganizing their finances and operations. The solvent railroads in the region feared that such subsidies would help their competitors and hurt them. Western and southern lines generally still opposed subsidies in principle. But they were concerned that massive closures on connecting eastern routes would deprive them of some of their own traffic. It was difficult for the industry to arrive at a common position on the specific remedy for the northeastern problem.[29] Eventually it decided it could live with a government-planned reorganization of the bankrupt northeastern lines if it were accompanied by subsidies to railroads outside the northeast as well. One point the industry had no trouble reaching agreement on, however, was that the time had come to go beyond regional measures. Whatever solution was chosen for the northeast, the industry was determined to press for a far-reaching revision of the whole federal regulatory framework administered by the ICC.[30]

FEDERAL RAIL POLICY IN THE 1970s

The Nixon administration wanted free enterprise solutions to the railroads' financial problems. Short of the drastic expedient of letting the railroads totally abandon passenger service and stop freight service to many communities across the nation, no free enterprise, income-based solution was to be had. One way or another the government would have to subsidize the railroads. The political problem of the administration was to find the least objectionable way to disburse these subsidies.

The first technique chosen involved allowing the railroads to unload (as the industry called it) their unprofitable passenger service (and hence a large part of their annual deficits) onto the public treasury. This was accomplished by the creation of a quasi-public, for-profit company, the National Railroad Passenger Corporation, or Amtrak. This company, according to the administration's original proposal, would receive government subsidies during a period of transition but would legitimize them by holding out the promise that it would one day make a profit and repay the money it had been lent by the government. Amtrak would not own any tracks or terminals, nor would it initially own any rolling stock. It would lease the equipment it needed from the existing rail companies on a basis that would guarantee them a profit on the service. The rail unions were assured that the choice was either Amtrak or the cessation of service in most of the nation. Congress was told by Secretary of Transportation John Volpe, "With sufficient capitalization, a new quasi-public corporation. . . has a good chance of becoming a sound and successful enterprise."[31] The administration's plan passed both houses of Congress without a roll call vote and was signed into law (PL 91-518) by the president on October 30, 1970. Amtrak ran its first train on May 1, 1971.

The legal character and the question of policy control of Amtrak are complex. The company's structure and relations with the government and the rail industry reflect the transaction that was the raison d'être for Amtrak, the unloading of the passenger deficit. The new corporation was authorized to contract with the private companies to assume their passenger service. For the privilege of unloading its deficit on Amtrak, a rail company was charged a one-time only buy-in fee in proportion to the size of its deficit.

In return for this entry fee, and in addition to relief from the deficits, the rail companies were offered either common stock in Amtrak or a tax deduction equal to the amount of the fee. Most railroads took the tax deduction; only four roads that had large carryover losses and did not need further deductions took the stock. Besides this common stock, which had a par value of $10 per share and was issued only to railroads, the law authorized the issuance of preferred stock at $100 per share to the general public if and when the company's profit picture improved enough to warrant it. None has as yet been issued. The United States government does not own any stock in Amtrak. Thus, to the degree that stock ownership indicates ownership, Amtrak may be said to be owned by the four railroads.[32]

But in the case of this quasi-public corporation, stock ownership does not indicate policy control. The law provided for a fifteen-member board of directors, later raised to seventeen. Four are chosen by the common stockholders, three presently vacant places will be filled by representatives of the preferred stockholders if there ever are any, and the president of the United States appoints ten, including the secretary of transportation, who is an ex officio board member. None of the appointees named by the president may have any direct or indirect relationship with any private rail company, and none of the railroad directors may vote on any proposal concerning any contract between Amtrak and any railroad. One presidential appointee must always be the secretary of transportation,and one must be a consumer representative. In addition to the president's power to appoint a majority of the board of directors, the Department of Transportation was given the authority to pick the routes to be included in the Amtrak system. Congress retains the right to confirm the president's nominees, appropriate monies, and change the details of the governing statutes, which they have done several times, as, for example, when they required Amtrak to operate a new experimental route every year.

Amtrak began operating trains on May 1, 1971, with initial grants from the federal government of $40 million and $300 million in loans and loan guarantees. The administration's optimistic expectations that the new quasi-public corporation would be cheap to operate were soon dashed with mounting deficits. Between 1971 and 1979 Amtrak received over $3.2 billion in public funds. The annual subsidy for 1979 alone was $755 million, which included $600 million for operating expenses, $130 million for capital expenditures, and $25 million for repayment of guaranteed loans.[33] The transportation results achieved by Amtrak were disappointing. While it did preserve the skeleton of a national rail passenger system, it did not achieve any dramatic resurgence of rail passenger transportation. Buses and airplanes continued to be far more important carriers of intercity fare passengers. Few travelers were diverted from automobiles onto Amtrak trains. By 1979 the Department of Transportation was forced to recommend sharp cutbacks in the route mileage and number of trains run by Amtrak in an attempt to hold down the mounting deficit.[34] How much of the route reductions Congress will allow remains to be seen.

Most of Amtrak's early expenditures flowed into the accounts of the private rail companies, but it did not seem to help the neediest among them very much. As rail earnings dropped, rail executives began sounding a new note in their public pronouncements—a financial crisis was at hand, and only federal action could bring relief to this vital but beleaguered industry. As if to underline the industry's statements, the giant Penn-Central corporation filed for bankruptcy in 1970, joining five other smaller northeast railroads. The problems in the northeast were hurting the more profitable roads in the south and west. It was unthinkable that the rail system in the region simply be liquidated—the communities affected would not stand for it. But there did not appear to be any income-based reorganization of the northeast system that could take place without massive public subsidies.

The individual states in the northeast were already subsidizing many of the commuter lines of the bankrupt roads in the area and were not prepared to deal with a regionwide problem of this sort. The attention of the highest policy-making circles of the executive branch was focused mainly on foreign policy, the forthcoming elections, and later on Watergate. Therefore Congress became the branch left with finding a solution to the rail crisis. That august body was pushed along at what was for it a breakneck speed by the events of the crisis itself. The Penn-Central management declared on several occasions that, unless public subsidies were forthcoming, they would have to stop service. At one point the federal bankruptcy court threatened the same stoppage because continued deficit operations were eroding the creditors' equity in the corporation.

Under this severe pressure from the bankruptcy proceedings, and amidst a rising clamor from the railroads, the rail unions, the financial interests, and the local and state governments of the region, Congress produced the Regional Rail Reorganization Act of 1973 (PL93-236), known as the 3R act, which extended the policy of unloading railroad costs onto the public treasury. In this instance the costs so unloaded were the costs of keeping the bankrupt railroads going until the reorganization could be accomplished, the costs of any dispute in the valuation of assets transferred to the reorganized corporation, some—perhaps most—of the costs of capital improvements in the northeast rail system over a period of years, the costs of operating unprofitable lines (these to be jointly paid by the federal and state governments), and the costs of the generous labor-protective provisions of the act.

This act created two new organizations. The first, the United States Railway Association (USRA), an independent federal agency, was authorized to carry out the reorganization of the bankrupt rail properties, the valuation and transfer of their assets, and the planning of the routes for the reorganized rail system in the northeast. The second, the Consolidated Rail Corporation, was to be a for-profit corporation that would eventually be just like any other railroad. But until its debt to the government falls below 50 percent of its total indebtedness, the president retains the power to appoint the majority of the corporation's board of directors. Conrail was to be funded by USRA loans; 1976 was fixed as the deadline for all reorganization work to be completed and for Conrail to be in business.[35]

The 3R act thus laid the foundation for a government-subsidized solution to the northeast railroad problem. Of course a great deal of detailed and intricate work needed to be done to actually implement the planned solution. The USRA reorganized the assets and finances of the bankrupt railroads and planned the new system. The Department of Transportation and the Rail Services Planning Office of the ICC reviewed the plans. The Supreme Court heard suits by the railroads' creditors and found the 3R act to be constitutional. Railroads in other parts of the country discovered they were in financial trouble too and requested their share of federal aid. Congress held hearings with a view toward enacting legislation that would prevent the Penn-Central palsy from spreading to the rest of the nation's railroads. During this upsurge in public activity in the rail policy area the industry itself wanted to make certain that the government did not try to use the subsidies it would be granting as the opening wedge of planning for a consolidated national rail system. Its position was expressed by Stephen Ailes, president of the Association of American Railroads, to a House subcommittee holding hearings on the USRA's final system plan:

It is important, however, that care be taken to see to it that financial assistance is not conditioned upon governmental conceptions and notions as to how the railroad system should be restructured or "rationalized"—how the railroad map should be redrawn, what mergers and consolidations should take place, etc. There is no doubt that restructuring and rationalization of the railroad industry is desirable and, in the long range, important. But financial assistance is needed urgently, without delay or inhibiting conditions. It should not be made contingent upon consistency with some "master" plan. . . . Congress should make it clear that the goal—the Congressional purpose—is a railroad industry in private hands and in good physical shape in 1980, and that maximum precaution in the expenditure of federal funds is not a primary consideration.[36]

How well Congress succeeded in obliging the rail industry can be seen in the provisions of the legislation it produced, the Railroad Revitalization and Regulatory Reform Act (4R act) of 1976 (PL 94-210). This was an important bill with an industrywide impact. It had three major purposes: to insure the private enterprise character of Conrail, to spread some federal subsidy money to other railroads outside the northeast, and to remove some of the aspects of the regulatory process believed to be hampering the profitability and competitiveness of the rail industry. To ensure a private enterprise character for Conrail, the 4R act made these changes: (1) the composition of the board of directors was changed so that a majority of its eleven members are now private rather than public individuals. The president now appoints only two members and the USRA three. Since the president of USRA is an ex officio member, Conrail's board has the semblance of a public majority, but in fact there is nothing to guarantee coherent policy-making control by any public authority. (2) Instead of financing Conrail exclusively through loans, the USRA was authorized to purchase preferred stock in the corporation; Conrail will not have to pay dividends on this stock until it becomes a profitable corporation. A total of $2.1 billion in start-up funds for Conrail was authorized. (3) The private creditors whose assets are being transferred to Conrail will be given certificates of value in addition to normal securities; these certificates will be guaranteed by the government to be worth the net liquidation value of the assets that went into the reorganized corporation.[37]

The second purpose, wider geographical distribution of aid monies, was achieved by authorization of several other spending programs:

• $1 billion was allocated for government guarantees of loans to railroads at rates of interest substantially below the market rate.

• $600 million was authorized to begin a program of assistance to marginally profitable railroads through government purchase of redeemable preferred stock when the railroad can certify that private financing is not available.

• $360 million was authorized to subsidize the continuation of branch line service that the ICC had approved for abandonment.

• $1.75 billion was made available to improve the facilities in the northeast corridor. Including the Conrail start-up costs, the total authorization of the bill was $6.5 billion.[38]

The third goal was embodied in the regulatory reform provisions of the 4R act. These reforms were designed to modify the way in which the ICC limited the railroads' ability to generate income.[39] In general Congress directed the ICC to develop new rate-making standards that would take better account of the rail companies' need for revenue. Specifically Congress told the commission it could no longer suspend any rate that contributed to the going-concern value of the railroad on the grounds that it was too low nor suspend any rate because it was too high, unless it determined that the railroad making the rate had market dominance in the area covered by the rates. Moreover as an experiment a two-year, no-suspend zone was created in which the commission could not block a 7 percent increase or decrease in rates on the grounds that it was too high or too low. The commission was also directed to allow the introduction of seasonal, regional, and peak period rates designed to raise rates and help prevent periodic shortages of rolling stock. The legislation provided that some services (for example, loading, unloading, reconsignment) which had been included in general tariffs and were not needed by every shipper, could be disaggregated and priced separately. It modified the powers of the railroad rate bureaus to encourage greater competition, gave the ICC the authority to exempt from regulation certain traffic for which competition from unregulated modes was strong, and introduced provisions requiring the commission to speed up its procedures in rate, merger, and service abandonment proceedings to reduce the cost of regulatory lag.[40]

The 3R and 4R acts did not solve the basic problem of the rail industry. Northeastern rail operations continued to be troubled. Conrail's deficit for 1977 was $367 million, and preliminary figures for 1968 indicated the corporation would be more than $400 million in the red. Congress had to appropriate an additional subsidy of $1.2 billion to tide Conrail over until 1983. The USRA warned that this would not be enough. It estimated that Conrail would need $2.6 billion more in subsidies.[41] The rail industry as a whole continued to be plagued with low earnings. In 1977 the industry's profits fell to $347 million, the lowest since 1932.[42] Eleven class I rail companies (excluding Conrail) showed deficits, and three were in reorganization. Spokesmen for the industry continued to preach the need for more legislative action on deregulation. They charged that the ICC had thwarted the intent of the 4R act by "a march toward more regulation" rather than pursuing deregulation as it was supposed to.[43] The cries of the industry were receiving close attention from policy makers as the Department of Transportation and Congress prepared for another deregulation effort in 1979.

The paradox of present-day rail policy is becoming clear: ever more government involvement in the rail industry is inevitable, even if the goal of policy is to free the industry from government restraint. Freedom from government restraint must take the form of reducing the authority of the ICC. But reductions in the commission's authority do not return a commensurate degree of policy discretion to the private companies or to objective market forces. Rather a good proportion of this policy discretion is transferred to other public agencies, such as congressional committees, the Department of Transportation, and the USRA. The real question is not whether government involvement will be minimized and market forces maximized but what paradigm will guide public choice and whose interests will be served. Will the protective proceduralism of the ICC be replaced by projective public planning? Or will the basically private interests of the rail companies and unions continue to provide the impetus and focus of public policy?

PRIVATE PRIVILEGES, PLANNING, AND PUBLIC POLICY

In *Politics and Markets* Charles E. Lindblom develops an insightful perspective on the manner in which business and government interact to produce policy decisions.[44] He points out that in private enterprise, market-oriented societies a large number of decisions affecting the allocation of resources, jobs, income, and so on, are delegated to businessmen who operate the market system; they make decisions for the whole society in the course of making decisions for their own businesses. The delegation of these decisions does not diminish either their importance or their public character. Hence government cannot be indifferent to how well business performs its functions. A major responsibility of government is to see that business performs its role to the general satisfaction of the community. In such private enterprise systems the government cannot simply command business to perform; it must offer inducements, even special privileges, that take the form of relative freedom from governmental constraint and the ability to exercise strong influence over any public decision affecting the business sector. Lindblom notes that there is often disagreement over the details and extent of the privileges to be accorded because business usually demands more privileges than it needs. Its strongest argument for privilege is that it can simply withhold its services and capital if sufficient inducements are not forthcoming. It rarely comes to that, however. Most of the time a compromise is worked out, since neither business nor government wish to destroy each other. The substance of these compromises slowly shifts over the decades in the direction of less privileged autonomy for business and more involvement and authority for government. At any given time businessmen "predict dire consequences when a new restraint is imposed on them, yet thereafter quickly find ways to perform under it."[45]

This seems to be an apt description of the rail industry's relation with the U.S. government. Railroads are a key service to the American economy. In the past their operation was left to the businessmen in charge of the rail companies. These were not a very savory lot in the last half of the nineteenth century. Partly because of their abuses, and partly because of the chaotic structure of the rail industry, some of the businessmen's privileges (rate setting, cessation of service, eventually union busting) were restricted by federal regulation. The political pressure which brought about regulation was generated largely by other businessmen, both outside (shippers) and inside (executives of weaker railroads) the rail industry. But on the whole businessmen in the rail industry retained many other important (and sometimes counterproductive) privileges. For example, they were permitted to choose to retain their autonomy as executives or owners of a hodgepodge of balkanized and inefficient companies by resisting government-planned consolidation. (If the reader doubts the importance of this privilege to remain on top in familiar corporate surroundings, let him review the story of the byzantine intrigues and the scrambling that took place for positions among the executives in the Penn-Central merger.)[46]

By the 1970s railroad management was demanding new privileges as a condition of continued performance. They had little trouble convincing the government and the general public that certain delegated tasks were not being accomplished satisfactorily: nationwide passenger service, freight service in the northeast and midwest, maintenance of way on many rail lines, and so forth, were all clearly declining to new lows. Rail industry spokesmen blamed the industry's poor performance on lack of sufficient inducements (government overregulation) and on privileges granted to their competitors (subsidies to trucks and barges). By and large the government was inclined to accept this reasoning and set out to restore some of the rail industry's vigor by offering it new privileges. This is the ultimate political meaning of the subsidies and deregulation actions of the 1970s. The political problems involved in extending these two different inducements were the mirror image of each other. Deregulation fit in quite well with general American attitudes toward big government and bureaucratic red tape. The problem was not selling deregulation to the general public but overcoming the opposition of the shippers, who feared it would cost them more money through higher rates, and the ICC which clung to its power and traditions and believed that part of its task was to protect the shippers. Together these two opponents managed to limit the practical impact of the first round of deregulation legislation in the 4R act.[47] Subsidies faced a different political problem. In the American policy paradigm subsidy is not as legitimate a privilege as freedom from regulation. Hence, when the various subsidy programs (Amtrak, Conrail, 4R act) were passed by Congress, it was necessary to pretend that they were only temporary expedients, transitional measures that would be eliminated once the industry was restored to sound financial health. Subsequent experience has shown that the transitional period promises to be of indefinite duration.

The 1980s will undoubtedly see an expansion and intensification of the business-government dialogue over rail policy that began in the 1970s. The report published by the Department of Transportation in October 1978, *A Prospectus for Change in the Freight Railroad Industry*, shows why the dialogue must go on. The Department of Transportation estimates that between 1976 and 1985 the railroad industry will fall between $13.1 billion and $16.2 billion short of the income it needs to provide adequate service.[48] The report finds that government is willing to help the rail industry make up the deficit by changing some of the regulatory policies that hold down the income of railroads and by continued public subsidies. The report also indicates, however, that government expects the rail companies to be more cooperative in responding to government initiatives toward the long-sought goal of consolidation of the industry into a leaner, more rational system and recommends an exemption from federal antitrust laws to any rail companies that join with the secretary of transportation to discuss consolidation plans. The report presented a variety of policy choices available, at least in principle, to remedy the basic weaknesses of the industry. These options were intended to stimulate discussion in the transportation community and to form the basis for hearings held by the Department of Transportation in the winter of 1978 to 1979 in several cities throughout the nation.

The report's options can be classified, as shown in table 3.4, according to the consequences they are likely to have for the rail industry and for the scope of government authority. The first dimension reflects whether the policy choice entails a high or a low degree of structural change within the rail industry. Structural change means changes in the corporate organization, ownership, mode of operation, and enterprise autonomy that would threaten the established privileges of the rail company executives, equity ownership, creditors, customers, and unionized employees. The second dimension is the degree of change in the scope of government authority needed to implement the policy. By scope of authority is understood not only the number and size of institutional

Table 3.4 Options for public policy in shaping rail industry outcomes

Degree of structural change in rail industry	Changes in scope of government authority	
	Low	High
Low	Regulatory reform	Effective intermodal coordination
High	Consolidation	Public ownership

changes to be brought about but also the number, nature, and political influence of the interests that will be affected by a given change. The entries in each cell are but shorthand labels for a number of different, but related, policy choices. For example, within the public ownership cell there are choices that involve different degrees of public ownership of rail facilities, ranging from full nationalization to regional public ownership to public ownership of the right-of-way but not the rolling stock and terminals. Under consolidation would be included such actions as mergers (side by side or end to end), market swaps, purchase of line segments from competing railroads, coordinated abandoments of service, and joint use of track and facilities. The intermodal coordination cell contains such policy options as increasing user charges to truck and barge operators, subsidies to the railroads for right-of-way costs, cutting state and local taxes on rail right of way, more stringent enforcement of weight limits, speed limits, and work rules in trucking, extension of ICC regulation to unregulated carriers, constraint of new technology that competes with the remaining rail traffic, such as coal slurry pipelines. The concrete measures subsumed under regulatory reform would include more streamlining of ICC procedures, provisions for retroactive collection of fare increases if such increases are approved after ICC hearings, a more liberalized definition of market dominance by the ICC, more exemption from antitrust provisions, more experimental no-suspend privileges for rail companies to raise or lower their rates to attract more traffic.

The rail industry's strong preference is for the options in the upper half of the table, choices that imply only a minimal amount of structural change within the rail industry. The industry has already achieved a large measure of satisfaction in the area of regulatory reform and can expect continuing progress as the deregulation movement continues to gain popularity with lawmakers. Rail spokesmen have no qualms about calling for greater government regulation of their competitors while demanding less regulation and more subsidies for themselves. They see higher taxes and more constraints on trucks and barges as only fair and justify their prescription in the name of equalizing the conditions of competition among the modes. Conversely they continue to be reluctant to follow the lead of public bodies in the direction of a governmentally planned consolidation of the rail system. Public ownership of railroad companies is still anathema and will be tolerated only as a last resort.

Policy makers in the Department of Transportation would prefer—on the evidence contained in the *Prospectus for Change*—to put most of their efforts into areas where the need for changes in the scope of government authority would be small but the promise of payoffs in improved transportation performance would be great. The department recognizes the immense political difficulties it would encounter if it were to try to shift the balance of competitive advantages away from trucks and

The United States: The Political Economy of Private Ownership

barges and toward railroads. It prefers choices on the left side of the table. It supports regulatory reform but feels that it alone will not be sufficient to restore financial health to the rail industry. Increasing revenues is not enough. Costs must be significantly decreased, and the only way to accomplish this is through significant consolidation measures. The department has indicated it will rely on the authority granted to the secretary under section 401 of the 4R act of 1976. This allows the secretary to develop plans for a more effective structuring of the rail system, to study the savings that would result under such a plan, and to convene, upon request by one or more railroads, conferences of rail and other interested parties to discuss implementation of such plans. Companies attending such conferences will be free of any antitrust liability. Agreements reached between companies as a result of these conferences must be approved by the secretary, who may then urge its adoption by the ICC.[49] The secretary has no power to compel the railroads to discuss consolidation. Whatever is accomplished will have to be purely voluntary and largely a product of the railroad's initiative. As in the past the rail companies can be expected to be reluctant to engage in any large-scale and far-reaching consolidation plans. Thus in the near future the rail policy options most likely to be chosen fall in the upper left-hand cell, regulatory reform. Some marginal policy choices may be made that fall under intermodal coordination, and some slight progress may be made in the direction of consolidation, but these options will be more costly to policy makers than regulatory reform in the sense that they will have to be purchased with concessions in other areas.

Does the comparison with the French rail policy experience hold any lessons that could be useful for understanding the consequences of the choices to be made in the United States in the near future?

Yes, the French experience demonstrates three things that may be valuable to U.S. policy makers. It shows that what might be called the piecemeal path to public ownership is possible, and perhaps even desirable. In France a gradually growing publicly owned system existed in harmony with a slowly shrinking private system for nearly fifty years. This was possible because of the authority with which public officials were able to plan the growth and consolidation of the French rail network to ensure the smooth working of the two components. In addition it shows that a substantial national planning capability can make the transition from a mixed rail system to a publicly owned one relatively smooth if it takes preservation of an extensive national rail system as its goal (rather than shrinking it down to profitable size), and if the planning process takes possible future nationalization into account. Lastly the French experience shows that public ownership does not mean the end of all market incentives and that planners do not have to abandon competition as a tool for achieving their goals. Just as in the United States transport policy makers in France are still attracted to the idea that free and equal competition between modes is the best way to determine the optimal allocation of transport resources. This was the idea behind the reform of the SNCF, the *contrat de programme,* the proposals for the equalization of the infrastructure charges, and the rest. But because of the greater strength of the technocratic tradition in France, officials in Paris know that a transport market unblemished by government intervention where all modes compete on an equal footing for the available traffic can never exist under modern conditions. The government is inextricably involved in the transport system. This does not mean that the ideal of competition must be abandoned. Rather it means that public policy must define the balance, set the conditions of competition, and monitor the operation of the system. To do this successfully requires effective political authority, the tools needed to hew out public policy. This is something the American political system has never readily conceded to transport policy makers in Washington. Ironically, the French with their long tradition of *dirigisme* and public ownership may be better equipped to foster effective and balanced intermodal competition in the transport system than the laissez faire, free enterprise-oriented Americans.

In modern, complex national transportation systems there will always be a dialectical interaction between the two decision-making modes of the market and public policy. No national transportation policy can afford to ignore either method. The market's advantages, when it is operating effectively, are that it is flexible and can adapt rather swiftly to short-term changes in supply and demand, and costs are borne by actors who more or less voluntarily agree to pay them. The recent success of airline deregulation is a good example of benefits of intelligent use of market competition to achieve savings to the public and increase the profits of industry. Public policy's advantages, when it operates effectively, are that it can provide the stability and the long-term perspective that can orient the behavior of others. It can shape and direct the outcome of market process toward the achievement of long-term common goals. The interstate highway system is an outstanding example of policy shaping the transport environment. If only the traditional market criteria were used to evaluate toll roads, most of the interstate system's mileage would never have been built.

Public policy making for the restoration and preservation of an efficient U. S. rail system may rightly make use of the reintroduction of market incentives through deregulation as part of a process of achieving a more desirable competitive balance. But U. S. policy should not stress deregulation at the expense of developing the consolidation and planning capabilities of the public authorities. In the nineteenth century it was tolerable to have a conception of the public interest in rail policy that amounted to little more than the maintenance—by market competition or regulation—of a balance of power between the rail companies and the shippers. Changing technology and changing social conditions have created the need for a broader vision of the public interest in transportation and for more effective public authority to achieve that interest. It will be necessary to go beyond shibboleths on the evils of nationalization and the virtues of competition. All the signs point to the fact that the public treasury is going to fund an increasing proportion of the capital requirements of the rail industry. The federal government should follow the French example and use this leverage to design a rail system that will serve broader publicly defined goals as well as the narrowly defined goals of the rail companies and unions. This will not be easy to do in a political system that lacks the traditions of technocratic planning and public enterprise present in France. The American tendency has been to temporize and stumble from one crisis to the next. The costs of this style of policy making are increasingly obvious. Whether the style can be changed without a new and greater crisis is not clear. It is reasonable to predict that the transportation environment of the twenty-first century will not be as forgiving of policy failures as in the past. Failure to make effective use of public authority now to adapt the rail system to national needs will probably bring on the crises that will force us to use that authority later.

II
MASS TRANSIT

INTRODUCTION TO PART II

Today European transit systems excite envy and admiration in American visitors accustomed to cities where the automobile is rampant and public transportation shoddy at best or nonexistent. The press is full of articles exulting the high quality of public transportation in Europe, and a field trip to the Paris metro or the Stockholm subway has become a relatively common perk for U.S. transit professionals.[1] It was not always so. Seventy years ago the United States led the world in mass transit development. There were more miles of track, more passengers, more revenues, more new equipment in America than anywhere, and study tours went to New York and Chicago, not London and Munich. The intervening years, the years of the automobile, have been cruel to the American mass transit system. The system was allowed to deteriorate shamefully, with very little public concern until the last ten or fifteen years. In the early 1970s the impetus to rebuild became widespread. However, some of the initial hopes for a rapid renaissance of mass transit were soon dissipated in public debates. The parties to the debate offer conflicting criticisms and policy recommendations depending on which of two paradigms of public choice they use to interpret the problem.

These two different paradigms may be identified as the market paradigm and the social subsidy paradigm. The market model, which was long paramount in America and still has a strong appeal, holds that transport services are economic goods. Where there is sufficient demand, investors and entrepreneurs will find it profitable to produce the services. When demand for a particular type of transport service declines, they will no longer risk their capital to produce it, and, if demand falls low enough, the service will eventually no longer be produced at all. If left to function according to its own laws, the market will make the optimal allocation of resources among different modes of transportation. The more competition among modes and among firms, the better off everyone, producers, consumers, and taxpayers, will be. Government attempts to continue providing transport services in the face of declining demand and rising costs are uneconomic and doomed to futility. Public intervention almost always causes transport to be more costly, less profitable, and less efficient than if the transport sector were left alone.[2]

The social subsidy paradigm holds that transport is too important to the life of the community to be left in the hands of private firms interested merely in making a profit. Given the scale of modern urban life, public transportation is an essential public service, like fire and police protection or public education, which should be made available to all citizens, especially those least able to afford or use private automobile transportation. Moreover public transport can be an effective tool for achieving other social goals such as regional development and environmental protection. Urban amenity requires that city dwellers not be forced to rely totally on the private automobile for mobility. The public authorities must intervene, by subsidies and other steps if necessary, to assure that public transport is available to aid the community in achieving its broader goals.[3]

Since the first urban mass transit act was passed in 1964, and especially since the $10 billion long-term federal aid program enacted under the Urban Mass Transit Assistance Act of 1970, the United States has moved toward adopting a version of the social subsidy paradigm for urban transit. Policy debate and persuasion led to some rather high expectations among the social subsidy model's proponents and perhaps in part of the public as well. These expectations, as outlined in the secretary of transportation's 1975 Statement of National Transportation Policy include "the enhancement of our cities as vital commercial and cultural centers, control of air pollution, conservation of energy, access to transportation for all citizens and particularly the disadvantaged, facilitation of full employment and more rational use of land."[4]

In West Germany the social subsidy paradigm has traditionally had much greater intellectual acceptance than in the United States, but its institutional expression had been confined to the local and Land ("state") level. Since the mid-1960s the West German federal government has also moved to assume important financial and policy responsibilities in the country's urban transit systems.

Its policies have been even more clearly derived from the social subsidy paradigm than those of the U.S. government. Nearly simultaneous decisions by the federal governments of these two urban, industrial, democracies to become more deeply involved in urban transit problems provides an instructive comparison for U.S. policy analysts. West Germany's experience with a federal urban transit policy based on the social subsidy paradigm can, with careful and skeptical analysis, offer useful lessons for U.S. policy. First, and probably least important, insofar as the West German government uses policy tools unfamiliar in the United States, we may better appreciate the benefits and drawbacks of those tools and the problems likely to be encountered if they were adopted here. More significantly, because the German experience has been more successful than the American, it can suggest organizational and socioeconomic conditions that are prerequisites for the success of urban transit policies. Finally, it can provide instruction on the political conditions that limit the application of even relatively successful urban transit policies.

4
WEST GERMANY: THE LIMITS OF SUBSIDY

WEST GERMAN PUBLIC TRANSPORTATION

Private industry played an important role in establishing the urban transit industry in Germany. Indeed the electrification of the *Pferde-Eisenbahnen* ("horse railways") provided the major impetus for the growth of the German electrical and electric traction industries that soon were exporting equipment all over the world. But the rights of private transit entrepreneurs were never so extensive nor so long-lasting as they were in America. When the German transit companies were established, they were given municipal charters for a long but fixed period, normally forty or fifty years. Upon expiration of the concession all of the fixed property of the enterprise (tracks, transmission lines, buildings) was to become the property of the city without any further payment. The city also retained the option to purchase all the movable property (streetcars, office equipment) at its fair market value as determined by a panel of impartial experts.[1] Thus the rights of property were seen as limited and contingent at the outset. The goal of the process was viewed as providing the city and its citizens with valuable transportation services and only incidently as opportunities for private gain. Profit would be permitted of course, but it would not be the ultimate yardstick by which the industry would be governed.

American observers in this period always remarked on this difference of outlook. One visitor wrote, "The thing that distinguishes the cities of the Old World from those of the New is a difference in point of view. European cities have a highly developed community sense. The rights of the public are superior to the rights of the individual. When a conflict arises, the community is paramount."[2] Even before World War I a number of German cities operated their streetcars as municipal departments. In the chaotic years that followed many more took total or partial ownership of their transit systems. By the time of the emergence of the West German Federal Republic in 1949 virtually every large- and medium-sized German city had a transit system under the control of local authorities rather than private entrepreneurs.

Today publicly owned transit firms move by far the largest number of passengers and have the greatest number of employees, as shown in table 4.1. Publicly owned transit companies operate under a variety of legal forms and control ranging from being outright city departments to mixed economy companies with a public body holding a controlling portion of the equity stock. They are organized into a national association called the Verband Öffentlicher Verkerhrsbetriebe (VÖV), ("Association of Public Transport Enterprises") which includes the commuter lines of the German federal railways, the rail and bus lines of 66 nonfederal but publicly owned railways, the federal post office bus service, and 168 publicly owned transport firms. There are 4,900 privately owned transport firms, usually small bus companies, that continue to play a role in some aspects of urban and especially interurban transport. The private firms are organized into the Bundesverband des Deutschen Personenverkehrsgwerbes ("National Association of German Passenger Transport Businesses"). Table 4.1 shows the sizes of the different components of the urban public transport sector in terms of the number of persons employed, the number of paying passengers, and the number of passenger-kilometers produced.

Table 4.1 The structure of the public transport industry in West Germany (1975)

Type of industry	Employees (thousands)	Paying passengers (millions)	Passenger-kilometers (billions)
Publicly owned municipal transport company	87.2	4,833.8	25,538.6
Federal railways	394.9	1,599.5	44,582.0
Commuter lines	—	324.0	4,182.2
Local lines (under 50 km)	—	582.6	10,914.5
Intercity (over 50 km)	—	94.2	21,617.4
Railroad buses	—	592.7	7,867.9
Post office buses	461.6[a]	427.8	5,628.1
Nonfederal railways	22.4	584.5	4,895.0
Rail lines	13.4	74.5	680.0
Bus lines	8.5	510.0	4,215.0
Private transport companies	31.1[b]	818.8	27,700.6
Total		8,258.4	108,344.3

Source: Adapted from Manfred Zachcial, *Unternehmensgrössenprobleme im Verkehrssektor* (Göttingen: Verlag Otto Schwarz, 1976), pp. 112–113.
[a]Total post office employees.
[b]Figure for 1973.

The major trend in passenger transport in West Germany, as in all western nations, has been the tremendous growth of individual automobile travel in recent years. Auto travel was fifteen times greater in 1974 than in 1950, as shown in table 4.2. A second important trend to note in this table is that despite auto travel growth public transit has more than doubled in the same period. This is a far cry from the public transport situation in the United States. This ability to increase substantially the number of passenger-kilometers it produces constitutes the remarkable achievement of the West German public transport system. It is true that much of the increase came in the 1950s and early 1960s when auto ownership was much lower than it is now, but even in the 1970s public transit's traffic has been rising.

Within the public transport sector there have been some significant shifts between transport modes. Passengers have stopped riding streetcars and started riding buses. Data from the VÖV show that, while the total number of public transport vehicles increased by a modest 6 percent between 1960 and 1975, the number of buses rose by 84 percent and the number of streetcars declined by 45.6 percent. In 1960 streetcars made up nearly half of the total vehicle fleet, but fifteen years later they constituted only one-fifth. Buses rose from 40 percent of the fleet to 70 percent.[3] The same picture holds true when the trend is measured in terms of vehicle- or seat-kilometers.

Even though the bus sector is the major growth area in West German public transit, it exhibits some interesting within-sector differences between publicly owned and privately owned bus transport enterprises. The vast majority of bus companies are privately owned. In 1972 this meant that 4,744 of the total 4,981 bus firms in West Germany were private. These firms were much smaller than the publicly owned ones, hav-

Table 4.2 Trends in passenger transport in West Germany (1950–1974)

Billions of passenger-kilometers				Percent of total		
1950	1970	1974	Transport mode	1950	1970	1974
85	491	560	Total passenger travel	100	100	100
57	107	118	Total public transport	67	22	21
32	38	39	Railroads	38	8	7
25	60	66	Streetcar, bus, and taxi	29	12	12
—	9	13	Airplane	—	2	2
28	384	442	Automobile and motorcycle	33	78	79

Source: Bundesminister für Verkehr, *Verkehrspolitik '76: Grundsatzprobleme und Schwerpunkte,* p. 18.

West Germany: The Limits of Subsidy

ing only 21.8 percent of the total number of employees in the bus sector, while the public firms employed 78.2 percent. Private firms received 31.2 percent of the total revenue generated by bus transport, however. The reason for this is not, as one might be tempted to suppose, that the free enterprise firms are more efficient and less top heavy with administrators and nonproductive personnel. The same study shows that public and private bus firms have about the same proportion of employees in administration. In fact the public firms have a slightly lower percent, 8.7 compared to 10.9 percent for private.[4] The big difference in income and profitability lies in the kind of transport service each firm specializes in. The public firms are required by law to operate regularly scheduled lines, as well as special schoolbus and workbus services. This type of bus service moves by far the bulk of passengers (89 percent of the total), but it produces only 46 percent of the revenue. What the Germans call *Gelegenheitsverkehr,* charter buses, holiday trips, package tours, and other tourist trade transport, carries only 11 percent of the passengers. But because of its higher load factor and longer average trip, this type of service produces 54 percent of the total income generated in the bus sector.[5] German transport regulations discourage publicly owned firms from concentrating their efforts in this lucrative field and hence private bus companies win most of this type of highly profitable business.

The financial situation of public transit has worsened considerably in recent years. In 1970 the total deficit of all public transit in West Germany was 2.6 billion DM. By 1974 this deficit had risen to 5.2 billion DM.[6] In view of the decline in rail-bound transit patronage it is not surprising that rail-related public transport is the biggest money loser in the entire transport sector. In 1974 the commuter railroads of the German federal railways lost 3.5 billion DM. Some of the 1.7 billion DM that was lost by the other German public transport association enterprises is attributable to their rail operation. In 1974 the receipts of publicly owned transport firms covered only 59 percent of their expenses. Of course a large share of the responsibility for this cash shortfall lies with the authorities who set fares and schedules. In the name of general mobility and urban amenity they often insist on maintaining unprofitable frequency in scheduling, and in the name of social concern they grant special discount fares to various groups in the community (the handicapped, school children, university students, apprentices, commuters, and so forth). One study calculated that a regular full-fare ticket covered 97.8 percent of its cost. At the other end of the spectrum, however, a school child's ticket covered only 37 percent of its cost.[7] While public power has been holding down the cost of tickets, and hence the total incomes of the transit enterprises, it has been ineffective in holding down costs. The main cost growth has been the cost of labor. Between 1963 and 1973 the average wage in the transit industry rose 113.2 percent, while the average income per passenger-kilometer rose only 36.5 percent.[8]

LOCAL GOVERNMENT'S RESPONSE OF
MORE COORDINATION

Since local governments were the first to feel serious financial pressure from transit's mounting deficits, they attempted to respond, within the limits of their authority, by more efficient coordination of transit operations and planning. One development along these lines that attracted worldwide attention was the institution of the *Verkehrsverbund* ("Transport Federation"). The aim of this new form of association was to overcome the fragmentation of transport enterprises and authorities that existed within the metropolitan areas of Germany, as it did in most U.S. metro areas. The undesirable consequences of fragmentation will be familiar to many readers, having been well described at great length in most of the U.S. transport policy literature: inefficiency, duplication of effort, lack of adequate area coverage, difficulties in agreements among the jurisdictions, and so forth. In West Germany transport planners could point to a need for coordination and integration of transport services as a precondition for providing adequate, not to say improving, public transportation. The *Verkehrsverbund* was seen as a very positive step in this direction. The first and most widely studied federation was created in Hamburg in the mid-1960s. Other German cities have since followed suit, but since Hamburg's has the longest- and best-documented experience in the field, we will consider its efforts in some detail.[9]

The free and hanseatic city of Hamburg is West Germany's second largest city with a city population of over 1.7 million and a metropolitan area population of over 2.5 million. Hamburg is also a German *Land* although its total land area is only 250 square miles. Its status as a city-state gives Hamburg several unusual advantages for transport planning and coordination. First, since it has the tax resources of both a city and a state, Hamburg already had a high degree of financial independence, all the more because Hamburg has the highest per capita income of all German *Länder*. Second, its relatively large (for a German metro area) geographical size meant that it already had a larger than usual suburban population within its borders, which reduced the need for cross-jurisdictional coordination. But this relatively favorable situation did not insulate Hamburg from the general transportation trends and problems that Germany experienced in the late fifties and sixties. During a fourteen-year period from 1954 to 1968 the number of passenger cars per 1,000 population increased five times, while transit riding, measured in terms of annual trips per capita, declined by 23 percent.[10] It appeared that Hamburg was on the threshold of a disastrous plunge in public transit usage, with the inevitable accompaniment of serious auto congestion and environmental degradation. Early in the 1960s city officials began negotiations with representatives of the area's transport enterprises, with a view toward creating a more integrated transport system. The major transit carrier, the Hamburg Hochbahn A.G., which ran the subways and elevated commuter lines, was controlled by the city government which owned 85 percent of its shares. The second largest carrier, the S-bahn, was operated by the German federal railways. Together these two carriers accounted for 94 percent of all the public transit passengers in the city. But despite this dominating position of publicly owned transit, the preparation of the legal, organizational, financial, and technical groundwork for the transport federation took nearly five years. The Hamburg Verkehrsverbund (HVV) came into existence at the end of 1965. The details of its organization are complex and have been well described elsewhere.[11] What is of concern here are the results achieved by this local level attempt to improve the situation of public transport through administrative reorganization and policy coordination. Data made available by the HVV indicate that despite a continued rise in car ownership the decline in public transit trips has been halted.[12] The number of transit rides has been stabilized at a level just below 600 million trips per year. Ridership figures show that the greatest success has been, as one would expect, in the area of bus transport, which increased the number of passengers carried by 43 percent between 1967 and 1975. Buses won more passengers than the streetcars lost and thus constitute the only significant growth area for the Hamburg transit federation.

Beyond mere numbers of passengers carried, most observers agree that the federation has made significant progress in modernizing transportation facilities and streamlining operations. It established a single fare system based on the distance traveled, regardless of how many different types of transport are used. Ticket sales have been automated, schedules coordinated, express bus services instituted, park and ride facilities created, and so forth. The transport federation may certainly be said to have facilitated the measures aimed at improving the marketability of public transport. But many of these same measures could have been carried out even in the absence of the federation. Against the indisputable achievements of making public transit more attractive and halting the decline of ridership, one must weigh the fact that the Hamburg transit federation has not been able to escape the universal trend to growing financial deficits. In 1975 the HVV's income was 340 million DM, but the expenses of its members amounted to 518 million DM. Thus despite an 18 percent increase in fares at the beginning of the year 35 percent of the HVV's operating budget had to come from public subsidies.[13] The federal government pays for the deficit of the federal railways, while the *Land* of Hamburg covers the remaining deficit.

In effect the Hamburg experiment with increased local level coordination can be said to be reasonably successful in transit ridership. This success has caused the transport federation device and related concepts to be widely studied and spread to other German metropolitan areas.[14] Nevertheless, the burden of financing these efforts to maintain high levels of urban transit services has become too heavy for local and state governments to bear alone. They have increasingly turned to the federal government for fiscal aid and policy leadership.

THE FEDERAL ROLE IN URBAN TRANSIT POLICY

The West German federal government's responsibility for the commuter rail lines of the German federal railways, as well as for the extensive system of railway and post office buses means that it was involved in urban mass transit policy from the time of the Federal Republic's creation in 1949. Nevertheless, it was not until the mid-1960s that the federal government began direct financial aid to municipal transport enterprises. The first step toward more direct federal contact with local transport enterprises and authorities was taken in 1961 with the creation of a committee of experts charged with examining the causes of mass transit's financial difficulties, which were beginning to become worrisome.[15] The report of this committee led to the creation of a permanent advisory body, the Joint Commission of Federal, State, and Local Organizations for the Improvement of the Situation of Local Transport, which was charged with making recommendations and trying to see that they were carried out. It had no powers to compel compliance, however.

When the Social Democrats (SPD) entered the federal cabinet for the first time in 1965 as part of the grand coalition with the Christian Democrats (CDU/CSU), they received the transport ministry as one of their portfolios and were in a position to press for more direct and substantive federal action on behalf of public transport. The mass transit system after all directly benefited the working classes, the larger cities, and the union members working in transit—all strong supporters of the SPD. The first result of the social democratic pressure appeared in the provisions of the Tax Amendment Law of 1966. This imposed an additional 3 pf per liter tax on gasoline. (At the rate of exchange then prevailing, this would amount to about 2.8 cents per gallon.) The proceeds from this new tax were earmarked (*Zweckgebunden*) for the dual purposes of financing improvements in local roads and aiding public transit. According to the guidelines laid down in 1967 for the use of these funds, 60 percent of the receipts were to go for road aid and 40 percent to aid public transit. Between 1967 and 1971 local mass transit firms received some 1.75 billion DM from these specially earmarked gas taxes.[16]

In 1969 the Social Democrats won enough new seats in the national elections to be able to break out of their role as junior partners of the Christian Democrats. They were able to form a majority with the smaller Free Democrats (FDP). This gave a strong impetus to policy reform in many fields of foreign and domestic policy, including transportation. The social democratic transport minister, Lauritz Lauritzen, was determined to meet Germany's urban transport need with an extension of the federal government's involvement in the area. The still-growing financial deficits were being piled up by urban transit systems, and the federal railways did not seem to present an insuperable obstacle to these ambitions. He was convinced that public transport's financial situation had to be viewed from a new perspective. In a position paper that proved to be a classic statement of the rationale for a social subsidy paradigm applied to urban transit, Lauritzen explained:

Financial profitability at any price and insistence on being able to compete in a market which does not truly exist in urban transport should not be set up as the general goals of public transport enterprises. Rather, public transport must be assigned a place in the democratically understood conceptions of modern city planning and land use planning. If this should lead to the need for greater public expenditures, it can be done by way of compensating public transport enterprises for the general social burdens they must bear.[17]

The first legislative expression of these sentiments was the Community Transport Finance Act, which took effect on January 1, 1971. This altered the allocation ratio for the earmarked gasoline taxes from 60:40 to 55:45, for local road projects and transit aid, respectively. The next step was taken with the Transport Finance Act of 1971. This act doubled the tax on gasoline earmarked for local transportation, to 6 pf per liter. In addition it again changed the allocation ratio in favor of public transit, to 50:50. (In 1977 the ratio was changed still further to 45:55 for mass transit.) It also provided that the federal government would pay up to 60 percent of the cost of construction of a new public transport facility, and in areas along the border with East Germany the federal government would pay 75 percent of the cost. The Social Democrats also promoted several other policy changes designed to aid transit. For example, public transit buses were exempted from paying any annual vehicle taxes, and federal legislation was passed making it easier for local communities to cooperate in forming transport federations.[18]

Federal aid funds earmarked for local transit under the Community Transport Finance Act increased by 430 percent in eight years, from 253 million DM in 1967 to 1.1 billion DM in 1975.[19] But this was only a part of the total federal expenditure for urban transit. The subsidies granted to the federal railways commuter lines and bus lines, as well as those to the post office buses, also must be counted as part of federal expenditures for urban transit. Table 4.3 shows the total subsidy effort being made by the federal, state, and local governments. The federal government pays out about two-thirds of the subsidies received by urban transit. The 9.1 billion DM received by the transit industry in 1975 represents approximately 150 DM for every man, woman, and child in West Germany. Expressed in terms of dollars at the 1975 rate of exchange, that is a total of some $3.8 billion, or $62.40 per capita. Compare this with the American 1975 effort to subsidize mass transit where all levels of government spent $5.6 billion, or some $26.14 per capita.[20]

Table 4.3 Subsidies to urban public transport in West Germany by type of subsidy and level of government (1975)[a]

Type of subsidy	Level of government		Total
	Federal	State and local	
Commuter rail	3,478	1,022	4,500
Tax exemptions for public transit firms	899	218	1,117
Coverage of operating deficits of public transit firms	1,525	2,000	3,535
Subsidies to private transit firms	—	Data not yet available	—
Total	5,902	3,240	9,142

Source: Bundesminister für Verkehr, mimeo sheet, 1977.
[a] In millions of DM.

Changing economic conditions soon called into question the German government's ability to finance its open-ended commitment to public transit. The oil embargo and subsequent business recession led to reduced auto traffic and increased reliance on public transit. But they also led to a virtual stagnation of the tax revenues on gasoline earmarked for public transit. The period saw what many German writers refer to as a "cost explosion" in public transport, fueled largely by the very rapid increase in labor costs which make up 65 to 75 percent of the cost of the average transport enterprise. Eventually the pro-transit Lauritzen was replaced by the more cost-conscious Kurt Gscheidle as SPD minister of transport. Gscheidle cut back the total amount of federal funds planned for capital investment in the urban transport sector in the period 1976 to 1985 from 14.3 billion DM to 11.0 billion DM.[21] The new transport minister was also much less sanguine about the prospects for improving public transport than his predecessor. In an interview with the German news magazine, *Der Spiegel,* he seemed to suggest that public transport's principal function was keeping enough potential auto drivers off the streets at rush hour to make it possible to keep traffic flowing:

. . . if we let individual (auto) traffic grow even further in built-up areas, it would block itself . . . the whole enormous subsidy, over a billion marks per year that the federal government gives to public transit, in addition to what the states give . . . is being paid in order to have public transportation available in metropolitan areas. Only in this manner can individual traffic be maintained at all.[22]

Minister Gscheidle clearly sees his duty as consisting of reducing the financial burden of transport on the federal budget in the face of a mounting fiscal crisis. His budget cuts have not been limited to urban transit, however. He has proposed plans for the financial cure of the federal railways and even gone as far as to slow down the construction of the *Autobahnen*. He sees the solution to the problems of urban transit not in even more subsidies from government but in reorganization of the legal, institutional, and organizational structure of urban transport to achieve more coordination and greater efficiency. The principal thrust of Gscheidle's plan is to be the creation of new regional transit associations (*Nahverkerhrsverbände*) that will further consolidate the planning, financing, and oversight powers for local public transport. Improving the quality and performance of public transit would be an important goal of these transit associations, but as a report on the proposal frankly admits, "Above all, the new organization should lead to a more secure financial basis and a limitation of public transit's financial losses, especially those of the federal railways and the post office."[23]

In West Germany's system the federal government cannot bring about such a reorganization and regionalization of public transport without the approval of the states. The states are afraid that Gscheidle's proposals will lead to financial relief for the federal government but not for them. They suspect that the plan is an attempt to shift the deficit of the federal railway's commuter trains and the post office buses onto their budgets. Then they will be forced to either subsidize ever-growing deficits or agree to widespread cessations of service. This may provide financial relief for the federal government but will not help the *Länder* much. In addition the *Länder* believe that the plan slights the goal of improving public transport in favor of the goal of saving money (which it does). It is not surprising therefore that Gscheidle has had a difficult time getting the plan accepted by the *Länder*.[24]

The Social Democrats' pursuit of the social subsidy model of transport policy appears to have reached an impasse. The mounting deficits are becoming politically indefensible, yet the solution of cutting back on service also creates serious political difficulties. Transport decision makers have fallen back on trying to save money through economic rationalization and organizational reorganization. But rationalization (efficiency measures) has already taken place in the bulk of transport enterprises and does not offer much help. Nor does reorganization seem to be a solution. A politically acceptable reorganization plan tends to become just a paper shuffle and thus has no substantial impact. On the other hand, if the plan does offer a substantial impact (for example, shifting the railways' deficits from the federal budget to the *Länder*), it is bitterly resisted by the interests and jurisdictions to be affected.

Except for a few months during the fall and winter of 1973 to 1974, West German governments, even socialist ones, have shrunk from any policies aimed at actively discouraging individual automobile use. Of course there are German critics of the auto who say that public power should be used to restrain the explosive growth of individual transport.[25] The social costs of automobiles in West Germany's congested, urban society are too great. The state should use its taxing power to make the purchase of private autos and fuel so expensive that people would increasingly turn to public transport because it would be so much cheaper. To such critics SPD Transport Minister Gscheidle responded:

I do not know what kind of a policy that is supposed to be, making autos so expensive that they could only be used by people with a lot of money. Of the 20 million auto owners in the Federal Republic, three-quarters are workers. . . . I do not believe that in a democratic state, in welfare society, we could tell a potential auto buyer that he may not own a car—after 20 million people already have one.[26]

In a major summary of the principles of transport policy followed under his administration Gscheidle named as the first and most fundamental principle "Free choice of transport mode." (The other principles were controlled competition between modes, optimal mobility for the citizen and the economy, and an economically sensible division of labor in an integrated total transport system.)[27]

At present the federal transport ministry projects a rather sharp slowdown of the rate of increase in automobile ownership, without the need for drastic government measures to discourage car owning. Its figures show that in the 1960s auto ownership increased 12 percent per year. In the first half of the 1970s this had already fallen to 5.6 percent annually. The ministry projects an auto growth rate of only 1.9 percent per year from 1980 to 1985 and 1.1 percent per year from 1985 to 1990. If these projections are borne out, they would leave the Federal Republic with a relatively low 385 autos per 1,000 population in 1990. This would enable the public transit sector to hold onto its present 19 percent share of the total passenger traffic.[28] Of course these projections are only as good as the assumptions on which they are based. One of the most crucial assumptions built into the ministry's figures is that auto ownership growth rates will sink significantly below the growth rate of the overall GNP, something that has never happened in the thirty-year history of the Federal Republic. It is based on a calculation that a saturation point for autos exists and that the country is now approaching this point. If these assumptions should prove to be incorrect, then public transit would be in for greater difficulties than are already foreseen for it.

No politicians or parties in Germany, indeed in the entire western world, want to take the responsibility for adopting explicit policies denying their citizens the opportunity to own automobiles. If a German social democratic government, with its close ties to the transport workers union and its more paternal and collectivist orientation, is unable to restrain automotive growth, what chance does an American administration have? Such a restrictive policy would be political dynamite which could be tolerated only in the midst of a grave national emergency. The ability to do without the automobile declines with each passing year and each rise in the level of car ownership.

In the past West German policy makers did not have to be concerned with restricting the amount of competition the auto could give the transit system. Not only low levels of auto ownership but also many other factors in the West German transport environments favored transit. Indeed these factors gave West Germany advantages that largely determined the success that transit had there. The absence of these factors in America will make the success of U.S. mass transit policy more difficult.

REASONS FOR TRANSIT'S SUCCESS IN WEST GERMANY

Compared to the United States, West German transport policy benefits from a number of important factors that make coordination and consolidation of mass transit operations easier and ridership more likely. These factors must be taken into account when attempting to predict the likelihood of American mass transit policy having a ridership success similar to West Germany's. If these factors can be duplicated in the American environment, then perhaps they will be preconditions for the success of U.S. mass transit policy. If they can not be duplicated, then perhaps a very pessimistic judgment concerning the future of mass transit in America is called for. The advantages that tend to structure the transportation environment in West Germany in favor of mass transit can be grouped into two classes: socioeconomic and policy-organization.

Socioeconomic Advantages

1. Higher population densities at both the national and the metropolitan levels. West Germany's 61 million inhabitants occupy a land area of 96,000 square miles, which gives the country a density of 637 persons per square mile. The population density of the United States is 60 persons per square mile.[29] To put it another way, the Federal Republic's territory is about the size of the state of Oregon, but its population is 31 times as large as Oregon's. German urban agglomerations have a higher population density as well. The West German federal statistical office has calculated that by 1980, two-thirds of the population will be living on just 7 percent of the land area, giving West German urban agglomerations a population density of about 6,000 inhabitants per square mile.[30] By contrast the U.S. Census Bureau reported that the population density of the urbanized areas in the U.S. was 3,327 people per square mile in 1970.[31]

2. Less advanced suburbanization of metropolitan areas. Table 4.4 shows that in the period from 1950 to 1970 West Germany's central cities

Table 4.4 Distribution of population in metropolitan areas in West Germany and the United States (1950–1970)[a]

	West Germany		United States	
Year	Central city[b]	Outside central city[c]	Central city	Outside central city
1950	65.5	34.5	56.9	43.1
1960	66.9[d]	33.1[d]	50.1	49.9
1970	62.6	37.4	45.8	54.2

Sources: Wanderungsmotive und Stadtstruktur, *Schriftenreihe des Städtebaulichen Instituts der Universitat Stuttgart,* vol. 6 (Stuttgart, 1976); *Statistical Abstract of the United States, 1971* (Washington, D. C.: Government Printing Office, 1972).
[a]Given is the percent of population of metropolitan areas. For the United States the metro area corresponds to the Bureau of the Census Standard Metropolitan Statistical Area (SMSA). For West Germany it is the Stadtregion used by the Bundesministerium für Raumordnung, Bauwesen und Städtebau.
[b]Central city = Kernstadt.
[c]Outside central city = Ergänzungsgebiete, verstädterte Zonen, Randzonen.
[d]These are 1961 figures for West Germany.

retained a larger share of their metropolitan area's population than did U.S. central cities. Between 1950 and 1961, when the suburbanization of American cities was already proceeding very rapidly, West German central cities grew faster than their suburbs and increased their relative proportion of the population. In the 1960s the growth of central cities slowed in Germany, and in the 1970s many West German cities experienced an actual decline in population, with suburban areas continuing to grow rapidly. In fact most West German central cities had negative migration balances among the native-born component of their population since the mid-1960s, but this had been offset by the influx of foreign workers. These guest workers tended to concentrate in the older sections of the central cities (and to rely very heavily on public transportation for mobility, incidentally). When the 1974 recession virtually shut off the flow of foreign workers to West Germany, and unemployment caused many of them to return to their homelands, the population of the central cities took a sudden sharp drop.[32]

3. A style of suburban development more suited to public transit. The decline in the proportion of the population living in central cities is still modest by American standards; the Germans are some thirty years behind the United States here. But even the very real trend toward suburbanization, or deconcentration, taking place is significantly different from the U.S. experience. German suburbs tend to have much higher population densities than American suburbs. 1970 census figures show that West German suburbs (*Ergänzungsgebiete*) had a population den-

sity of 2,605 people per square mile.[33] This is because the single-family detached house is not as dominant in newly built German suburbs as it is in America. It is true that German families, like American families, dream of owning their own home someday. But despite rising real incomes they are not as able to afford a single-family detached home as Americans traditionally have been. Land prices, especially in metropolitan areas, have increased tremendously since the beginning of the 1960s. This has led to a decline in the already low percentage of single-family houses being built in the country and an absolute decline in the number of such houses constructed in cities over 100,000 in population.[34] On the other hand, there has been a boom in the construction of medium- and high-rise buildings specializing in apartments and condominiums (*Eigentumswohnungen*) which are more affordable by the mass of German families. This style of suburb that features high-rise apartments clustered around some stores, shops and a bus stop, and a kilometer of open field followed by another housing cluster is much more suited to the operation of public transit services than the typical American suburb.

4. A lower level of automobile ownership. By world standards West Germany is indeed a highly motorized nation. In 1977 ownership of private automobiles stood at 290 per 1,000 population. U.S. auto ownership in the same year was 500 per 1,000 population. But this high level of motorization is of rather new vintage. As recently as 1960 the number of automobiles per 1,000 population was 81, a level comparable with the U.S. level of 1921.[35] Even West Germany's present automobile ownership does not exceed that of the United States in the mid-1950s. These differences in degree and timing of mass motorization are very significant elements in shaping an environment favorable to mass transit.

Policy-Organization Advantages

1. Greater ease of metropolitan reorganization of local governments. Two of the great themes of the U.S. literature on local government and intergovernmental relations are the difficulties posed by the fragmentation of jurisdictions in metropolitan areas and the slow pace of attempts to overcome this fragmentation. In the Federal Republic metropolitan reform has proceeded much faster. By the early 1970s seven of the eleven German *Länder* had completed or were in the process of carrying out general local government reorganization plans oriented primarily toward the governmental and service delivery needs of metropolitan areas.[36] This has made coordination and consolidation of public transport services easier to achieve in West Germany than in the United States.

2. A longer tradition of public ownership of urban transport enterprises. Most commuter rail lines in Germany came under public own-

ership when Bismark nationalized the Prussian railways in 1878. By the end of the First World War most of the streetcar companies were owned by the municipalities and/or *Länder* they served. As bus transport became increasingly important, publicly owned enterprises entered this field as well. This meant that most key public transit enterprises in Germany were already publicly owned at a time when the vast bulk of the population had no realistic alternative means of transportation. These publicly owned systems and officials to whom they were responsible took it as a matter of course that the public transit would provide a high level of service. They continued to do so even as levels of motorization increased. By contrast, most transit enterprises in the United States now publicly owned were privately owned until the 1960s or 1970s. In 1948 there were only 36 publicly owned urban transit firms in the United States, and these firms accounted for only 25 percent of the industry's total revenue.[37] Today there are nearly ten times as many publicly owned transit enterprises, and they produce almost 90 percent of the industry's operating revenues and nearly 90 percent of the total passenger miles.[38] Public ownership came after a period of sharp decline in ridership, revenue, and service and has often been unable to do more than slow down the decline slightly.

3. A much higher tax on gasoline. This has the effect of raising the marginal cost of operating automobiles to a higher financial and psychological level than in the United States. In 1977, for example, the average price of regular gasoline in West Germany was 86 pf per liter. This equals about $1.42 per gallon. Sixty-one percent of this price was made up of taxes (86.7 cents per gallon compared to an average of 11 cents tax on a 60-cent gallon in the United States—4 cents federal tax and 7 cents state tax). Not only does this raise the cost of operating a car but it also provides the public authorities with more user taxes that can be earmarked for public transit. In the case of West Germany in 1977, 4.8 percent of the total gas tax receipts were earmarked for public transit.[39] This meant that some 4.16 cents per gallon went to public transit—more than the total amount of the 4 cent per gallon federal gasoline tax in the United States.

Thus the performance of the West German urban transit system over the past thirty years has been clearly superior to the record of the American system. Since 1950 the number of riders carried and the number of passenger-kilometers produced by public transit in West Germany have more than doubled. In an age of rapidly expanding auto ownership, simply holding onto riders is an accomplishment. Increasing them is a veritable triumph. Moreover the Germans have been able to modernize the infrastructure of their system and package its product more attractively than is the case in most American cities. They have been able to make use of the full panoply of transport modes from heavy rail commuter trains through light rail, buses, and taxis, in such a way as to offer a viable alternative to the private auto in German cities down to the level of

50,000 population and below. Maintaining this high level of service in the face of rapidly rising costs has become a serious burden on the public treasury, however. The federal transport ministry is attempting to slow the growth of public transit's deficits without cutting back service too drastically. This is proving very difficult to do, and hard choices remain to be faced in the future.

The examination of the West German experience with mass transit policy enables us to conclude that the use of the social subsidy model of urban transport policy makes good sense when it is applied in a timely manner to an urban transit system characterized by high levels of ridership and service in an environment of relatively high population density and low to medium levels of automobile ownership. In this situation a little subsidy can go a long way. It can make the difference between being able to maintain high levels of service and the onset of a declining service, declining patronage spiral. The German experience shows that high levels of ridership can be maintained even in the face of rising auto ownership, although the costs of doing so will rise rapidly too. But the subsidies must be begun before the transit system deteriorates to such an extent that people's travel habits, location decisions, and living patterns adjust to doing without public transport. Once the transit system declines precipitously, it is much more difficult, and much more expensive, to rebuild both the system infrastructure and the habits of reliance upon public transit essential to a high-quality transit system.

5
THE UNITED STATES: SICK TRANSIT, GLORIOUS MONEY

TRANSIT'S DECLINE: DID IT FALL OR WAS IT PUSHED?

The same factors that shaped the development of the railroads influenced the growth of the urban transit industry in the early 1900s: the availability of a new transportation technology, the lack of strong competition from other transport modes, a tendency toward ruthless and unbridled financial speculation and manipulation on the part of the industry's entrepreneurs, and relatively feeble attempts by public authorities to regulate the abuses while preserving the basic free enterprise framework of the industry. Both the nationwide and intercity (street) railroads provided the opportunity for self-enrichment. The problem for public policy was to prevent profit-making from interfering with the ostensive purpose of providing essential transportation services.

At the beginning of the electric era the major mode of regulation of the new electric traction companies continued to consist of the charters that cities had been issuing to horsecar companies which specified routes, fares, and responsibilities.[1] The greater capital requirements of electric traction led to widespread consolidation of companies within a given city and then to the growth of holding companies which acquired control of the transport firms of many different cities. This process often resulted in the parent company being seriously overcapitalized. In other words, its stock was watered to the point where its debt far exceeded the value of its assets. The shaky financial structure of the industry held up as long as prices and costs remained low enough to be covered by the standard nickle fare enshrined in most of the city charters and as long as patronage continued to grow.

These conditions generally prevailed in the pre-World War I era, which can now be seen as the golden age of the streetcar, when this form of public transit had a major impact on shaping the urban cityscape. Service was frequent, fares were low, and the streetcar was used by people of all social class and income levels. The public transit oriented city was a compact city, focused on the central business and shopping district and growing on the fringes as the streetcar lines were extended outward into the open land on the city's fringe. Often the growth of these streetcar suburbs was planned by private developers with financial interests in the transit company. They would buy land and then promote its development by running a streetcar line out to serve it.

World War I brought in an era of rapidly rising costs, and also at this time came the beginning of mass automobile ownership. The result was financial disaster for the overcapitalized transit firms of the country. By 1918 half the street railway mileage in the United States was in bankrupcy.[2] Just at the time when public transit had to face its most severe competitive challenge as a mode of urban mobility, the automobile, it was left starved of capital resources and deprived of the means to expand its service and improve its quality. Ridership growth slowed dramatically in the 1920s and began to sink steadily in the 1930s, as table 5.1 indicates. Transit lost its role as city shaper to the automobile. Instead of extending subway lines and upgrading streetcars by providing them with their own right of way, the transit firms stuck with their existing infrastructure and added only a few buses to their fleets. The car shortages and gasoline rationing of World War II gave the industry one last shot in the arm, and then came the deluge. From 23.3 billion total passengers in 1945 ridership dropped to 17.2 billion in 1950 and then to 9.4 billion in 1960. During these years of transit's decline little was done by the public authorities to halt the plunge. Urban development moved decisively away from transit's influence. It even lost its ability to help preserve the central business districts it had once created. The verdict of the market

Table 5.1 Trends in transit in ridership by modes and selected years (1907–1977)[a]

	Streetcar		Rapid transit		Bus[b]		
Year	Riders	Percent of total	Riders	Percent of total	Riders	Percent of total	Total riders
1907	8.9	94	0.7	7	—		9.5
1920	13.7	88	1.8	12	—		15.5
1930	10.5	67	2.6	17	2.5	16	15.6
1940	5.9	45	2.4	18	4.7	36	13.1
1945	9.4	40	2.7	12	11.1	47	23.3
1950	3.9	23	2.3	13	11.1	55	17.2
1960	0.5	5	1.8	19	7.1	68	9.4
1970	0.2	3	1.9	26	5.2	71	7.3
1977	0.1	1	2.1	28	5.4	71	7.6

Sources: American Public Transit Association, *Transit Fact Book 1977–78* (Washington, D.C., 1978), p. 27. Data from 1907 to 1940 are from Wilfred Owen, *The Metropolitan Transportation Problem,* rev. ed. (Washington, D.C.: The Brookings Institution, 1966), appendix table 16. Figures may not always add to totals because of rounding.
[a]Billions of total passengers.
[b]Includes trolley coach passengers.

appeared to be that the automobile was the form of urban transportation preferred by the vast majority of Americans.[3]

There was more involved in the decline of transit than just the public's desire for automobiles and suburban living, however. Decisions taken by private owners of transit firms obviously had a material impact on the way in which the industry operated. In the context of severe competition from the automobile and the prospects of a secular decline of the transit industry, the incentives the market offered to private ownership all pointed in the direction of reaping short-term profits rather than risking money on long-term investments to try to stem the decline. There is much profit to be made, even in declining industries, if one knows where to look for it. The fact that decisions made in pursuit of such profits may contribute substantially to the further decline of the industry is, according to the market paradigm, of no concern to the private entrepreneur. In this connection it is interesting to take note of the report prepared by Bradford Snell for the Senate Subcommittee on Antitrust and Monopoly in 1974.[4] Snell pointed out that in the late 1930s and 1940s General Motors decided that the only way it could create a market for its city buses was to organize the conversion from streetcars to buses itself in a number of cities. It created a company that bought up the transit lines in Kalamazoo and Saginaw, Michigan, and Springfield, Ohio. Then it dismantled the trolley lines and replaced them with GM buses. It was censured for this by the American Public Transit Association. But several years later GM formed a new company in partnership with Standard Oil of California and Firestone Tire and Rubber Company. This company, National City Lines, acquired control of the transit firms in forty-five cities, including New York, Philadelphia, Baltimore, St. Louis, Oakland, and Los Angeles, replacing their streetcars with buses. In 1949 GM, Standard Oil, and Firestone were convicted in Chicago Federal Court of having criminally conspired to replace electric trolleys with buses. GM was fined $5,000, and its treasurer was personally fined $1. Snell's report caused quite a flurry of excitement among critics of the auto industry when it appeared, but it would seem to be exaggerated to place the blame for the demise of public transit on a conspiracy by GM, Standard Oil, and Firestone. Their actions undoubtedly sped up the transition from electric rail traction to gasoline and diesel road vehicles. But the economics of the declining transit industry would have dictated much of this switch in any case, since buses were cheaper to purchase and operate (in the short run) than trolleys.

It did not take illegal conspiracies by giant corporations to induce private management to put profits before public service. Local businessmen were more than willing to do that. As ridership declined, financial wheeling and dealing became ever more frenzied. Sharp operators were determined to wring the last dime of profit out of the hulk of transit firms by selling off their assets, skimping on maintenance, cutting back service and employment. Transit companies were sold back and forth faster than baseball owners trade utility infielders. For example, the transit operation in Kansas City, Missouri, was sold to a Dallas financier and his Chicago-based partner in 1957. Two years later it was sold back to a group of Kansas City businessmen which included William Morris, a future lieutenant governor of Missouri. This group declared a stock dividend in 1961, even though the firm was operating at a deficit and its ridership was one-third of what it had been in 1946. Then between 1961 and 1966 the assets of the company were transferred first to the Sovereign Western Corporation of Nevada, then to the Westgate California Corporation, and finally back to the same group of local businessmen that had acquired the firm in 1959.[5] No comprehensive national studies exist, but one suspects that Kansas City's experience was rather typical of many small- and medium-sized cities in the midwest and west and a few large ones as well.

The final stage in the decline of the private transit industry was reached when owners began dumping the gutted relics of their firms into the laps of the public authorities. In many small towns the city fathers simply permitted the transit system to go out of existence. In others arrangements were made to operate a skeletal system under public ownership. The passage of the Urban Mass Transit Assistance Act in 1964 made funds available to local authorities to acquire their transit systems. Table 5.2 shows the sharp upward turn in the number of publicly owned transit firms since the mid-1960s. Public firms now dominate the American industry as they long have in Germany. Despite the fact that they constitute only 45 percent of the total firms, public transit enterprises produce nearly 90 percent of the passenger miles, earn 90 percent of the operating revenues, and employ nearly 90 percent of the workers.[6] This stands in sharp contrast to the industry thirty years ago. In 1948 there were only thirty-six publicly owned transit firms in the whole nation, and they accounted for only 25 percent of the industry's total revenue.[7] Thus there has been a radical transformation in the nature of

Table 5.2 Private versus public ownership of U.S. transit systems (1959–1977)

Year	Private	Percent of total	Public	Percent of total	Total	Percent
1959	1,173	96	52	4	1,225	100
1964	1,073	93	79	7	1,152	100
1970	938	87	141	13	1,079	100
1975	614	65	333	35	947	100
1977	553	55	455	45	1,008	100

Source: American Public Transit Association, *Transit Fact Book,* appropriate yearly editions.

the urban transit sector. It is no longer essentially a private affair in which market demand and decisions by private capital determine what kind of transportation services will be produced. Today it is a complex constellation of local, regional, and federal authorities that makes that decision. Private capital's role, while not negligible, is more indirect and sophisticated. But the paradigm that once governed thought about urban transit still lingers in the minds of many voters, politicians, and policy analysts. The new public owners of the nation's transit systems find themselves somewhat baffled and perplexed about what to do next.

LOCAL AND STATE GOVERNMENT
RESPONSE: TOO LITTLE, TOO LATE?

The historic relationship between the city and its transit company oscillated between apathy and antagonism. When fares were increased, or service cut back, it was good politics to be critical of the company. When deficits threatened, or investments had to be deferred, officials tended to remain indifferent to the plight of what was after all a private business. The mere fact that the transit company became publicly owned did not eliminate all such attitudes. Frank Colcord has studied the institutional changes in transit operations in many U.S. cities, and he maintains that most local officials in the 1960s continued to believe that the new public transportation enterprises "should be operated like private corporations as much as possible, including showing a primary concern for balancing expenditures with revenues."[8] Local policy makers felt that once publicly owned transit firms had been exempted from local property taxes, from state and federal excise taxes, and allowed to rationalize and consolidate their operations they should and could operate in the black. The new transit authority was publicly owned but largely on its own in terms of revenues, at least in the beginning. The feeling among city leaders was that the obstacles to an effective solution to transit's problems—jurisdictional fragmentation, narrow revenue base, lack of coordination, and so forth—could only be overcome with active assistance from other levels of government.[9] Consequently much of the action taken by local officials was to support transit lobbying efforts at the state and federal levels. The gradual success of these lobbying efforts generated funds that made the transit system into a more interesting object of politics and also induced city governments to step up their financial support of the transit system. As the federal and state governments took over funding a large proportion of the costs of capital improvements the cities were able to use their financial aid for operating assistance. Table 5.3 shows that in 1977 city subsidies accounted for 19.8 percent of the U.S. transit industry's revenue for that year. This represents the second largest source of revenue in the industry (behind passenger revenue), although local operating assistance is surpassed by the combined total of state and federal aid.

Table 5.3 Transit industry revenue by source (1977)

Source	Amount (millions of dollars)	Percent
Total operating revenue	2,280	53.6
Nonoperating revenue	73	1.7
Local operating assistance	841	19.8
State operating assistance	478	11.2
Federal operating assistance	584	13.7
Total revenue	4,257	100.0

Source: American Public Transit Association, *Transit Fact Book 1977–78* (Washington, D.C., 1978), pp. 18–19.

In chapter 7 we will see that state governments play a crucial role in financing the highway system, earmarking twice as much money as the federal government. How does the role of state government in mass transit funding compare with its highway role? There are two principal points to make in this regard. One is that state funding of mass transit is much more recent than state funding of highways. The states began building roads with general revenue funds in the 1890s, and they began earmarking gas tax revenues in the 1920s. States did not really begin to spend significant amounts of money on urban mass transit until the 1960s, after innovation had begun at the federal level. The benchmark in state funding of transit probably came with New York's $1 billion bond issue for capital grants to transit in 1967. The 1960s also saw both Pennsylvania and New Jersey pay transit-operating subsidies, and Massachusetts begin to pay 90 percent of both the debt service on MBTA transit bonds and commuter rail subsidy costs.[10] Once the states began to move in on transit finance, state funds became a significant factor. By 1975 twenty-four states were providing aid to transit. This aid was put to a variety of uses: for example, capital improvements, operating assistance, technical planning, and special projects. Most of the state funds for transit are derived from general revenue sources. A few states (six) have established state transportation funds to finance transit as well as other modes. Several other states (four) use special taxes or revenue sources (sales taxes, cigarette taxes, lotteries) earmarked to transit.[11] The total state level funding for transit in 1975 amounted to $779,856,000, compared to a total federal aid of $1,410,076,000.[12]

The second point to be made is that state funding of transit is not nearly as broadly based as state road funding. Not only do less than half the states have a transit aid program but also most of the twenty-four states that do aid transit do so at very low funding levels. Just eight states—Pennsylvania, California, New York, New Jersey, Illinois, Maryland, Massachusetts, and Connecticut—account for 87 percent of the total state transit aid funds.[13] These states contain or are adjacent to very large cities which can make use of fixed route transit systems, especially commuter rail trains which receive the bulk of the state funds.

Clearly then state and local governments have responded to the problem of preserving the public transportation systems of urban regions. But their responses came rather late in the cycle of decline. Such responses would not, in and of themselves, have been sufficient to halt the system's deterioration. In any case much of the financial support that cities and states have given to public transportation over the past fifteen years has been stimulated by federal programs and would probably not have been given in the absence of federal aid matching requirements. Thus it would appear that federal policy holds the key, if there is a key, to preserving and restoring public transportation in America.

FEDERAL RESPONSE: THE POLITICS OF BALANCED TRANSPORTATION

In the early and mid-1970s federal aid to public transportation was one of the fastest growing of all federal programs. Aid distributed through the Urban Mass Transportation Administration (UMTA) went from a mere $147 million in 1969 to over $1.4 billion in 1976.[14] What were the programs financed by these funds? What accounts for the dramatic change of commitment to the urban transit sector on the part of Congress and the president? Most interesting of all, how should we evaluate what the program has accomplished so far, and what are the prospects for the future?

Let us begin with a brief overview of the milestones in the growth of federal urban transportation policy.[15] Its origins may be traced back to the Housing and Urban Development Act of 1961, which contained an emergency loan provision designed to help the nation's commuter railroads. In addition to the $50 million in loans for the railroads, it made available $25 million for mass transit demonstration projects. This small amount of money was not expected to produce any startling results. It was a compromise that provided the railroads with some extra income and the nation's transit backers with a foot in the door of the federal policy process. Perhaps equally important for the long-term development of federal policy was a report prepared the same year by the Institute for Public Administration at the direction of the Department of Commerce. This report was subsequently published under the title *Urban Transportation and Public Policy*.[16] President Kennedy accepted it as embodying the democratic administration's new outlook on transit problems and commended it to the Congress. It advocated increased emphasis on mass transportation, planning for a more balanced transport system, and a view of transit as more than just a private, profit-making business. Transit should be seen as a public service program that often cannot be a profit-making enterprise. This was to be the direction in which policy planning for mass transit would evolve, away from the idea that it must pay its own way with farebox receipts and toward the European social service model of transit as an essential component of an urban community.

President Kennedy was unable to get Congress to increase the level of funding for transit. His Urban Mass Transportation Bill perished in the House Rules Committee in 1962. But the idea of a federal role in transit had gained considerable support. Transit supporters formed the Urban Passenger Transport Association to help the administration lobby for its transit legislation. Their efforts paid off under the Johnson administration with the passage of the Urban Mass Transportation Act of 1964. This was more than just a foot in the door. It has been called the cornerstone of the federal transit program.[17] This act added an important new element to the federal transit aid program: capital grants to public transit enterprises. These grants, financed from general revenues, covered up to two-thirds of the net cost of a transit project. To be eligible for a capital grant, a city had to have a coordinated transit program. Only public bodies could receive money, but the funds could be used by public authorities to acquire ownership of transit firms. The act continued the program of low-interest loans begun in 1961 and the demonstration projects as well. It authorized $75 million for fiscal 1965 and $150 million each year for 1966 and 1967. Finally, section 12 of the act limited the amount of grants that any single state could receive to 12 ½ percent of the total funds disbursed in any given year.

During the next several years there was much legislative attention devoted to urban transport problems but little increase in the level of funding. The High Speed Ground Transportation Act of 1965 authorized a three-year $90 million program of research and demonstration projects. That same year Congress authorized the construction of a subway for the District of Columbia. Legislation was needed to transfer the administration of the Urban Mass Transit Assistance program first to the Department of Housing and Urban Development and then to the Department of Transportation after it came into existence in 1967. Extensions and amendments to both the 1964 and 1965 acts were passed. But the total amount of federal funds authorized in the period 1962 to 1970 did not exceed $800 million, or an average of less than $90 million per year.[18] Table 5.4 shows the growth of federal transit aid from 1962 to 1976.

The year 1970 marked the next surge ahead for federal involvement in transit. At the request of the Nixon administration, Congress passed the Urban Mass Transportation Assistance Act of 1970 which authorized $10 billion in federal aid over a twelve-year period. This marked the coming of age of mass transit aid. The strong support given the bill by the Republican administration was surprising since transit legislation had always been regarded as a ward of the Democratic party, and congressional Republicans had voted against the 1961 and 1964 legislation. Nevertheless,

Table 5.4 Growth of federal urban mass transit assistance aid (1962–1976)

Combined fiscal years	Total UMTA aid (dollars)	Percent of fifteen-year total
1962–64	33,707,100	0.5
1965–67	298,983,200	4.2
1968–70	465,224,700	6.5
1971–73	1,971,805,300	27.7
1974–76	4,330,728,900	60.9
15-year total	7,104,943,100	100.0

Source: Calculated from data given in U.S., Department of Transportation, Urban Mass Transit Administration, *Statistical Summary* (Washington, D.C.: Department of Transportation, n.d.), p. 1.

President Nixon and his transportation secretary, John Volpe, worked closely with Democratic leaders in Congress to get this legislation adopted. The bill passed the Senate by 84 to 4 and the House by 327 to 16, which indicated a high degree of bipartisan support.[19]

One problem not dealt with by the 1970 act was the perennial question of how to assure the stability and continuity of funds for this stepped-up transit aid program. Congress was still required to appropriate the funds every year from general revenues. Transit's supporters felt that an effective long-term program required a more secure source of funds, and they joined with other elements of the antiautomobile coalition to try to get the Federal Highway Trust Fund opened up to transit. By 1972 this pressure was strong enough to prevent passage of any highway aid bill at all. The next year the highway and transit forces chose to compromise. The Federal Aid Highway Act of 1973 authorized, for the first time, the use of some highway trust fund money for mass transit. The compromise legislation provided that in 1974 cities could buy buses or subways with general revenues, with this spending being offset by freezing an equal amount in the highway trust fund. In fiscal 1975 local governments were permitted to use this same method of exchanging highway trust fund entitlements for general revenue funds to be spent on transit projects up to a national limit of $600 million. In addition they were authorized to tap the trust fund directly for up to $200 million, but this money was restricted to bus-related projects. Beginning in 1976 the act allowed cities to use up to $800 million of highway funds for capital spending on either bus or rail related transit projects. It also gave cities and states that chose not to build a segment of the interstate highway system the option of trading their trust fund authorizations for the cancelled segment for an equal amount of general revenue funds to be spent on a mass transit project instead. Finally, the act raised the federal share of transit capital-spending projects from two-thirds to eighty percent of the net cost.[20]

Once a high level of authorizations for capital assistance had been

The United States: Sick Transit, Glorious Money

reached, trust fund exchange money made available, and the federal share of the project's net cost raised, the last remaining barrier to be overcome was the prohibition against using federal funds for operating assistance. This was perhaps the highest psychological hurdle of all. It was one thing to persuade legislators to fund badly needed capital improvements, but to ask for operating subsidies was more difficult. Many policy makers felt that providing federal funds to cover a transit enterprises's day-to-day operating deficit would encourage poor business practices, complacent management, and avaricious labor union wage demands. Transit's supporters argued that careful monitoring of the aid program could limit these undesirable effects, and that it was unreasonable to expect the industry to pay its own way from farebox receipts, given the rapidly rising costs of operation and the low levels to which ridership had fallen. They again carried the day. In 1974 the National Mass Transportation Assistance Act established the principle that federal funds could be used for operating subsidies. The act also authorized an $11.8 billion program of federal assistance to run from 1975 through 1980. Included in this was $500 million for transit aid to nonurban areas, designed to gather broad-based support for transit aid in the Congress.

Having completed our brief overview of the evolution of federal policy, let us now turn to the question of how this policy evolution came about. Why should it be easier and less controversial for the federal government to spend large sums of money for urban transit in the late 1970s, when the U.S. transport system is more dependent on the automobile than ever? As Altshuler points out, federal aid to urban transit began as a program pushed by the liberal Democrats and their big city oriented supporters. It came into its own and saw its greatest growth under two conservative Republican presidents, with widespread bipartisan support in the Congress.[21] How did transit go from a special interest, big city affair in the 1960s to what became a safe issue in the early 1970s?

There are several factors that help explain this transformation. First, as the nation grappled with a growing number of domestic problems, it appeared that transit could be a part of the solution of many of these problems. This broadened its appeal. Such crises as the decline of the cities, the need to provide new jobs in our urban areas, the pollution of the atmosphere by auto emissions, lack of mobility for the handicapped, and the energy crisis seemed to call for improved public transportation as remedies. Whether transit was or can ever be an effective solution to these ills is another question. The point is that to a large number of people it appeared to be a remedy. Transit aid was less divisive and controversial than many other more radical remedies being put forth. As Altschuler has observed, even though the Nixon administration was striving to distance itself from the big-spending, pro-black, welfare state image of its predecessor, it felt comfortable promoting an increase in federal aid to transit:

Transit turned out to be an ideal centerpiece for the urban policy of a conservative administration. Though clearly of high priority to urban spokesmen, it did not stir class and racial antagonisms. Quite the contrary, it attracted support from every portion of the urban ideological spectrum.[22]

A second development was the overcoming of transit's narrow geographical base of support. Congress finds it difficult to get majorities behind programs that benefit only a few of its constituencies. Most transit rides take place in just a few large cities. Eight metropolitan areas produce nearly two-thirds of the country's total transit rides. The New York area alone accounts for one-third. This solution is reflected in the figures on the distribution of transit aid across the country. Despite the UMTA efforts at seeding new buses in small- and medium-sized towns around the country, from 1964 through 1976 just five urban areas received 57.8 percent of all capital grant funds, and ten areas received nearly 80 percent.[23] This inherent geographical concentration of transit is a political weakness overcome only after long years of struggle. Some observers claim to have detected what amounts to a bargain between the narrowly based transit lobby and the broadly based highway lobby.[24] Throughout the 1960s transit and highway forces had been enemies. Revolts against the construction of urban expressways seemed to imply support for transit. Transit forces were thus allied with those groups that wanted to end earmarking of road user taxes for highway construction. When the strength of the antihighway faction grew great enough to block passage of the highway aid bill in 1972, the highway forces concluded that the best way to protect the trust fund would be to give the transit lobby a piece of the action. This was the breakthrough of the 1973 legislation: it removed the transit lobby's incentive to continue opposition to the earmarking of road funds. In this manner the highway advocates have found an effective means of protecting their own vital interests. The bargain struck in 1973 has not only helped transit overcome its narrow geographical base but also contributed to the reestablishment of near unanimous congressional support for the highway program. Further it has solidified the political base for funding transit programs and improved the range of options available to local governments when they plan future transportation investments.

Finally we come to the question of what all of the stepped-up government spending, especially the federal aid, has accomplished. Obviously the first and most important goal of this great infusion of money had to be to halt the decline in transit ridership and, if possible, to bring about an increase in patronage. Without success in the ridership area none of the other benefits sought from transit—energy savings, cleaner air, saving the cities, for example—could be achieved. The ridership decline was halted, and the trend was reversed, although not as quickly or as easily as was initially hoped. The figures in table 5.5 show that transit patronage continued to decline throughout the late 1960s and early 1970s. Only

Table 5.5 Trends in urban passenger travel in the United States (1940–1975)

Year	Transit passengers (billions)	Transit passenger miles (billions)	Automobile passenger miles (billions)	Percent transit
1945	19.0	112	240	32.0
1950	13.8	84	403	17.0
1960	7.5	46	627	7.0
1970	5.9	37	1,089	3.3
1975	5.6	35	1,341	2.6
1977	5.7	36	1,465	2.5

Sources: Alan A. Altshuler, Changing Patterns of Policy: The Decision Making Environment of Urban Transportation, *Public Policy* 25 (spring 1977), p. 174; revised and reprinted as, The Decision Making Environment of Urban Transportation, in *Public Transportation: Planning, Operations and Management,* edited by George E. Gray and Lester A. Hoel (Englewood Cliffs, N.J.: Prentice-Hall, 1979), esp. table 3-2, p. 42. The 1977 transit data are from American Public Transit Association, *Transit Fact Book 1977–78* (Washington, D.C., 1978), p. 27. Auto data calculated from Federal Highway Administration, *Highway Statistics 1977,* table VM-1.

when very substantial federal aid funds became available in the mid-1970s did the decline of ridership bottom out and begin to creep upward again. More increases in the national ridership figures can be expected in the next few years as new rapid transit systems or extensions open in cities such as Washington, D.C., Baltimore, and Atlanta. Increased patronage will not bring about a transportation revolution overnight, but, if it continues steadily over many years, it could be very significant. At the rate ridership has been increasing since 1973, for example, the 1945 level of ridership will be reached by 1998. Of course it remains to be seen whether the increases of recent years can be sustained.

THE FUTURE OF URBAN PUBLIC TRANSPORTATION

Despite the ridership increases of recent years the future of urban public transportation is by no means assured. Indeed the troubles that lie ahead for transit are potentially so serious that Altshuler believes "transit is in some respects as endangered today as it was a decade ago."[25] The main storm cloud on the horizon is financial. How long can transit aid from all levels of government continue to increase at the rate required to rejuvenate the system in an age of fiscal austerity and post-Proposition 13 retrenchment? There is a danger that public transportation programs will come to be seen by policy makers and policy analysts imbued with the spirit of the market paradigm as just another big government boondoggle that deserves to be consumed by the fires of neoconservative budget slashing.

Transit's financial demands are quite serious. During the decade from 1965 to 1975 the total national operating deficit of the transit industry increased by 1,700 percent, from $0.01 billion to $1.7 billion. If this rate of growth should continue for another ten years transit's deficits by 1985 would be approximately $10 billion, exclusive of debt service and capital grants![26] It is possible that in the future the burden of transit subsidies will call the whole decade of federal urban transit policy into question. Indeed the Carter administration's support for transit aid increases has been lukewarm at best. If this continues, and federal aid is reduced or remains stagnant in an era of rapidly rising costs, it would result in another spiral of decline in the quality and quantity of the country's urban public transit services, wiping out most of the gains achieved up to the present.

The intellectual justifications for this cooling off of federal executive enthusiasm for transit were expressed in a number of studies published by economists and political scientists in the mid-1970s. George W. Hilton's critique was one of the earliest and best known among demurrers.[27] Economists like Hilton are by profession strong proponents of the market as a mechanism for social allocation decisions. Hilton recognizes that the special circumstances involved in federal transit programs prevent profit from being the guide, but he still demands that federal aid programs be cost-effective, that inputs of aid should produce outputs of increased ridership and related spin-off benefits. At the time of his writing no such ridership increases had come about, and Hilton thus judges the UMTA program a failure. Moreover he charges that UMTA is devoted to preserving cities of the traditional type, with a large central business district and a radial pattern of movement to and from work. This requires huge investments in rail technology which constitute subsidies to high-income suburban commuters and are not really effective in stopping the process of urban sprawl and decentralization. UMTA cannot make driving more costly to individual motorists, and its new transit facilities are not attractive enough to lure them out of their automobiles. Hilton's general conclusion was that the UMTA program was a failure that wasted several billion dollars worth of capital and actually aggravated the problems it was supposed to solve. The policy implications from such conclusions are obvious: slow down or stop massive federal investment in transit.

The problem with such analyses and recommendations, say transit's defenders, is that they are literally too shortsighted. Hilton's data on the lack of ridership increases were outdated before his studies ever appeared in print. He allowed for only three or four years of the post-1970 step-up in mass transit investment to make itself felt, and he was not able to take the changed conditions brought on by the Arab oil embargo and OPEC price increase into account. This suggests that there is a longer lead time between transit investments and ridership increases than the conventional time horizon of policy analysis takes into account. The proper time frame for evaluating public transit investments is decades, not just two or four years. Only with such a long-term perspective will the full ridership benefits of transit investment become manifest and thus susceptible to meaningful cost-benefit analysis.

A second element in the critique of transit disputes the claim that increased reliance on public transportation can save substantial amounts of energy and thus help the country overcome its dependence on imported petroleum. Charles A. Lave, among others, has challenged the simple arithemetic behind this claim.[28] He specifically debunks the idea that construction of new rail rapid transit systems is a way to save energy. He maintains that, when the energy used to construct such systems is taken into account, not just the energy used to operate them, the balance sheet is distinctly unfavorable to transit. In his energy analysis of the Bay Area Rapid Transit (BART) system he found that the energy expended in construction is so large, and energy savings in the operation so small, that it would take between 168 and 535 years to earn back the original energy investment, depending on what assumptions one made concerning patronage and load factors. Altshuler agrees with Lave with respect to new rapid rail systems. After reviewing the evidence for all major transit modes, Altshuler states that he has been able to identify only two situations in which transit could guarantee energy savings over the automobile: reducing or eliminating fares while holding vehicle mileage constant, thus increasing load factors and instituting express bus service in special lanes in severely congested corridors, providing no new construction is needed to get the lanes.[29]

Many of the ridership and energy savings claims made for mass transit, especially expensive rapid rail systems such as BART, assumed that the very existence of such new systems would not only attract riders from automobiles but also lead to changes in land use and population density. It was hoped that newly constructed systems would create the same kind of relatively high density, transit-dependent land use patterns that grew up around existing rail transit lines. This expectation by and large has not yet been fulfilled, and thus transit's payoffs in ridership and energy savings have been disappointing. Reporting on a study of housing patterns and land use along BART's Concord line in suburban Contra Costa County, Denis J. Dingemans found that "only a small share of the many new townhouses constructed since BART was planned have clustered near the stations, and access to BART does not appear to have been the dominant influence on the townhouse location process."[30] Andrew M. Hammer agrees, pointing out that the impact of local rail transportation on the distribution of metropolitan growth was greatest when transportation access was a very scarce resource before the coming of the automobile. "Today, in developed areas, incremental improvements in accessibility cannot be judged to have the same type of controlling influence exhibited in the past."[31] In U.S. metropolitan areas, with their high levels of automobility and good road systems, accessibility to public transportation is simply no longer very important in land use decisions, and it can no longer shape the cityscape as it did when people needed to live within walking distance of transit stops. In his study of BART impact on housing developments, Dingemans recognizes this and concludes: "In future cases it would be wise to secure control over land use development in the transit station areas before vast amounts of public funds are spent to construct suburban rapid transit systems."[32]

This brings the analysis close to the nub of the problem. What are the chances that the U.S. political system could produce a set of land use controls that could change the pattern of land use to one more favorable to public transportation usage? Is there any prospect of being able to change the thrust of metropolitan area development away from auto-dependent growth and suburban sprawl toward a more transit-supportive pattern of planned higher density development? Altshuler, while conceding that land use controls could help public transportation achieve some of its goals, is quite skeptical about the likelihood of their widespread adoption: "The evidence seems overwhelming that most Americans prefer low-density living. To our knowledge, moreover, no American state or region (let alone the national government) has adopted increased urban density as a policy goal."[33] Clearly the buying and selling of land is one of the most fundamental aspects of our free enterprise economy. It would be naive not to recognize that many very powerful segments of our society are ideologically opposed to increasing land use controls, have an interest in the continuation of sprawl development and have more than enough political influence to block any clumsy attempts to impose land use planning and thereby shift the pattern of metropolitan growth toward higher density development. American political institutions at all levels are singularly ill-suited to the growth of such coordinated and purposeful public power, even if a popular majority were in favor of it.

Does this mean that public transportation is doomed never to fulfill any of the bright hopes it held out in the late sixties and early seventies? Must it remain a marginal mode that plays a role only in a few large, increasing obsolete northeastern cities? A real possibility is that the affluent suburban American way of life may not hold. Prudence suggests that at least some provision must be made for a less affluent future. This might be termed the bomb shelter argument for public transit. Petroleum shortages, international political developments, and other crises may suddenly deprive the nation of adequate gasoline supplies. Or a technological breakthrough to replace the internal combustion engine may not be ready when the oil finally runs out. Or some other, at present unforeseen, development may make the sprawl pattern untenable. An effective public transit system and land use pattern will enable the society and economy to continue to function with a minimum of disruption.

Action now to preserve and extend transit systems and a transit-supportive environment is a necessary hedge against an increasingly uncertain future.

Given all the political obstacles to effective land use controls, how can policy makers begin to move toward planning for a more transit-supportive metropolitan area environment? The first step is to realize that it is not necessary to plan for very high population densities. As Mathew J. Betz points out, there has been a "lack of clarity in much of the U.S. urban transportation-planning literature" because it typically considers only two combinations of land use density and dispersion. The high-density concentration found in the centers of older eastern cities and the low-density dispersion of suburbia and post-World War II urban development.[34] But in fact, Betz notes, there are two other possible combinations of density and dispersion, as illustrated in figure 5.1. Cells 4 and 1 of the figure represent the traditional patterns just mentioned. Cell 2 shows a dispersion of high-density activities such as might occur when regional shopping centers and high-rise apartments are spread out instead of being clustered. Cell 3 would be the least common in the contemporary American experience. Low-density activities are concentrated in one portion of an area, with the remainder undeveloped. Cell 3's ability to function as a transportation corridor is obvious. Pushkarev and Zupan have calculated that the threshold of transit-supporting density, one that allows at least half-hourly local bus service, is seven dwellings per acre.[35] This density can be achieved with single-family homes on 60 × 100 ft

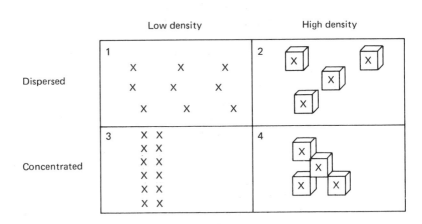

Figure 5.1 Theoretical patterns of land use density and dispersion (Source: Mathew J. Betz, Land Use Density, Pattern and Scale as Factors in Urban Transportation, *Traffic Quarterly*, 32, April 1978, p. 265).

lots. The density of attached homes and garden apartments is about fifteen dwellings per acre which can support a wide variety of transit services, including express bus service, light rail, and rail rapid transit, if this density can be maintained in a corridor leading to a significant downtown area. The key factor is to plan communities with a public transportation corridor in mind and locate facilities that attract trips near transit.

In educating the public about planning and land use controls designed to support transit, planners must make it clear that the results will not be New York style densities. But this in itself is not likely to remove all the political barriers to land use controls. What other factors are there that might help make corridor planning more acceptable? Demographic and economic trends may be on the side of the planners for a change. While no one expects the thrust to suburban and exurban growth to collapse completely, significant countertrends are already emerging that can be exploited for transportation-planning purposes. The rise in the number of single-person households, childless couples, and elderly households suggests that the dream house of the future will not always be a single-family detached home on a large wooded lot. In addition, as housing prices escalate to the point where the dream house becomes unreachable in any case, anything that can bring down the cost of housing is likely to be well received by buyers, sellers, and public officials. *The Costs of Sprawl* study commissioned by the U.S. Council on Environmental Quality, the Department of Housing and Urban Development, and the Environmental Protection Agency, and carried out by the Real Estate Research Corporation, concluded that the capital costs of a planned, higher-density community (nineteen dwellings per acre) would be 44 percent lower than the costs of an unplanned low-density sprawl development.[36] The major savings were in the cost of land, streets, and utility installations. Moreover operating costs were estimated to be 11 percent lower in the planned community. Additional benefits would be derived from lower air pollution and lower energy consumption. (These estimates were based on analysis of model, not actual, communities, and, as the disclaimer goes, actual savings may vary.)[37] The point is that planned communities will not automatically be excluded from competing with unplanned ones because of higher costs imposed by government red tape. They may in fact be more competitive. The home-building industry and local public authorities, whipsawed between inflation and a simmering tax revolt, may soon come to look on planning as an all-American management device to cut the cost of providing homes rather than as a socialistic attempt to suffocate free enterprise. This is particularly likely to be the case if they are offered financial incentives to engage in coordinated transportation and land use planning.

The federal government would have to take the lead in coordinating policies in this area. Coordination is the operative word. It would be undesirable, and probably impossible, for the federal government to plan directly urban land use or to compel state and local governments to do so. Proper coordination of incentives could make it attractive, however. The broad outlines of what needs to be done are clear. They were sketched in a report by the congressional Office of Technology Assessment (OTA).

Federal actions could seek to establish strong linkages between existing community development programs and transit programs in order to effect a coordinated national urban growth management policy. . . . Capital grants for sewerage systems and water supply systems could be tied to the availability of transit services. . . . Mortgages and subsidies for community development in fringe areas could be oriented toward multi-use, clustered activity centers related to transit. . . . Organized and systematic policies for public investment in infrastructure . . . could serve as an effective lever to guide and manage growth.[38]

In the early years of this century transit planning and land use planning were often closely linked, and this linkage made them into potent city shapers. The linkage was accomplished by private interests, however. Traction magnates became wealthy not so much from revenues from their nickel trolley fares as by acquiring, developing, and selling the real estate opened up along their routes.[39] The task of public transportation policy makers is to see that the transit-land use planning linkage is restored. Public purposes will play a larger role in the process than in the old days, but the goals will be remarkably similar: a cityscape well suited to the use of transit facilities.

The goal of such coordinated planning should not be to coerce future metropolitan growth into a procrustean bed of administratively dictated high-density development. It is to change the framework of costs and incentives by which private land use decisions are made. Only then will administrative coordination be truly effective. Altshuler notes that, while people may not object to new transit facilities, they will resent and resist attempts to force them to use such facilities. They prefer the carrots of inducements to the sticks of compulsion.[40] Wildavsky, reflecting on the experience of the social programs of the 1960s, expresses much of the same point:

When public policy has tried to alter basic patterns of individual behavior involving large numbers of people, this effort has failed; but when citizens have sought to get government to reallocate resources, they often have succeeded. . . . We find it easier to command government to change than to change ourselves.[41]

A gradual long-term shift in the way governments support and encourage private development, coupled with market forces moving in the same direction, is thus the most likely way to restore significant, viable public transportation to most major U.S. metropolitan areas. The construction industry anticipates that between now and 2000 half as many new buildings will be built as were in the entire history of the United States.[42] The question is whether they will continue to be built in the sprawl pattern or in a pattern that favors public transit and minimizes automobile travel.

As we pointed out in chapter 4, West German metropolitan areas have achieved this goal. The Germans were fortunate in beginning transit subsidies before the onset of mass automobile ownership. Timing was the crucial factor in the success of German public transportation. This should not be seen as a counsel of despair to Americans, however. It will take at least several decades to begin to rehshape the U.S. metropolitan areas, but it still can be done if the people act now to lay the legal, financial groundwork and the mass transit infrastructure. While there are real difficulties and obstacles today, the longer the process is delayed, the more costly and disruptive the change will be. Clearly we cannot expect metropolitan communities to rely only on public transportation. No West German city does. But we must plan for these communities substantially larger public transportation operations, both ongoing and emergency backup, than at present.

III
HIGHWAYS

INTRODUCTION TO PART III

The automobile was the first and most important product of the second phase of the industrial revolution, the consumer goods revolution. Originally the industrial revolution involved the production of capital goods— things to make other things—such as steel mills, power looms, and machine tools. The consumer did not often see these things, only the eventual end products such as textiles and cheaper food shipped by rail. But with the coming of the motor car the stimulus for industrial growth shifted from producing capital goods to producing goods for direct use by individual consumers. Many products of this second industrial revolution required an extensive investment in supportive infrastructure to function efficiently. For example, washing machines required plumbing and electricity. These in turn required water mains, sewer lines, generating plants, and transmission lines. The private market could produce some of these infrastructural investments. But often private industry could not do the job fast or cheaply enough, or on terms acceptable to the community at large. In these instances the government moved in to do the job instead.

Highways are a classic example of how authority rather than the market was exploited to secure the infrastructural investment needed for the full use of a new product and the rapid expansion of a major new industry. An individual could buy his own motorcar, but he could hardly build his own roads to drive it on, for the cost of doing so would have been prohibitive. In the early days of motoring there was no feasible way to use the market mechanism to sell roads to buyers in the same way that cars were sold. Toll roads would not work because the points they could serve were too limited and early traffic volumes were too low. The full benefits of owning an auto (the attractiveness of the auto as a consumer product and hence the potential for profits and expansion in the auto industry) could be realized only through a virtually infinite expansion of accessible points by means of a general upgrading and improvement of the publicly provided road and street system. Thus the use of public funds and public works departments to improve the roads was strongly desired by motorists and motor car manufacturers. Not everyone was eager to see public funds used in this way, however. Motorcars were owned mainly by the rich and well-to-do. Why should people who did not own cars pay taxes to pave the way for a few wealthy joy riders?

Representatives of the motorists then pointed out that the automobile represented not just an occasion for expenditure but a source of revenue as well. License fees and taxes on automobiles and automotive products could generate enough revenue to relieve the general treasury of having to pay out anything at all for the roads. In Britain and America the motorists and the public authorities derived from the prevailing paradigm of public choice the notion of earmarking the revenues from motor vehicle taxes to be spent exclusively for highway construction and improvement. Earmarking proved to be a very powerful and appealing notion to motorists and their allies, precisely because it served their interests at the same time it appeared to be the quintessence of democratic theory applied to the solution of an important public policy problem. It had its roots in a Millsian belief in individual liberty and a Lockean sense of social contract between taxpayer and the public authorities. Proponents of earmarking maintained that an individual has a right to own and operate a motor car. This right can be limited only to protect the rights of others; for example, safety laws are legitimate protection for other drivers and pedestrians. Motorists will agree to have their vehicles and fuel taxed, but only if the proceeds are used to build roads that expand the car owner's right and ability to exploit the full potential of the vehicle. In this way the motorist and the government make a compact that earmarks motor vehicle tax revenue for highways. In addition earmarking could also be seen as an effort to use governmental authority to recreate a pay-as-you-go market mechanism for financing road construction investments. The tax method that allows the motorist—the major beneficiaries of such investment—to bear the bulk of the costs of the road program.

For all these reasons earmarking became more than just a simple public finance mechanism. Over the years it became a symbol of an important public commitment. For some groups it became a rallying cry and a political credo. Later it became a target for other antiroad groups. There is no doubt that earmarking and the manner in which it was institutionalized became an important factor in shaping the national transportation systems and in accounting for the uneven developments in these systems. In Britain and America earmarking formed the basis for highway finance policy early in the automobile age. But the practice was implemented in different ways, and in consequence the problem of highways and their roles in the total transportation system are quite different in each country. Chapters 6 and 7 will focus on the ways in which earmarking fit into the institutional context of transportation policy making in Britain and America and how this in turn helped shape the two nation's paradigms of public choice and transportation policy outcomes.

6
GREAT BRITAIN: TRAFFIC IN TROUBLE

THE AUTOMOBILE IN BRITISH SOCIETY

In the spring of 1907 the British chancellor of the exchequer, Herbert Asquith, was asked in Parliament for his opinion on taxing the growing number of private motorcars in Great Britain. Such a measure, Asquith replied, would be an "almost ideal tax, because it is a tax on a luxury which is apt to degenerate into a nuisance."[1] Nothing could have been more typical of the British upper-class attitude toward the automobile in the early decades of this century: it was unlikely that the private car could become widely owned by the middle classes and unthinkable that it should or could be owned by the lower classes. Whatever motoring would be done by men of humble station would be as chaffeurs and lorry (truck) drivers. The more adventuresome among the wealthy would continue to use their new self-propelled playthings for weekend pleasure trips in the country.

At about the same time as Asquith's remark was making the rounds of London society, an American businessman wrote a letter to a U.S. trade journal, giving his views on the future of the motorcar in the United States:

The assertion has often been made that it would be only a question of a few years before the automobile industry would go the way the bicycle went. I think this is in no way a fair comparison and that the automobile, while it may have been a luxury when first put out, is now one of the absolute necessities of our later day civilization. The bicycle was a recreation and a fad. The automobile, while it is a recreation, is in no way a fad.

The letter was signed "Henry Ford."[2]

Not only were British perceptions of the future of the motor car very different from those of their American cousins, but the socioeconomic matrix into which the motor car had to be introduced was quite different as well. As early as 1840 American levels of per capita income had greatly surpassed the British. By 1909 Americans were on the average more wealthy than Englishmen and could afford to contemplate mass ownership of automobiles.[3] Further, British automobile production methods lagged far behind American ones. Every school child knows how Henry Ford revolutionized industry by introducing mass production of the famous Model T Ford. But it was more than just the conveyor belt and overhead hoist that gave the U.S. auto industry its lead over the world. In

America the engineering industry as a whole had evolved a system of standardization and parts interchangeability coupled with a heavy reliance on subcontracting. This allowed the American manufacturer to use his capital more efficiently by increasing his vehicle assembly capacity and at the same time to purchase low-cost component parts produced by outside specialists. In Britain manufacturers usually made most of their own parts and components. This added to the capital requirements for entering the motor industry. It meant that the U.K. firms produced fewer cars at higher prices. In view of the lower per capita income in Britain, it meant a much more restricted market for cars.[4]

Even before the outbreak of the First World War Britain's lag in diffusing ownership of automobiles was substantial. In 1913 there were 34,000 motor vehicles produced in Britain and 485,000 produced in America.[5] The war simply increased America's lead. Table 6.1 shows that by 1920 auto ownership levels in the United States had reached a level that Britain did not attain until the mid-1950s. Growth of car ownership in Britain continued to be sluggish in the 1920s. Indeed the return to the gold standard and the general strike of 1926 produced such gloom that the British motor industry believed growth would be even slower than it was. In 1927 the Society of Motor Manufacturers and Traders made some calculations on the cost of buying and keeping a car, estimated the groups in British society that could afford such costs, and concluded that the saturation point for auto ownership would be reached when registrations reached a total of one million.[6] A year later the *Economist* suggested that "the time is past when any startling increase in annual registrations may be expected."[7] In fact registrations reached one million in 1930. Despite the depression the two-million mark was reached in 1939.[8] This was a far cry from the 27 million American cars then on the road, but it illustrates something characteristic about the relationship be-

Table 6.1 Growth of automobile ownership in the United States and Great Britain (1910–1970)[a]

Year	United States	Great Britain
1910	5	1.7
1920	76	5
1930	187	23
1940	208	51
1950	263	47
1960	342	108
1970	434	215

Sources: U. S., Department of Transportation, *Highway Statistics: Summary to 1965*, p. 23; U.S., Department of Commerce, *Statistical Abstract of the United States 1975*, p. 570; British Road Federation, *Basic Road Statistics* 1973, p. 2.
[a] Private cars per 1,000 population.

tween planning and forecasting (private and public) and the automobile in Britain. Despite the fact that the full impact of the motor car on British society was delayed for many years, it seemed as if there was never enough provision made for the inevitable and foreseeable consequences of mass motoring when it did arrive. Whereas the American lifestyle and landscape had a chance to evolve with and adjust to the changes wrought by the automobile during a period of more than sixty years, British towns and living patterns persisted in their old, preauto mold much longer. Not until the early 1960s did the growth of auto ownership begin to cause serious disruption and dislocation in Britain. In spite of the fact that the British could study the mistakes made in the course of the American experience in great detail (most were appalled), efforts by planners and politicians to avoid or alleviate the worst consequences of automobility were seriously hampered by the overwhelming demand on the part of the common man to get behind the wheel of his car and drive where he pleased.

In the years since 1955 the long-cherished dream of owning a car has become a reality for many members of the middle- and working-classes in Britain. The extent of the motor car's penetration down to the lower levels of the social hierarchy can be seen in the results of a survey carried out by the Automobile Association. It showed that of those who had owned cars prior to 1945 nearly 70 percent were in the top social classes. But of those who had purchased their first car since 1956, more than 60 percent were in the two lowest social brackets.[9] Ownership of an automobile was one of the most concrete manifestations a worker could make of a claim to equality with social betters. As one commentator put it:

Car ownership became the new liberator in democratic terms; it was the new emancipation for the lower-middle class and the new skilled worker. Place in society is reflected too obviously with other possessions; one's home and residential area too clearly reflect one's earning power and status. But the car is different: the driver of a typical family saloon can be (and frequently is) drawn from very wide sectors of society; his station is unknown and unknowable; the car is at once a concealer and a herald of his stake in mid-mass. As a democratizing medium it is a passport to a social recognition formerly denied him; as a destroyer of traditional class barriers it is supreme.[10]

Problems arose, however, when the burgeoning number of automobiles brought with it the inevitable side effects of noise, congestion, pollution, and general disruption of urban amenities. British towns are older and more compact than American towns. Thus despite the lower levels of car ownership British society began to experience many of the same auto-related problems and disputes America was also undergoing in the 1960s and 1970s. A segment of the British middle class, symbolized and led by urban planners, sociologists, and social critics, became disenchanted with the effects of the auto and sought to restrict the use and possibly even the ownership of motor cars. This set the stage for a political struggle against a transport policy that would allow unlimited growth of automobile travel.

We will examine the evolution of a major part of British policy toward the automobile: the provision of the roads essential for the auto's operation. We will see how social conditions, particularly the delay in achieving mass motorization, combined with the nature of British institutions to produce a public policy that put fewer resources into roads than was the case in America. We will then notice that the consequences of such a policy can be evaluated as both good and bad: good in that there is still a chance for Britain to enter the last two decades of the twentieth century with a more balanced and economical transportation system than America's, bad in that the lower classes in Britain must pay a higher share of the costs of this balance in the form of more restricted use of automobiles than either their social superiors in Britain or their car-owning lower-class counterparts in America.

THE RISE AND FALL OF THE ROAD FUND

Early in this century the central government in London had little to do with the roads, which were the responsibility of local government. Local authorities financed their roads from the rates—local property taxes. This made sense because most of the traffic on Britain's roads at the time was local traffic. Travelers going any substantial distance took the train. Freight, except for local deliveries, was also handled by the railroads, supplemented by some canal traffic and coastal shipping. There was no formal network of national thruways. Intercity routes followed the same paths as the king's highways of the late middle ages, or the traces of the turnpikes of the early nineteenth century. Turnpike companies, private enterprises with government charters, had flourished briefly between 1800 and 1840, but the roads they built had been designed for the ox cart and horse-drawn wagon. With the coming of the railroads, they lost most of their traffic and went bankrupt. The turnpikes themselves were then either abandoned or taken over by the local authorities and maintained at an even lower standard. Beatrice and Sidney Webb described the condition of the roads at the time: "A more or less yielding or gravelly surface, formed of imperfectly consolidated broken stone, in which the horse's hoof could find, alike in wet weather and dry, in summer heat and winter's frost, a firm foothold."[11]

For horse traction such roads were quite sufficient. Motor traction was another story, however. In 1904, when there were only 8,500 private cars in use, there was already a growing volume of complaints by motorists about the poor condition of the country's roads.[12] Dust and congestion due to pedestrians, bicyclists, and horse-drawn vehicles were the major summer problems; mud was the bane of winter driving. Naturally the vast majority who did not own cars were not at all eager to pay more taxes to improve the roads for the benefit of a few wealthy scorchers (speeders).

It soon became clear to motorists' organizations such as the Royal Automobile Club and the Automobile Association that the solution to the problem of providing better roads had to be sought at the national level. After several years of discussion and the creation of a royal commission to look into the problem, the motorists put forward a proposal. They advocated a national road fund to be administered by a central highway department and used to maintain and improve the roads. A representative of the automobile club told the royal commission that motorists would be willing to pay more toward the cost of the roads, provided the money collected from them was spent for roads and not for other purposes.[13] This approach was eagerly accepted by the government as the basis of its plan. In his budget speech to Parliament in 1909, the new chancellor of the exchequer, Lloyd George, proposed to make the road system virtually self-financing. The government would impose a graduated horsepower tax on automobiles and a tax of 3 pence per gallon on imported petrol (gasoline). The proceeds of these two new taxes, less the cost of collecting them, were to be administered by a central authority and spent on the roads. Lloyd George's proposal was soon embodied in the Development and Roads Improvement Funds Bill laid before Parliament that same year. During the course of the parliamentary debate on the bill Lloyd George explained the bargain the government had struck with the motorists:

They [the motorists] are willing and even anxious to subscribe to such a purpose, so long as a guarantee is given in the method and control of expenditure that the funds so raised will . . . be devoted exclusively to the improvement of the roads. . . . I want to make it clear . . . that expenditure undertaken out of the fund must be directly referable to work done in connection with the exigencies of the motor traffic of this country.[14]

Here was the notion of earmarking motor vehicle and motor fuel revenues being proclaimed in Britain years before its first appearance in the United States. But there was a crucial difference between this British style of earmarking and the subsequent American methods. The promise to spend motor vehicle and motor fuel tax revenues only on roads was made in Parliament and was thus on the public record, but it was not written into the law! The actual text of the law created a Road Board and a Road Fund that would receive the revenues from the motor taxes and spend them on roads. But nowhere in the law was it stipulated that the Road Board had to spend all the funds it received. Nor did it explicitly prohibit the government from withdrawing some or all of the unspent road funds and using them for other purposes. In other words, the earmarking of road revenues was a political and not a legal obligation. At the time the British motorist associations were quite content with Lloyd George's assurances. During the royal commission hearings an automobile club spokesman was specifically asked if he was concerned that the treasury might take over the revenue for the Road Fund. He replied, "Any recommendation made by this commission would probably carry such very great weight that no chancellor of the exchequer would venture to disregard it."[15] Thus at the time it appeared inconceivable that His Majesty's government would violate its solemn and public promise to earmark motor revenues for the Road Fund.

In fact the government did keep its promise for the next fifteen years. The Road Board officially came into existence in 1910. But it was not a true road-planning and road-building authority because the House of Lords had feared such an authority might encroach upon local government's powers. They amended the bill to ensure that the Road Board was little more than a conduit for funds flowing to local governments. The board made grants to local authorities, who were free to spend them on their roads with a minimum of supervision from the board. As a result there was no comprehensive planning or reconstruction of the British road system, and almost no new road construction at all. More than 90 percent of the grants made by the Road Board went toward small scale improvements in road surfaces.[16] The board's major accomplishment was to subsidize the paving of Britain's existing road network. Tar replaced dirt and gravel at the expense of the motorist instead of the local taxpayer.

Had the spread of automobile ownership been as rapid in Britain as in America, the deficiencies of the Road Board would have been clear from the start. Even so it was not long before motorists were complaining about the slow pace of the board's grant program. The board was virtually an extension of its chairman, Sir George Gibb, who had previously been the general manager of the North-Eastern Railroad, and chairman of the Underground Electric Railways Co.[17] Perhaps because of this background Gibb proceeded to distribute the Road Board's funds with agonizing slowness. By the end of its first year of operation the board had made grants worth just over a quarter of a million pounds. But it had received so much revenue from the proceeds of the new taxes that it had accumulated a surplus of nearly two million pounds. By March 1915 the surplus had mounted to six and one-half million. The board worked quite unsystematically; throughout its entire lifespan of eight years it met only forty-one times.[18] It was not long before exasperated local governments began to petition the exchequer to allow them to receive direct payments from the treasury, rather than have to wait for Road Board grants.

In retrospect it is clear that this British attempt to institutionalize the practice of earmarking differed in two major respects from later American efforts. First, there was no ironclad earmarking procedure written directly into the law. This invited the treasury to poach on road funds without having to seek parliamentary approval. Second, the manner of operation of the Road Board and the personality of its chairman did not permit it to develop into the nucleus of a national highway department, like the American Bureau of Public Roads, which could come to constitute a nexus of political power by linking local highway departments, motorists, and the business community into a powerful coalition-supporting highway construction. In the end these two differences proved the undoing of earmarking in Britain, and therefore had a major impact on the development of British highways and the degree to which the country adopted the automobile as its primary passenger transport mode.

The informal procedure for earmarking established by Lloyd George in 1909 was dismantled piecemeal during the 1920s and 1930s. After World War I the several departments relating to transport were reorganized into a new Ministry of Transport which was preoccupied with railroad problems and dominated by men with railroad backgrounds.[19] The previously independent Road Board was abolished in favor of a Department of Roads within the new ministry, despite the opposition of the motorist groups. In addition one of the principal sources of road revenue, the petrol tax, was abolished. The Road Fund continued to exist and receive revenues from vehicle fees and taxes, but without the petrol tax revenue the fund's growth was much slower than it otherwise would have been. Soon even this modest growth was impeded by the financial exigencies of the times. The general strike of 1926 gave the treasury the excuse it had been looking for to break the bargain of 1909 and divert road revenues into the general fund. The Conservative chancellor of the exchequer at that time was Winston Churchill, and he had for some time been considering the best way to go about raiding the Road Fund. He was in favor of aiding the still privately owned railroads by cutting back the amount of public money that was in effect subsidizing their competition, the lorry and the bus. Apprehensive motorists groups bombarded Parliament with pleas that the government was morally bound to uphold its part of the bargain of 1909 in which they voluntarily submitted to taxation in return for a pledge that the revenue raised would be spent only on the roads. Churchill would have none of this argument. In blistering, typically Churchillian language he thundered back:

There can be no question of the power of Parliament to sweep away the whole system of taxation and reimpose new taxation. . . . Whoever said that motorists were to contribute nothing for all time to the general revenue of the country, or that, however great their luxury and wealth, or the inroads they make on the convenience of pedestrians they were to be exempt for all time through their character of motorists from the smallest contribution to our revenue? Entertainments may be taxed; public houses may be taxed; racehorses may be taxed; the possession of armorial bearings and manservants may be taxed—and the yield devoted to the general revenue. But motorists are to be privileged for all time to have the whole yield of the tax on motors devoted to roads. Obviously this is all nonsense. Whoever said that, whatever the yield of these taxes, and whatever the poverty of the country, we were to build roads, and nothing but roads, from this yield? We might have to cripple our Trade by increased taxation of income; we might even be unable to pay for the upkeep of our Fleet. But never mind, whatever happens, the whole yield of the taxes on motors must be spent on roads. . . . Such contentions are absurd, and constitute at once an outrage upon the sovereignty of Parliament and upon common sense.[20]

Mr. Churchill announced that in his 1926 budget he was taking £7 million from the accumulated surplus of the Road Fund and applying it to meet current general obligations. He also proclaimed a new policy whereby each year one-third of the tax on automobiles would be regarded as a luxury tax and transferred to the treasury. The next year Churchill made an even larger raid on the Road Fund, taking the entire unspent balance of £12 million. He took a further step in the direction of divorcing motor vehicle taxes from road spending when he reintroduced the petrol tax but provided that its yield be paid directly to the treasury rather than to the Road Fund. This left the fund with a much narrower revenue base and the precedent that unspent balances could be taken by the treasury at any time.[21]

When the great depression struck, there was further pressure to use road revenues for relief and other social welfare measures. The earmarking principle swiftly lost much of its remaining support in the Commons, as successive committee reports called for bringing all public expenditure under parliamentary scrutiny. For example, a report of the National Expenditure Committee in 1931 decried the "heavy outlay on what we have termed 'amenity development' largely serving the needs of pleasure traffic insofar as it is required at all." The committee went on to remark that the Road Fund had become little more than a "convenient means of financing grandiose projects without the inconvenience of obtaining parliamentary approval and providing for the cost in the annual budget."[22]

Finally in 1936 the Conservative chancellor of the exchequer, Neville Chamberlain, announced that not only was he expropriating the Road Fund's balance again that year, but also, beginning in 1937, the Road Fund would finally lose its last shreds of financial independence. It would have to submit annual estimates like any other government department and would receive its budget from annual appropriations by Parliament. "Surely," reasoned Chamberlain, "when a chancellor has to wrestle with a task so formidable as that in front of me, he ought to be able not only to survey the whole field of expenditure but also all his sources of revenue, so that he can direct them where they are most needed."[23] Now the roads budget would have to compete with welfare spending, defense spending, subsidies to other forms of transport, and the like. The legal existence of the Road Fund lingered on for twenty years after its practical demise; it was formally abolished by the Miscellaneous Financial Provisions Act of 1955.[24] Thus the British attempt at earmarking came to an end, not with a bang but with a whimper.

THE SHORT, HAPPY LIFE OF THE
MOTORWAY BOOM

One of the consequences of failure to secure increasing resources for the roads through earmarking was that spending on highways in Britain stagnated for more than twenty years. In 1930 the central government had spent £20.5 million on roads while local governments spent £44.9 million. In 1939 the figures were virtually the same. In 1950, taking account of inflation, they were even lower (see table 6.2). Naturally World War II, with its draconian petrol rationing and six-year hiatus in civilian auto construction, had a severe impact on road spending. In fact K. M. Gwilliam has calculated that in 1949 the total British road expenditures were, in real terms, less than in 1911, despite a twentyfold increase in vehicles using the roads.[25] This situation could not continue indefinitely. Indeed during this long period of austerity a number of important legal and administrative changes took place that were to have a very significant impact on highway policy in later years.[26]

The postwar years were a period of vaulting hopes and nagging frustration. The new Labor government made public an ambitious set of plans for the roads. They envisaged a ten-year period during which the main national roads would be comprehensively reconstructed and a start made on building a network of motorways (superhighways). The central government was to spend £80 million in the first year alone, with steadily increasing expenditure thereafter. But the plans were never put into practice. With no automatic mechanism to ensure long-term financing, the roads fell victim to Britain's severe postwar economic crisis. The roads budget was an easy item to sacrific compared to Labor's cherished

Table 6.2 Central and local government spending for highways in Great Britain (1920–1975)[a]

Year	Central government	Local government	Total
1920	3.5	23.1	26.6
1930	20.5	44.9	65.5
1939	20.6	44.0	64.6
1946	9.1	34.2	43.3
1950	25.9	53.2	79.1
1955	39.5	60.7	100.2
1960	98.9	89.2	188.1
1965	209.4	146.1	355.5
1970	334.4	276.5	610.9
1972	404.2	399.2	803.4
1975	541.0	583.0	1,127.0

Source: British Road Federation, *Basic Road Statistics 1975,* pp. 1, 27.
[a]In millions of pounds.

social welfare programs. There was no strong bureaucratic spokesman within the government to oppose the treasury's slashing of the road budget. The Ministry of Transport was again preoccupied with rail problems, this time the nationalization of the railroads, and it was content to let local government do what it could to patch up the roads. Derek Aldcroft pointed out that the transport ministry "seemed scarcely aware of the pressing need to spend large sums on new roads . . . the ministry was still under the impression that traffic problems could be solved largely by patchwork improvements and judicious control of traffic at crucial points."[27]

Not until the mid-1950s did the economic situation permit this picture to change significantly. Road expenditure by the central government doubled between 1955 and 1960, and in 1959 the amount spent by the national government exceeded the sum of local road expenditure for the first time. Moreover, central government spending on new construction, mainly motorways, was rising much faster than spending on maintenance and minor improvements. In 1959 the first sections of motorway, the Preston bypass and the London–Birmingham motorway were opened to traffic. Road spending doubled again between 1960 and 1965, and by 1970 the central government was spending more than eight times as much on highways as in 1955 (see table 6.2). The increase in spending was barely able to keep up with the automotive explosion that took place during those same years. From a relatively uncongested road net with only 2.3 million cars in circulation in 1950, Britain's highways were changed into a congested system with over 11.6 million cars in 1970.[28]

What kind of policy impact did the rise of mass auto ownership have on British highway spending? The data in table 6.2 show that the absolute amount spent on roads has been rising over the years. But what about the trend in highway spending in relation to highway revenues? In other words, in the absence of an earmarking plan did British governments continue to spend about the same proportion of highway revenues on the roads, or a smaller proportion? The answer is apparent in table 6.3 which shows that in 1940 nearly three-quarters of the revenues collected from automobiles were spent on the roads. By 1950 this percentage had dropped below two-thirds. By 1970 barely one-third of the highway-generated revenue was being spent on roads; the rest went into the general fund. Thus, even though road spending did rise rapidly in Britain after 1955, it did not rise as fast or as far as it would have if all, or even a fixed proportion, of the motor taxes had been earmarked for highways. The motorists organizations never tire of pointing out this fact to justify their requests for more highway spending. But the British government, once having established the principle that motor taxation is no different than any other tax, is not going to reinstitute any form of earmarking. All the more so, since motor taxation has come to constitute

Table 6.3 Road-user tax revenues and highway expenditures in Great Britain (1940–1972)[a]

Year	Road-user tax revenues	Highway expenditures	Expenditures as percent of revenues
1940	87	65	74.7
1950	131	79	60.3
1965	895	355	39.6
1970	1,797	611	34.0
1972	2,102	785	37.3

Source: British Road Federation, *Basic Road Statistics 1973*, p. 35.
[a]In millions of pounds.

fully 12 percent of the total national tax revenue, it is far too valuable a source of income to be spent merely for roads.[29]

The growth rate of road spending began to slow down in the 1970s. Even more important was the fact that the growth of central government road spending slowed down faster than the growth of local government road spending. This meant that a smaller percentage of the total road budget was going for motorways—which are 100 percent financed by the national treasury—and more was being spent on improving and upgrading existing roads—which are jointly financed by central and local governments. In fact, as table 6.2 indicates, by 1975 local road spending had once again surpassed national spending. This signaled the end of the motorway boom, an event brought about by the potent combination of fiscal pressures and citizen discontent with the extension of motorways into urban areas. It is to a dramatic example of that citizen discontent that we now turn our attention.

THE MOTORWAY BOX REBELLION

Britain has long been a predominantly urban nation. Its cities were shaped long before the invention of the automobile. The narrow, winding streets of British towns, with their closely packed rows of homes, shops, and pubs that American tourists find so fascinating, become clogged with traffic much faster and by fewer cars than American streets. London, as the largest urban complex in Britain, has always faced serious transportation challenges. In the nineteenth and early twentieth centuries London developed one of the most effective public transport systems in the world. A vast network of commuter railroad lines, subways, and bus routes extended London's commuting hinterland thirty or more miles from the center of the city. Despite this excellent public transport system the prosperity of the 1950s and 1960s brought with it a tremendous growth in the number of private automobiles being used in the city. Car registrations in London tripled between 1950 and 1966; by that year one out of three families in central London and one out of two families in the suburbs owned at least one car.[30] This caused problems. The city's streets simply lacked the capacity to handle such a volume of automobile traffic. Average speeds for crosstown journeys plummeted, and congestion became a serious impediment to the quality of life in London. Marginal improvements such as one-way streets, no parking zones, and more offstreet parking did not improve the situation. Londoners and the local authorities stood therefore at an important turning point in the development of their city. Should they attempt to preserve the historic environment of the city by somehow limiting the use of the motorcar? Or should they modify substantially the character of London by building a system of urban highways designed to accommodate the existing and foreseeable traffic?

For a while it appeared that the choice might be to build the roads needed to accommodate the traffic. The 1960s were years when urban motorways seemed to be the only solution. Road building was part of the spirit of the times and was articulated into a comprehensive transportation-planning philosophy. This trend was best expressed in the report of a task group at the Ministry of Transport, *Traffic in Towns*.[31] (The report was widely referred to as the Buchanan report, after Mr. Colin Buchanan, the principal author.) In an earlier book on the social impact of the automobile, entitled *Mixed Blessing,* Buchanan had shown that he was well aware of the high cost to society entailed in increased automobility.[32] In the Ministry of Transport study he and his colleagues indicated that this cost would have to be paid and spelled out in detail how the automobile and the city should be reconciled in Britain.

The report started from the proposition that traffic and towns were inseparable. The human activities in urban areas would inevitably generate traffic. At the same time, however, the amount of traffic that a given urban area could tolerate without the loss of many of the amenities of city life was limited. To preserve the character of many residential and shopping areas, some restraint on the growth of traffic in these areas was essential. The best way to do this, the report argued, was to delimit those streets whose purpose was clearly of local nature—to enable people to drive to and from their homes, or to neighborhood stores, cinemas, businesses—where thru traffic was clearly deleterious to the environment, and keep the thru traffic off such local streets by channeling it onto a few major arteries that would bypass the local streets altogether. Buchanan's scheme called for a hierarchy of roads, ranging from district streets to primary, regional, and national roads. In many urban areas roads as far down in rank as primary roads were to be built to motorway standards. This would leave local streets less congested, better able to serve the local uses that they were designated for.

The Buchanan report had an immediate impact on traffic planning in the United Kingdom and indeed in the world. (An abridged paperback version of the report had a very brisk sale, and the book has been translated into six foreign languages.) It was not that the report was strikingly original that made it so influential but rather that it summarized many ideas that had been current for some time but never related to one another in a systematic fashion. Perhaps the aspect of the report most enticing to the traffic planners was the authors' feat of demonstrating that the urban environment could best be preserved and protected by constructing an extensive network of motorways. It was this point that cities could have both environmental protection and motorways, indeed that without motorways to channel thru traffic there could be no effective way to protect local neighborhoods from the rising tide of cars, that made *Traffic in Towns* into the intellectual justification for an ambitious program of motorways in London.

In fact plans for an extensive program of urban motorway construction had been gathering dust in the county hall since they had been drawn up by Patrick Abercrombie in an urban renewal program produced during the wartime blitz. Redrafted several times over the years, the plans called for a system of three circumferential ringways connected by twelve radial motorways. Ringway 1, known as the motorway box, was planned to cut through the residential areas of inner London. Ringway 2, about seven miles from the center of the city, would cut through the interwar surburbs (suburbs that grew up in the 1920s and 1930s, between the two World Wars), and ringway 3 would circle the built up area about twelve miles from the center.[33] But although the traffic planners cherished these projects, there had not been much active political support for them in the organs of local government in London. In the mid-1960s local government in London had been reorganized into a two-tiered arrangement consisting of, at the bottom, thirty-two boroughs with an average population of 250,000 and the Greater London Council (GLC) at the top. The GLC's jurisdiction extended over some 620 square miles and included a 1970 population of 7.6 million. It was designated the strategic planning authority for the greater London area, with a wide variety of competencies, including the planning of major road construction.[34]

Shortly before the 1967 elections to the GLC the leader of the Conservative group on the council, Sir Desmond Plummer, decided to make the issue of the slow pace of road construction in London one of the main planks of the London Tories electoral platform.[35] The Labor group which was in control of the council was too sluggish in this area. Londoners were fed up with the impossible traffic situation in their city. We have to get London moving, physically moving, he said. The planned road projects have to be moved off the drawing boards and out onto the ground. The Conservatives, if elected, would see them built. This was a promise.

The Conservatives won the 1967 GLC election, and the 1970 election as well, although it is hard to say if the roads issue was a major factor in the voters choice. But Sir Desmond treated his victory as a mandate to push hard for motorway construction in London. The vast bulk of the finances for such motorways would have to come from the British treasury of course. That was Sir Desmond's main problem in the beginning. The full system of ringways was estimated to cost approximately £2 billion ($4.9 billion) at 1970 prices.[36] This represented something like £800 for every family in London and made it the single most expensive public works project in British history. The inner ringway, the motorway box, would cost more than £20 million ($48 million) per mile to construct. Nevertheless, Sir Desmond persevered, and construction gradually began to get underway.

No public works project of this magnitude could be carried out without arousing opposition. Urban superhighway construction projects often seem only slightly less controversial than nuclear reactors. In the case of the motorway box the baseline of protest was created by the fact that it would entail the destruction of 15,000 to 20,000 homes in a city chronically short of housing. This natural constituency for rebellion was reinforced by a rapidly growing variety of environmental concern groups that became active in Britain (and in the United States as well) in the late 1960s and early 1970s. These organizations ranged from primarily London-based groups such as the London Amenity and Transport Association and the Pedestrian Association to national bodies such as the Transport Reform Group, the Motorway Action Group, and the broad coalition represented by Transport 2000, which was an alliance not only of transport and environment groups but also included representatives from the British Railways and the three major unions.[37] The leadership and much of the rank and file of these groups tended to be well educated, middle class, and slightly socialist in orientation. They drew upon the expertise of sympathetic planners and social scientists at such institutions as the London School of Economics to help prepare impressively documented briefs against the motorways.

The opponents of the motorways asked the GLC to demonstrate what benefits the new roads would bring. Wouldn't they simply generate more traffic, as had happened with other expressways in other cities? This would leave local streets still congested because the traffic had to leave the motorways at some point. In addition the city would be short 15,000 houses and probably more because the £2 billion that the project would cost would, given the financial pressures on British government, be taken away from other spending programs such as public housing. Wasn't too little thought being given to better coordination of public transport? Wouldn't the same £2 billion invested in public transport yield the same goal of increased mobility and access without the drawbacks of destruction, disturbance, and disamenity involved in the motorway scheme?

These arguments, repeated over a period of years and given publicity by an official public inquiry into the GLC's plans for future transport development had a definite impact on public opinion.[38] The London Labor party, searching for an issue they could use against the Tories who controlled the GLC, seized on the motorways and made a promise to abandon the whole scheme into the major plank in the 1973 electoral platform. When Labor did win control of the GLC in that year, the new administration of Sir Reginald Goodwin withdrew the GLC support of the program, which effectively cancelled it.

To symbolize the change in policy thinking about how to deal with the motor car in London's transport environment, Labor appointed Michael Thompson of the London School of Economics and leader of one of the major antimotorway groups to be the GLC's consultant on transportation. Thompson was able to draw on the thinking and planning of a wide variety of antimotorway intellectuals whom he brought with him to the GLC's transport department. The policy principles followed by this group were substantially different from those held by their Tory predecessors. The differences were spelled out in a special report, *Transport Policies and Programme 1975–1980,* issued by the GLC shortly after Labor came to power.[39] The report rejected the notion that more and better transportation is an end in itself, or even an end worth achieving if it entails sacrificing other important values. New transport undertakings must be viewed skeptically. "The aims of transport are secondary to the general social aim of improving the quality of life in London and the proposals must be judged in this light. Certainly no simple monetary measure or economic evaluation can of itself be a sufficient guide to the worthwhileness of the proposals as a whole."[40] Londoners should not be hindered unnecessarily from moving about, but neither should they be unduly troubled by traffic nuisance or road construction projects. Most new transport funds should go to public transport improvement. Efforts should be made "to restrain the use of cars particularly at the busiest times. For some of the journeys which cannot be made by car, because of traffic restraint, public transport will provide an alternative; for others it cannot, and these journeys will not take place."[41] This would have been heresy to conventional traffic planners. The GLC proposed to restrain traffic in central London, at least at first by such measures as restricting the amount of on- and offstreet parking, higher parking charges, keeping public car parks closed until 11 AM, creating exclusive bus and taxi lanes, and pedestrianizing many streets. The next step would be requiring cars entering central London to obtain a special license, and after that they would begin to license and tax private parking spaces.

With such an outlook on the automobile there is not much need for further development of the road system. The report flatly stated, "the building of a network of urban motorways is no longer acceptable in London."[42] It also rejected large-scale upgrading of existing roads but did recognize that this may be necessary in some situations. Road im-

provements were henceforward to be evaluated according to a new set
of criteria, which are rather different from the ordinary. A road scheme
may be judged disadvantageous and hence not be adopted if it

• increases general road capacity and therefore encourages more
traffic,

• needs a large property or land take, especially housing or open
space,

• is detrimental to areas of high amenity (conservation areas) listed
buildings,

• produces a section of the network out of balance with the rest (which
means the next section must be done, and the next, and so on),

• causes severance to communities,

• is very costly in terms of the benefits achieved.

A road project may be judged advantageous if it

• is part of a scheme to restrict commuter traffic from inner London or
major shopping centers,

• enables pedestrianization or partial pedestrianization to take place,

• improves the movement of public transport,

• improves public transport interchange facilities,

• reduces pedestrian/vehicle conflict or accident risk,

• enables environmental improvement to be achieved, environmental
areas to be protected or created,

• provides for the needs of areas being redeveloped,

• enables freight to be moved by the most appropriate route or the
mode of transport least damaging to the environment,

• improves amenity and convenience for pedestrians,

• maintains standards of structural safety (such as dealing with weight
restricted bridges),

• provides a staged solution to the ultimate solution but with benefit in
its own right.[43]

The motorway box rebellion represents a significant turning point in
the continuing development of transport policy in the United Kingdom. It
was a revolt not only against a specific set of roads but also against an
entire philosophy of road building. The rebellion was carried out by a
well-educated, middle-class minority of intensely concerned and active
citizens who claimed to be representing the best interests of the vast
majority of Londoners, even those who owned cars but did not wish to
see the charm of their city destroyed. There was more than just the negative accomplishment of stopping the roads. The process of formulating,
and then beginning to apply an alternative philosophy or paradigm of

transport planning, put renewed emphasis on public transport and greatly reduced the future growth prospects for the automobile/highway complex. The rebellion meant, as one English observer put it, that "the day of the large-scale urban motorway, at least in London, is now over. . . . London will probably end this century with fewer miles of motorway than any other major city in the world."[44]

Considering London's key position as the fulcrum of the political, economic, transportation, and communication systems of the British Isles, events there are bound to have widespread repercussions throughout the entire country. Indeed citizen protests against road schemes have been felt in many other British towns and cities. In addition dissemination of the alternate paradigm emphasizing traffic restraint and reliance on public transport was given a strong impetus by the conflict over the London motorway box. The paradigm was spelled out for planners and specialists in works such as Stephen Plowden's *Towns against Traffic,* the title of which indicates it is an answer to the policy recommended in the Buchanan report.[45] The paradigm has even been popularized in paperback bestsellers such as *Changing Directions,* a report published by the Independent Commission on Transport.[46]

Motorist groups, which still represent a growing proportion of the British population, will undoubtedly counterattack and attempt to get the road-building program back into high gear.[47] But the very fact that public opinion and the policy-making elite are split on the issue of how far to develop highways in urban areas makes it easier for the central government to divert funds away from roads to other urgent priorities. This was exactly what was happening in the mid-1970s. As the pound

Table 6.4 Length of superhighways and motor vehicles per mile of road in selected countries

Country	Miles of superhighways (1974)	Motor vehicles per mile of road (1973)[a]
United States	35,431	30.7
West Germany	3,404	64.4
Italy	3,160	80.5
France	1,506	33.8
Great Britain	1,063	72.1
Japan	943	38.5
Netherlands	849	70.5
Belgium	628	45.9

Sources: Herbert Gröger, Die Verkehrsstrukturen in den Ländern der EG, *Internationales Verkehrswesen* 5 (September–October 1976), p. 278; Hirotada Kohno, The Development of Japan's Road Network, *The Wheel Extended* 6 (summer 1976), p. 13; British Road Federation, *Basic Road Statistics 1975,* p. 28.
[a]Includes superhighways, main roads, secondary roads, and other roads.

declined, and the inflation rate rose, successive governments found it useful to push back the completion dates of road projects under construction, postpone planned roads, and scale-down projected motorway networks. This could be justified in the name of environmental concern as well as economy. Whatever position one takes with regard to the merits of the automobile, it is clear that the way in which the British have financed their road system has forced policy makers continually to weigh the importance of highways against other social goals. This weighing process has led them to place far less importance on roads than is the case in the United States, and less than is the case in most other highly industrialized, highly motorized democracies. Only Italy has more cars per mile of road, and only Japan, with a much lower per capita ownership of cars, has a shorter network of superhighways. Even the Benelux countries, if taken together, have substantially longer superhighway systems (see table 6.4). Virtually alone Britain has chosen not to develop enough road space to meet the demand but instead to let congestion act as a form of traffic restraint and an impetus for individuals to choose public transport over private. In this respect Britain is indeed the "odd man out."

7
THE UNITED STATES:
THE IMPORTANCE OF BEING
EARMARKED

THE ROLE OF THE STATES IN AMERICAN
HIGHWAY POLICY

It has often been said that the automobile was European by birth but American by adoption. Europeans such as Gottlieb Daimler, Karl Benz, and Emile Constant Levassor may well have pioneered the technology of the automobile, but millions of ordinary American citizens changed the motorcar from a technical curiosity and plaything of the rich into an everyday mode of transportation. The giants of the U.S. auto industry—the Fords, the Durants, the Sloans, the Olds—are fabled, and their feats of production and salesmanship are well known. Less known is the remarkable effort of political persuasion that had to take place all across America to get governments to build the roads necessary for the automobile to assume its dominating place in the American transportation system. Europeans such as John L. McAdam, John B. Dunlop, and James Young may well have contributed the technology of hard-surfaced roads, pneumatic tires, and refined petroleum, but the American people put these things together, mixed in a little politics, and created an ever-expanding supply of the most potent road-building material known to man—money. This chapter tells the story of how the American political system enabled them to do it and of the difficulties involved in trying to get them to stop doing it.

As in Britain late nineteenth-century America relied on local governments to provide roads, which were paid for out of local property taxes. The voters saw to it that these taxes remained low. The quality of roads provided in this manner was low also. It is generally agreed that American roads in this period were much poorer than their British counterparts. Barely adequate for horse traction in ideal weather, they became a swampy morass of mud with the onset of the rainy season. But the popularity of the bicycle and then the automobile created a demand for better roads that soon exceeded the ability of local governments to provide.[1] In America, unlike Britain, the demand for better roads frustrated at the local level did not then shift to the national government but to the state governments. The existence of this intermediate level was to lead to important policy differences between the two English-speaking nations. American state governments were able to assume the main responsibility for financing the roads without being subjected to all of the competing.

financial pressures that British national government had to face and were thus able to go much further in meeting motorists' demands for more and better roads.

In 1891 New Jersey became the first state to appropriate funds to aid local government in road construction.[2] New York imposed the first motor vehicle registration fee in 1910 and showed the other states that the automobile could be a source of revenue as well as an occasion of expenditure. With new funds flowing into state coffers from license fees, the states did not remain content just to aid local governments but began to create their own highway departments to build their highways. Despite this increased state activity, road building continued to lag behind the growth of automobile ownership. Americans, wealthier, and at the time more rural, than their cousins across the sea, adopted the car with amazing rapidity. Auto ownership rose from 5 cars for every 1,000 people in 1910 to 76 cars per 1,000 people in 1920. Britain did not reach a comparable level of car ownership until the mid-1950s (see table 6.1). But while the number of cars in use was increasing 1,600 percent between 1910 and 1920, the length of paved roads increased by only 82 percent. By 1920 some 447,000 miles of road had been paved, but over 3,160,000 miles remained unpaved.[3]

It was clear that a new method had to be found to finance the roads. It had to be acceptable to the motorists, the property-owning taxpayers, and the business community. It had to be stable, not subject to periodic swings from rags to riches. Above all, it had to bring in much more money than existing fees were doing. The motor fuel tax seemed to be the obvious answer. Oregon imposed the first gasoline tax in 1919—one cent per gallon. The other states followed suit, and by 1929 all 48 states had a gasoline tax, which became and remains the most important highway-user tax in the United States.[4] The gasoline tax was so successful that states soon began to siphon off its revenues to fund other state programs. This diversion of highway revenue was no more acceptable to U.S. motorists than to British motorists. But the American motorists were notably more successful in doing something about it. Coalitions of state automobile clubs, taxpayers associations, and road-user groups, aided by their national affiliates and groups sponsored by the auto industry itself worked to promote ironclad earmarking. Their favorite device was to insert an amendment into the state constitution. Minnesota, in 1920, was the first state to adopt such an earmarking amendment. It was followed by Kansas in 1928 and eventually by fifteen more states, the last being Utah in 1962.[5] Once such devices are in a state constitution, it is virtually impossible to get them out again.[6] In states where an amendment was not possible, earmarking schemes based on normal legislation were introduced. In 1974 forty-six of the fifty states had specially earmarked highway trust funds.[7]

To encourage the adoption of earmarking in the states, the motorists groups worked on the federal level as well. They supported legislation linking federal road aid to the earmarking of funds at the state level, a link embodied in the Haydon-Cartwright Act of 1934, which states:

Since it is unfair and unjust to tax motor vehicle transportation unless the proceeds of such taxation are applied to the construction, improvement, or maintenance of highways, after June 30, 1935, federal aid for highway construction shall be extended only to those states that use at least the amounts now provided by law . . . for the construction, improvement, and maintenance of highways and administrative expenses in connection therewith . . . and for no other purpose.[8]

This position seemed reasonable to most state legislators and, as far as can be known, to most of the voters as well. The notion of earmarking had become an accepted and institutionalized part of the paradigm of public choice in U.S. transport policy. The philosophy behind earmarking was laid out by a distinguished transport economist of the period, Charles L. Dearing. He held that a diversion of highway-generated revenues "in effect constitutes a breech of faith with road users. Either the user rates have been fixed so high that they produce more revenue than is required to maintain the road plant in satisfactory condition, or the plant is being permitted to deteriorate because of the diversion of road funds to other purposes."[9] Dearing went on to say that a user tax is only equitable if the amount collected is immediately related to the service rendered. It is not equitable if it is imposed as a special tax on one segment of the public with no corresponding benefit. Highway taxes were only justified if the taxpayer got a direct return for his money in the form of better roads, more safety and convenience, and reduced driving time and costs. There were few politicians in state government (certainly none of Churchill's stature) who were prepared to argue with the assumptions that underlay this paradigm.

Even today the practice of earmarking state highway revenues for the roads constitutes the bedrock foundation of highway finance in America. This is sometimes lost sight of because most contemporary critics of highway policy have focused their attention on the federal government's highway trust fund. But one should remember that the state funds collect and earmark twice as much money as the federal fund. In 1972, for example, the states collected $11.2 billion in highway-user taxes, while the federal government collected slightly less than $5.4 billion (see table 7.1). Most of the federal money goes out to the states in the form of grants, so the states actually spend the lion's share of all the highway funds in the country. Control of revenues on this scale has made the states, especially their highway departments, into one of the bulwarks of the prohighway forces in America. They are the crucial nexus that connects the other groups in the highway lobby to the federal government's executive and legislative branches.

Table 7.1 also shows that both the federal and state governments get their highway revenues from user taxes, while local governments fund their roads mainly with property taxes, which do not increase as fast as motor vehicle and motor fuel revenues. The existence of these ever-growing state funds of earmarked highway revenue has perpetuated a highway-oriented transport system much longer than would have been the case if road finance responsibility had been shared between the central and local governments, as in Britain. The role of the states in U.S. transportation policy then has been to increase reliance on highways and act as a brake on policy flexibility in the search for a more balanced transport system.

FEDERAL AID AND INTERSTATE HIGHWAYS

For many years the federal role in highway finance was very limited. The Federal Aid Highway Acts of 1916 and 1921 set the early pattern of federal-state relations. The states were required to designate a certain portion of their total road mileage (7 percent), which then became eligible for federal aid on a 50–50 matching basis. The federal government in this manner was able to coordinate state highway planning to create an interconnected system of main highways. It did not order the states to plan and build according to a preordained national scheme, but rather it encouraged them to cooperate through its grants-in-aid, accompanied by sets of standards that had to be adhered to in return for the aid. The level of federal aid stayed at the $75 to $90 million per year throughout the 1920s. In the depression it rose significantly with the New Deal pump-priming policies, reaching a peak of $353 million in 1936. To fund this in-

Table 7.1 Sources of funds for U.S. highways by level of government (1972)[a]

	Level of government			
Source of funds	Federal	State	Local	Total
Highway-user taxes	5,370	11,200	363	16,933
Property taxes and other assessments	592	340	3,197	4,129
Investment income	313	353	280	945
Bond issue proceeds	—	1,672	700	2,372
Grand total	6,275	13,564	4,540	24,379
Percent of total	25.7	55.7	18.6	100.0

Source: U.S., Department of Transportation, *1974 National Transportation Report: Current Performance and Future Prospects,* p. 28.
[a]In millions of dollars.

creased effort, the federal government imposed a one cent per gallon gasoline tax of its own as part of the Revenue Act of 1932.[10]

World War II, while temporarily hurting highway finance, helped expand the federal government's legal role in the road sector. The Federal Aid Highway Act of 1944 rearranged the federal aid roads into the so-called ABC system of primary, secondary, and urban arterial extension roads. The ABC roads continued to receive funds on a 50–50 matching basis. The same law also authorized the construction of "a national system of interstate highways, not exceeding 40,000 miles in total extent, so located as to connect by routes as direct as practicable, the principal metropolitan areas, cities, and industrial centers, to serve the national defense, and to connect at suitable border points with routes of continental importance in the Dominion of Canada and the Republic of Mexico."[11]

But while the act did hold out the glittering promise of an integrated national network of superhighways, it did not change the funding ratio of the superhighway system, which remained at 50–50. Since at the end of the war there was already a great backlog of work to be done on the ABC system, and the construction of a new superhighway was much more expensive than the repair or upgrading of an existing road, there was little incentive for the states to begin work on the interstate segments located within their borders. The federal highway funds appropriated by Congress were nearly all used for the ABC system, and the interstate system languished.[12]

To keep up with the rising tide of postwar automobility—private auto registrations rose from 28 million in 1946 to 40 million in 1950, and then to 52 million in 1955—some states turned to toll roads as a means of financing multilane, limited access highways.[13] A veritable turnpike boom hit the country in the late 1940s and early 1950s, which saw the construction of over 3,000 miles of toll road in thirteen states at a cost of some $2 billion.[14] These roads performed quite well. They moved vehicles at higher speeds with fewer accidents than the ABC system, and nearly all of them had no trouble earning sufficient revenue to pay off their bonded indebtedness. This ticket-tollbooth method of highway finance had many advantages but one great disadvantage: it simply did not build enough roads. Toll roads had to be economically viable and good credit risks. They had to be built along routes with a high level of demonstrated traffic. They could not risk waiting until they generated their own traffic because that would hamper their ability to repay their creditors.[15] Even at the height of the turnpike boom only 8,000 miles of construction had been planned. This was a far cry from the 40,000 miles of proposed interstate system that could not get off the drawing boards for want of adequate financing.

Few politicians of the day disputed the need for more and better roads. The problem was to find a way of paying for them without raising federal or state taxes, and without unbalancing the federal budget. It was then that President Dwight D. Eisenhower stepped into the unaccustomed role of policy initiator.[16]

Eisenhower had Vice-President Nixon address the 1954 session of the National Governor's Conference and propose vastly increased federal aid for highways, especially interstate highways.[17] The initiative was very well received by the governors, but it was deliberately vague as to where the money for such aid would come from. It soon became clear that, if there was general agreement on the need for new highways, there was no clear consensus on how to finance them. There ensued nearly two years of maneuvering and coalition building before Eisenhower's initiative was enacted into law.

The president first appointed a special commission headed by General Lucius D. Clay to consider the options. The Clay panel's report clearly favored freeways over toll roads. It said a toll road system would violate the principles followed by federal aid highways since 1916. Besides toll roads would precipitate a revolution in the western states. It recommended financing the interstates by means of thirty-year bonds issued by a new Federal Highway Corporation. These would be returned by dedicating or earmarking the thirty-year revenues from existing federal gasoline and tire taxes.[18] This proposal was defeated in Congress, however, largely because Senator Harry F. Byrd (D., Va.), the chairman of the Senate Finance Committee preferred a pay-as-you-go system which would not incur any interest obligations.[19]

The rubber industry, the American Automobile Association, and the oil industry took the position that, since the interstates were also defense highways, they should be financed from the general revenues. The administration opposed this and insisted that the spending program be accompanied by a revenue-raising program as well. But a bill sponsored by House Public Works Committee Chairman George Fallon (D., Md.) which incorporated a pay-as-you-go revenue scheme based on increased gasoline, tire, and vehicle taxes was defeated by a nonpartisan vote in the House because of the bitter opposition of the industries which would have carried the increased tax burden.[20]

Over the recess between the 1955 and 1956 congressional sessions supporters of stepped-up federal highway spending organized lobbying and educational efforts on its behalf. The interests that had opposed the increased taxes were given time to rethink their positions. The federal and state highway departments designated where the urban segments of the interstate system were to be built. Representative Fallon changed his user tax proposals to make them more acceptable to the affected interests. The result was that the highway aid and user tax legislation was much more politically acceptable than in the previous session.[21] The new proposals were embodied in a two-part legislative package, the Federal Aid Highway Act of 1956 and the Highway Revenue Act of 1956.[22] These bills proposed to take the revenues from the existing federal gasoline tax, together with the receipts from a one cent per gallon increase in the gas tax and new excise taxes on tires and heavy vehicles, and channel them into a specially earmarked Federal Highway Trust Fund. In addition, to ensure that the construction of the interstate system got under way as quickly as possible, they raised the federal share of interstate construction costs to 90 percent, while keeping the federal share of ABC roads at 50 percent. Once the groundwork of compromise had been laid, Eisenhower's highway plan became politically unassailable.[23] It rolled through the 1956 session of Congress like a tractor trailer on a downgrade—a voice vote in the House and an 89 to 1 approval of the combined bills in the Senate. Thus the earmarking principle was at last enshrined at the very peak of U.S. highway policy. Nearly all of the nation's land transportation dollars were to be spent on highways, and nobody was inclined to ask embarrassing questions about the possible consequences of this one-sided emphasis. Treasury Secretary George M. Humphrey expressed the prevailing sentiment about the proper balance in transportation policy when he said, "America lives on wheels, and we have to provide the highways to keep America living on wheels and keep the kind and form of life we want."[24]

The impact of the new federal-earmarking program was impressive. Federal road spending rose from an average of $460 million a year in the period 1946 to 1956 to an average of $3 billion a year in the decade after the fund's creation. By 1973 total federal expenditures for highways were running well above $5 billion per year. About two-thirds of this was going to the interstate system, the rest to the ABC system and other road uses.[25] By September 30, 1975, some 37,125 miles of the now projected 42,000-mile interstate system had been completed. As we saw in table 6.4, the earmarking of highway funds has given the United States the financial capability to build a superhighway network that is several orders of magnitude above anything done abroad. America has more superhighways than the rest of the world combined. Beyond that her total road net is one of the most congestion free in the world, if measured in cars per mile of road. Other transport modes such as rail service or urban mass transit may have declined into an awful state for lack of public subsidies, but America's highways are second to none. This in the final analysis is the importance of being earmarked.

Earmarking was thus both a symbol and a source of the strength of the prohighway forces in America. It was in pursuit or defense of the symbolic linkage of taxation and expenditure that the diverse elements of the highway lobby were most often and most easily united and mobilized at the state and federal levels. It enabled them to appeal to the mass of motorists concerned with their highway tax dollars at work and make the argument that highways paid their own way. Thus it was also a source of strength when the highway program was challenged. It gave the highway forces an added edge because they were in the position of defending what appeared to be a conservative, self-financing mode against advocates of a mode (transit) that was always asking for a handout.

For a decade the trust fund mechanism functioned smoothly, but in the late 1960s two developments took place that plunged the whole notion of earmarking into political controversy. The first was the Vietnam war, with its rising federal deficits and inflation. In 1966 President Johnson cut federal spending by $5.3 billion. Included in the cuts were $1.1 billion of highway trust fund money that Congress had already appropriated. Johnson's impoundment of these funds brought cries of anguish from the states and sharp pressure from Congress. The president soon relented and released the money.[26] Later President Nixon resumed the practice of impounding highway funds; he was not swayed by protests. The states had to take their case to the courts. By 1972 Nixon had impounded over $2.5 billion in highway funds, and there were more than thirty suits pending against the administration on the issue. The Justice Department urged the Supreme Court to consider a case and settle the impoundment issue on broad constitution grounds. The Supreme Court declined to do so and returned all the cases to lower federal courts, which generally ruled against the administration. The first and only test of the issue at the appeals court level came in *State Highway Commission of Missouri v. Volpe.* Here the Eighth U.S. Circuit Court of Appeals ruled on April 2, 1973, that the administration had illegally withheld money apportioned to Missouri under the 1956 Federal Aid Highway Act. The court declared that funds appropriated by Congress under this law "are not to be withheld from obligation for purposes totally unrelated to the highway program."[27] Thus did the system of separation of powers and judicial review protect the earmarking of road funds from the financial pressures of inflation and budget deficits and poaching by the executive that have so long plagued the British roads budget.

THE FREEWAY REVOLT

The second problem to threaten the security of the Federal Highway Trust Fund was an upsurge of popular protest against the construction of the urban segments of the interstate highway system. Public works always stimulate opposition from individuals whose private interests are adversely affected. When public projects such as highway construction proceed naturally, incrementally by means of the gradual widening and upgrading of old roads, controversy can be kept within manageable bounds. It is when there is a radically new element in road construction such as the creation of a major urban highway where none existed before that the potential for serious outbreaks of protest is created. Building the urban interstates contained all the ingredients for a confrontation between the public authorities bent on getting the roads through and the citizenry who did not want their familiar environment disturbed for the sake of the dubious benefits conferred by the roads. The predictable protests were unpredictably strong, however, and came as quite a shock to highway officials. By 1970 freeway revolts had broken out in a dozen U.S. cities: Hartford, Washington, D.C., Chicago, Shreveport, Baltimore, Boston, New York, Cleveland, Philadelphia, Providence, San Francisco, and Seattle. The Department of Transportation announced that it considered construction of these urban segments "completely essential to an integrated national system" but conceded that local opposition could result in their not being built.[28] We cannot examine each of these freeway revolts individually, nor do we need to. A brief look at two of the better-documented controversies will suffice to illustrate the dynamics of such revolts.

San Francisco led the parade of U.S. cities in revolt against their freeways. The fight started as early as 1954 when opposition to the Western freeway began to develop. The objectors lost this battle but then switched their fire to the Embarcadero freeway which was scheduled to cut across the foot of historic Market Street. The original plans for the Embarcadero freeway called for a six-lane elevated expressway. Traffic planners demonstrated that this would be insufficient to meet the projected 1980 traffic demand, and the plans were revised to call for an eight-lane, double-decked elevated expressway that threatened to block the city's view of one of its most charming waterfront vistas. The Federal Highway Administration and the California State Highway Department refused to pay the additional cost of putting the road underground, as city officials requested. Citizen complaints and opposition had been building up, and the decision to keep the double-decked concrete monster above ground touched off an explosion of protest. Finally, in what has been described as one of the wildest San Francisco Board Meetings on Record, the city's Board of Supervisors voted to stop the project cold.[29]

Antifreeway sentiment continued to run strong in San Francisco, and in 1966 the city chose to renounce over $240 million in federal aid highway funds to keep the freeways out. The raised stub of the partially built Embarcadero was left standing, forlorn and purposeless, unless it was to be seen as a war memorial to freeway fighters. City officials were able to channel much of the aroused opinion into constructive public support for the bond issues for the BART system, which was fifteen years in the making and lacked any federal funding for most of the early years.

Another freeway revolt took place in Boston against an eight-lane expressway known as the inner belt that was to circle the city's core through Roxbury, the Fenway, Brookline, Cambridge, Somerville, and Charlestown, and link up with a segment of Interstate 95 in a five-story interchange in lower Roxbury. At first the prospects for stopping the roads appeared quite dim. Massachusetts law did not offer the option of local veto of road schemes that had been available to the San Francisco protestors. The two men who were governors of Massachusetts during the period of protest, John Volpe and Francis Sargent, had both previously been directors of the State Public Works Department and were apparently firmly committed to the freeways. Sargent was quoted as saying of the inner belt: "This road is the key to the entire Massachusetts transportation system. It has to be built."[30] Volpe had gone on to become federal Secretary of Transportation and was pushing the road from that end.

The opposition to the roads gradually coalesced into umbrella groups such as the Save Our Cities Committee and the Greater Boston Committee on the Transportation Crisis. Community leaders, clergymen, neighborhood groups, civil rights groups, and blue ribbon panels of intellectuals from the area's many universities came together and kept the issue in the news. Eventually Boston's mayor, Kevin White, was won over to the antifreeway cause. White was considering running against Sargent for governor, and this threatened to inject the freeway issue into partisan politics. In February 1970 Sargent went on television to announce that he had decided to reverse himself on the highway issue. He proclaimed a road moratorium. In November of that year Sargent was re-elected but continued to oppose overreliance on highways in transport planning for Massachusetts. He dramatized his change of heart by appointing a new Massachusetts secretary of transportation, Alan Altshuler, a political scientist from MIT who was a transport policy expert critical of overreliance on the automobile.

The publicity that was generated by the freeway revolts in San Francisco, Boston, and other cities was valuable for two reasons. First, it helped to make the general public aware of some of the issues involved. Second, it served to legitimize the protest against a highway-dominated transport system by creating an image of the masses rising in wrath against the greedy, insensitive road builders. It gave the efforts being made at the national level to break the highway trust fund the aura of a popular crusade of good against evil, of the average man against the entrenched interests, the little people against the powerful highway lobby. In fact the antiroad coalition that emerged in the late 1960s and early 1970s included many more interests than just the little man. It had to if it hoped to be effective. The forces now working for the opening up of the highway trust fund included big city mayors and councils, the rapidly growing number of publicly owned transit companies, private transit companies, transit workers unions, and many city planners.[31] Their national goal was not aimed at stopping all urban freeway construction but rather at modifying federal policy so as to give local officials a choice in their transport planning between private and public means of transport. The group was as much pro-transit as it was antiroad, perhaps more.

The national level coalition's first success came with the Federal Aid Highway Act of 1970, which permitted the states to use some money from the highway trust fund for the construction of highway-related transit support facilities such as exclusive bus lanes, passenger shelters, and parking areas. But this same legislation extended the trust fund until 1977. By 1972 the transit lobby had grown strong enough to persuade the Senate to write a highway bill that permitted trust fund money to be used for the purchase of buses and subway cars. The House refused to agree to this, however, and as a consequence no highway aid bill was passed that year. Pressure built up on the House to agree to a compromise in 1973, for many states were running low on highway funds. The 1973 Federal Aid Highway Act was a major step away from the exclusive earmarking principle. It authorized the states, beginning in 1975, to use up to $200 million (one-quarter of the amount of trust fund money earmarked for urban highway systems) for the purchase of capital equipment in bus-related projects. The act also authorized up to $800 million in 1976 for the purchase of bus and rail capital equipment. Moreover it allowed an increase in the proportion of federal aid to transit projects from 66.7 to 80 percent of the net cost of a mass transportation facility and authorized the states to substitute a mass transit line for an urban expressway if the state highway department and the U.S. secretary of transportation approve.[32]

This constituted a rather serious breech in the defenses of the trust fund. Highway advocates were now clearly losing ground. Even the Republican administration seemed to be turning against them. In 1975 President Gerald Ford, once a staunch defender of the trust fund, proposed legislation that would have virtually abolished the fund. His bill would have given the trust fund only one cent of the four-cent federal gasoline tax. Two cents would have gone to the treasury and the remaining one cent to the states. In the message that accompanied the bill, Ford said the highway trust fund was "a classic example of a federal program that has expanded over the years into areas of state and local responsibility, distorting the priorities of those governments."[33] The highway lobby proved strong enough to block this legislation. In part this was because they now had help from their traditional enemies, the transit lobby, who felt it would be foolish to abolish the trust fund as transit was finally getting a share of the fund's revenue. In April 1976 Congress passed a highway bill that extended the life of the trust fund for two more years. The bill allowed states, with the approval of the secretary of transportation, to reject completion of nonessential segments of the interstate highway system and receive equivalent revenues for transit projects instead.[34]

With the coming of Jimmy Carter the antiearmarking forces had high hopes of making further inroads into the trust fund, perhaps abolishing it altogether, because of President Carter's expressed preferences on energy conservation and eliminating gas guzzlers from the highways. They were disappointed in the Carter administration's policy positions as they were made public, however. Key administration officials admitted that the trust fund's original purpose, construction of the interstate highway system, had been largely fulfilled. But they said the fund should be kept in existence to finance the maintenance and repair of the interstate system which was becoming increasingly expensive and burdensome to the states. In August 1978 the Senate overwhelmingly rejected an amendment offered by Senators Edward M. Kennedy and Lowell P. Weicker which would have abolished the fund.[35] In November 1978 the House and Senate passed, and the president signed, a highway bill that extended the trust fund through fiscal 1984 and made trust fund expenditures for resurfacing and repair of interstate and other federal aid highways a major new thrust of the federal highway program.[36]

OLD SOLUTIONS, NEW PROBLEMS, AND POLICY FLEXIBILITY

Comparing the results of British and American highway finance policies, it is clear enough that the American system was better at building highways. Even if one controls for the difference in geographical size and the different levels of car ownership in the two countries by measuring the highway construction effort in terms of vehicles per mile of road, the United States is seen to have made twice the effort of Britain (as shown in table 6.4). The way in which the United States institutionalized the principle of earmarking is in large measure responsible for this outcome. As highway officials never tire of pointing out, effective highway development programs require a steady, assured flow of funds over many years. Long-term investment programs required by highway systems cannot be turned on and off like a water faucet. To insure this steady flow, highway funds must be protected from politicians' whims and the vagaries of the budgetary process. They must have legal protection and broad political support. The U.S. style of earmarking provided this protection and support. America had lower-cost cars to begin with and therefore a more rapidly growing, more democratic market for automobiles. People who were car owners, or potential car owners, regarded high motor vehicle and fuel taxes as antidemocratic and compelled the politicians in state and federal government to keep these taxes low. Earmarking of the taxes on motor vehicles was essential if enough revenue was to be provided to build a good road system. Earmarking did its job in an almost painless fashion. For many years motor vehicle taxes represented a small, declining amount relative to the rising income level of the general population. But because of the rising levels of car ownership, the total amount of revenue from road use taxes was more than adequate to build the world's best highway system.

Alas, as so often in life, this fabulous mechanism for building roads had the vices of its virtues, and they became more obvious as the U.S. highway system became more extensive. Earmarking solved the problem of financing a huge continental highway system only too well. But when it was adopted, neither the politicians nor the people were able to foresee that such a solution to financing the highway system would help undercut the market solutions to railway and urban transit problems and hence create a new set of problems for transport policy to grapple with. Earmarking built the roads and kept the taxes on motorists low, but it also kept the growth of public resources and capabilities in nonhighway transport modes minimal. The vast bulk of the tax revenues generated by motor vehicles, which represented the vast bulk of all transportation-generated revenue, had to be spent on roads and could not be diverted to other areas of need. Over the years this resulted in a great imbalance in the development of the different transport modes. In Britain, where diversion of motor vehicle taxes left British highway planners relatively poverty-stricken compared to their American colleagues, they were forced to make do with less. When traffic became too heavy for a given road, the British system encouraged more reliance upon traffic control and restraint measures and upon public transportation. Earmarking produced affluence for U.S. highway planners and encouraged the adoption and continuation of a highway-oriented transportation policy. If existing roads did not meet traffic requirements, then the solution was to build more and better roads. The money was there to pay for them. There was no need to think about rationing road space or limiting traffic access to certain areas at certain times or diverting part of the traffic to public transport. In America physical engineering has always been easier than social engineering.

The 1960s saw the once sacrosanct principle of earmarking come under fire from critics of the unbalanced transportation system it was providing. The controversy over breaking the Highway Trust Fund was, from one point of view, about finding ways of getting motorists to pay for some of the external costs of over-reliance on the automobile. These critics charged that the decline of public transit and the financial sacrifices needed to preserve and restore it were really costs imposed on the community by motorists, and therefore motorists should pay for these costs by allowing a portion of their motor taxes to be diverted to public transit. The 1970s saw a compromise between the highway and transit forces that did permit the diversion of a portion of the highway trust fund's revenues to transit. This compromise was an important beginning, but it is not likely to be a long-term solution to the problem of restoring balance to the transportation system. The reason for this is the tremendous inflation in the cost of both highway construction and maintenance and in construction and operation of public transit facilities. Recently the Department of Transportation launched an investigation into the extraordinary price escalation in federally aided highway projects. Its statistics showed that highway construction costs in the third quarter of 1978 were 37.1 percent higher than in the same quarter in 1977.[37] Costs of transit projects are rising much faster than the general inflation rate as well. Revenues from motor vehicle and fuel taxes are not rising fast enough to meet these costs. With a dramatically more fuel-efficient fleet of cars in store for the 1980s the prospects are dim that motor vehicle tax revenues—at present low rates—will be able to catch up with highway and transit costs.

Thus it would appear that a substantial increase in motor vehicle and motor fuel tax rates will be required. It will not be easy to win public acceptance of these increases, however. For most of our history the cost of owning and operating a car has been falling relative to personal income. Now, because of the general rate of inflation, publicly mandated safety and pollution standards, OPEC oil price hikes, and so on, car costs are rising relative to income. Public resistance to raising them still further (by the imposition of higher gasoline taxes, for example) is likely to be stronger in the present circumstances than in the past. Highway forces in several states have already tried to get voter approval for gasoline tax increases and have failed. In hindsight it is clear that the federal and state governments "missed the bus" in the fifties and sixties when they did not raise gasoline taxes to keep them at the same level proportional to income as they had been. Now the highway trust funds of the federal and state governments risk "running out of gas" because their dollars will not buy enough roads anymore. In such a situation the highway forces may resist fiercely any more diversion of funds to nonhighway uses.

It is therefore imperative to find a revised solution to the old problem of highway finance. The new solution should be one that permits the maintenance of a high-quality highway system. After investing so many hundreds of billions, it would be folly to allow the system to deteriorate seriously. But more important the new solution, unlike the old, should not tip the balance in favor of one transportation mode over all others or interfere with the solution of new problems. It must enhance public capabilities to deal with highway-generated problems such as financial weakness in urban public transit, neighborhood disruption, environmental pollution, and energy overconsumption. It must give policy makers sufficient resources and flexibility to shift public investments in transportation facilities toward establishing a more balanced transport system.

The most flexible solution of course would be to adopt the British system of putting all of the highway revenues into the general fund and appropriating money according to perceived needs. Under such a system it is unlikely that highways would be destitute of funds. The entrenched influence of the highway lobby remains too powerful to permit that. Indeed the highway lobby's power is such that under most foreseeable circumstances it will be impossible to abolish earmarking altogether in favor of the British system. We are left then with the need to find a solution that increases flexibility without too directly challenging the power of the highway lobby. The creation of a general transportation fund would seem to be such a combination of policy flexibility and political feasibility.

Since highway policy makers will probably experience serious resistance if and when they ask for user tax increases, they may well need new allies and arguments to win their case. By coupling the creation of a general transportation fund with a significant increase in gasoline taxes, they could win over many groups that normally oppose the road lobby. The transit lobby could be enticed with the promise of a larger share of the added revenues, for example. In this manner policy makers could achieve a new measure of policy flexibility for themselves, while offering increased revenues to major components of the passenger transportation system.

Would the American public be likely to accept such a dilution of the earmarking principle? It appears that public opinion is shifting away from earmarking and toward approval of the concept of a general transportation fund. According to a national survey carried out for the Department of Transportation, 50 percent of those asked approved of the creation of a general fund, while only 41 percent preferred earmarking.[38] Moreover, when the sample was broken down by age, the general fund idea was seen to be much more popular with younger respondents than with older ones. Sixty-three percent of those under 25 years old and 57 percent of those between 25 to 34 approved of the general fund idea. Only among people over 50 did more people prefer earmarking to the general fund. This suggests that the heyday of popular support for earmarking is ending and that the general fund idea is the coming thing. Older people had their ideas formed in an earlier, simpler age when the problems facing policy makers and the public were quite different from today. Young people are used to the complexity of modern transport policy problems and are less prone to see earmarking as a sacred compact between citizen and government. The object here is not to examine such a plan in all its precise details but rather to argue that the general principles outlined ought to guide policy makers in formulating their response to the needs of transportation finance in the 1980s.

What will the politics of a general transportation fund be like? The experience of President Carter's failed gasoline tax increase offers some instruction. In March 1980 the president announced that he was going to use his executive powers under section 232(b) of the Trade Expansion Act and the Emergency Petroleum Allocation Act to impose a $4.62 per barrel fee on imported oil.[39] He proposed to collect this fee only on gasoline, however. The other two branches of government acted swiftly to block the president's initiative. In May a federal judge ruled that the president had exceeded his authority by directing that the fee be collected only on gasoline, which would inevitably include domestically produced fuel as well.[40] In June the Congress voted overwhelmingly to reject the fee and then voted to override the president's veto of their fee rejection.[41] It was the first time a Democratic Congress had overridden a Democratic president's veto since Harry Truman left the White House. Carter's attempt to raise the price of gasoline at the pump through an import fee came at a time of relatively abundant gasoline supplies. The revenues would have gone directly into the general fund, with no provisions for rebating the money to consumers and no firm assurance that other taxes would be lowered to offset the import fee. The goals of the fee were said to be conservation and general revenues to balance the budget, not improvements in transportation finance.

It would appear therefore that a future increase in the federal gasoline tax will have a much better chance of enactment if it is closely tied to real transportation finance needs, rather than being presented as a conservation measure (although it might have some conservation effects, depending on the size of the increase). The strategy of selling a tax increase will likely involve pointing out that failure to raise revenues to meet the growing burden of highway maintenance will jeopardize the achievements of the past several decades.[42] It will also involve creating a broad coalition of interest groups capable of persuading the Congress to take a step it is demonstrably reluctant to take. A renewal of the squabble between the highway lobby and the antitrust fund forces would threaten to delay or prevent the formation of the coalition. This could give the forces seeking to weaken the earmarking system important political leverage. It is impossible to predict how strong that leverage will be and exactly how it may be used. It is unlikely that exclusive earmarking would be abolished outright. Perhaps some or even all of the revenue from the tax increase could be put into a general transportation fund, while leaving the highway trust fund with exclusive claim only to the revenues from the previous four cent per gallon tax. Whatever the specific arrangement, such a change would increase public policy's capability to adjust transportation policy in ways more consistent with overall national goals, while at the same time protecting the highway system which is the supreme achievement of earmarking.

IV
THE AUTOMOBILE

The automobile is the most convenient, flexible, and sought after form of mechanized personal transportation ever developed. Americans spend far more money on automobile travel than on all other forms of passenger transportation combined. Automobile travel gives individuals such a degree of personal mobility, such liberation from the restraints of place, that the slogan that headlines the ad campaign of the New Car and Truck Dealers of America is all too true: "Your driver's license plus your wheels equals freedom."[1] Americans seem to realize that in down-to-earth practical terms their right to drive is more important, or at least more useful, than their right to vote. In any case more adult Americans drive than vote. It is widely recognized that the automobile is more than just a means of transportation. As John B. Rae observes, "The total effect of motorized highway transportation on the growth and structure of present day society is so vast and so complex that definitive measurement is out of the question. The combination of motor vehicle and paved road is one of the mightiest forces to emerge in and influence our civilization."[2]

Yet, as we know from Hegel, anything that achieves such power and influence is bound to contain inner contradictions and generate its own opposition. That the automobile is such an integral part of our society means that society's problems are its problems. In an era of widespread social malaise the automobile becomes a highly visible focal point for many of the problems that beset modern society. The energy crisis is dramatized by the long lines of cars at the gas pumps and the soaring prices of motor fuel. Environmental pollution problems are brought home to the public when catalytic converters suddenly must appear on their cars and they have to pay more for unleaded gasoline. The social problems of alcohol and drug abuse show up as accident reports in the morning paper. Inevitably the car becomes the target for an increasing amount of criticism, and in recent years it has been deluged with literature pointing out its negative aspects. We have become aware that the car brings bad as well as good to our society.

In all fairness it should be pointed out that it is not the car per se that causes all these problems but rather the way in which it fits into our society, economy, and political system. How our values and institutions organize the production, distribution, and use of automobiles reveals both our strengths and weaknesses as a people. On the positive side there is the tremendous productivity, the prosperity, the mass consumption of material goods pioneered by the auto industry and still largely sustained by that vital sector of the national economy. On the negative side, however, there is the awful wastefulness of resources, land, human lives as well as the selfishness, the privatism, the shortsightedness that seems to be stimulated by overreliance on the automobile.

In a perverse way it seems as if the very success of the automobile transportation system is the source of its major problems. A few cars do not pollute much or consume too much oil. A hundred million cars do. This problem is neither unique to the automobile system nor unprecedented in historical experience. Garrett Hardin has reminded us of the historical precedents of what he calls the tragedy of the commons.[3] In medieval European villages small herds of cattle were owned by individuals, but the pastures where the cattle grazed were held in common by the whole community. In a situation where the cost of raising cattle was borne by the community, each individual had an incentive to increase the size of his herd beyond what he could have afforded if he had had to bear the full cost of feeding all his cattle. As more and more individuals tried to maximize their own profits in this manner, the total number of cattle came to exceed the capacity of the pastures, and the precious resource held in common was destroyed by overgrazing. Hardin points out that selfless individual decisions to limit the size of one's herd would have been illogical, since that would simply have allowed the most avaricious and least public-spirited citizens to reap more (temporary) private profits. Only some sort of authoritative mechanism that assigned costs to individuals in such a way as to deter from abusing the privilege of using the commons could have preserved the benefits of the commons.

The situation of the automobile is analogous to that of the commons. For each individual motorist the benefits of using a car greatly outweigh the costs of doing so. Once a person has bought a car, the extra individual costs of any given trip are minimal in comparison with the gain in mobility and accessibility. The extra costs of increased auto travel are to a very great extent borne in common: congestion, air pollution, depletion of oil resources, expansion of intrusive highway systems, and the like. The incentives are structured in such a way that it makes little sense for any given individual to forego a trip by auto and switch to transit or stay at home. The least public-spirited citizens would then be free to make even more trips themselves. Thus a spiral of increasing reliance on the auto and increasing degradation of the common resources of air quality, urban amenity, and other public goods sets in. The existing market mechanism in automobile transport is revealed to be seriously flawed because it does not assign the costs of consuming common resources to the individual drivers who benefit from their depletion.

Coping with the car in societies where transportation is based on mass motorization thus involves attempts to use authority to guide and restructure the outcomes of market processes to prevent a tragedy of the commons. How much authority will be used, what specific purposes it will be used for, and who will have to submit to such authority are questions that have the potential to arouse great disagreement and perhaps even serious political conflict. In America the attempt to use authority to cope with the car calls for a series of changes in our traditional paradigm of public choice that are neither simple nor popular. We have been so accustomed to orienting our social existence around the unlimited expansion of the automobile transportation system that ways and means of changing this state of affairs are hard to accept and a little frightening. Thus in many respects there is a keener interest in the United States than in Europe in developing the intellectual rationale and the bureaucratic capability for such a shift. This is because the United States has farther to go in adjusting its paradigm. The need is more urgent in the United States because mass motorization has progressed farther than in Europe. The traditional European paradigms and policies still contain many provisions that, although they are historical relics, are more suited to coping with future problems than the more modern paradigms based on maximization of growth and individual freedom of choice now proving deficient.

8
EUROPE AND THE UNITED STATES: COPING WITH THE CAR

THE CAR CULTURE AND ITS CRITICS

In the not so distant past we preferred to "accentuate the positive" aspects that the car brought to our society and "eliminate the negative," or at least overlook them. As the automobile triumphed as a shaper of our world, that became harder and harder to do. Today it is impossible not to see the negative consequences. We find ourselves struggling to deal with these consequences in a way that will enable us to preserve some of the positive benefits of automobility. The historian James J. Flink has suggested a sequence for portraying the changes in public attitudes concerning the car and its consequences. He writes that there have been three distinct stages in the development of American automobile consciousness.[1] The first stage ran from the invention of the motor car through the pioneering era of motoring up to the time Henry Ford began mass production of his Model T in 1910. This stage was characterized by the rapid development of social attitudes favorable to the motor car, as well as the growth of business and governmental institutions that laid the groundwork for the rapid expansion of the automobile system. The second stage, from 1911 to the late 1950s, saw "mass idolization of the motor car and a mass accommodation to automobility" that transformed the American lifestyle into the car culture. The third stage was inaugurated in the late 1950s, when it became apparent to keen observers that "automobility was no longer an historically progressive force for change in American civilization."[2] Since the onset of what might be called automobile consciousness III, the motor car has been seen by those whose consciousness has been raised as more of a problem than a solution.

In Europe the stage of mass motorization and mass idolization was not reached until the early 1950s. This relatively late accession to automobility gave European public opinion and public policy several advantages over their U.S. counterparts. First, Europeans had the clear example of American excess as a warning of what lay ahead if accommodation to the car was allowed to proceed unhampered. (They did not always take full advantage of this, but it undoubtedly helped them to avoid the worst.) Second, the Europeans had two generations of experience with a situation in which public policy treated the private automobile as an expensive luxury (in both private and public terms) not as a necessity of daily life. High taxes on such luxuries were easy to justify to mass publics forced to ride buses and subways. European governments entered the automobile age with most of the harsh, restrictive policy tools (such as graduated horse power taxes and high gasoline taxes) that U.S. policy makers have had great difficulty getting enacted into law. Finally, the late European start in automotive growth meant that its explosive, unplanned stage would be relatively short. Because of the older, more compact nature of European cities, auto-generated problems of congestion, pollution, and urban disamenity became evident at much lower levels of car ownership than in the United States.[3] The energy crisis of 1973 to 1974 reawakened European governments to the international economic and political costs of automobility after only one generation of auto growth rather than three as in America. These factors, as well as the cultural and institutional differences between Europe and the United States help account for the different manner in which their respective political systems have attempted to cope with the car.

The first American converts to automobile consciousness III were inevitably intellectuals. Only a few of the voluminous antiauto authors and titles will be cited here. Urbanologists such as Lewis Mumford and Jane Jacobs warned of the impact of the auto on the city.[4] Essayists such as John Keats attacked *The Insolent Chariots*,[5] and A. Q. Mowbray warned of the *Road to Ruin*.[6] Helen Leavitt blasted superhighways as superhoaxes,[7] and one aroused author saw an apocalyptic struggle of *Autokind v. Mankind*.[8] Even transportation insiders began to turn against the car, as when Ben Kelley blew the whistle on *The Pavers and the Paved*[9] and John Burby decried *The Great American Motion Sickness*.[10] These critical books were followed by works that claimed to offer solutions to the ills of the car culture. One of the more interesting books of this type was entitled *Beyond the Automobile*.[11] In it Tabor R. Stone offered a popularization of some current architectural and engineering thinking on how to reshape the transportation environment to reduce dependence on the auto. Social scientists K. H. Schaeffer and Elliot Sclar analyzed the land management techniques needed to provide *Access for All* by restraining the growth of the car in urban areas.[12]

In Europe the densely inhabited and land-conscious Netherlands was the first nation to see widespread public awareness that the cost of mass automobility might be too high. A book entitled *The Selfish Automobile* appeared in 1953 and warned that Holland, still adding to its tiny land area by winning back land from the sea, could not afford the kind of sprawl that accompanies the automobile.[13] (Today the Dutch have the lowest per capita car ownership in the European community.) By the 1960s intellectuals throughout western Europe were sounding much the same theme. In France the respected demographer Alfred Sauvy noted that life in French cities was being *immobilisé par la mobilité*. He decried the effect of the motor car on the traditional French way of life and sighed ruefully, with Appollinaire, "*Adieu Montparnasse, il fallait que les autos passent.*"[14] In West Germany Hans Erb blasted the aggressive drive of Volkswagen, BMW, Ford, Mercedes-Benz, and other firms, to conquer the masses for their products in his biting book, *Auto, Auto, über Alles.*[15] Several years later Hans Dollinger registered the auto makers success with his book, *Die totale Autogesellschaft* ("The Total Auto Society").[16]

The criticisms of the car culture written in the 1960s tended to have a helpless, despairing note to them because one of their major complaints was car makers and highway lobbyists were powerful enough to flatten any opposition. In the 1970s, however, the critics became more optimistic about making progress against the automobile. The rise of an important environmental movement and above all the energy crisis added weight to their side of the argument. The new theme emerging is that the automobile age is ending. It is doomed because the internal contradictions of the automobile economy can no longer respond to the external challenges it faces. In her book, *Paradise Lost: The Decline of the Auto-Industrial Age,* Emma Rothschild portrays the American automobile industry's dilemma as one of mounting problems with labor productivity combined with increasing saturation of the auto market with the kind of product Detroit turns out.[17] The industry is wedded to outmoded Fordist assembly line production methods and equally outmoded Sloanist marketing techniques of planned obsolescence and nonutilitarian frills on cars. The power of Detroit to capture the fancy of the buying public is waning and so is its influence on American civilization. James J. Flink takes up this theme in the final chapter of *The Car Culture.*[18] He judges, "By the early 1970s automobility also was no longer a historically progressive force for change in American civilization."[19] The power of the auto industry remained strong in the U.S. economy, still providing one job in six, but its hegemony was being eroded by the growth of government, which exceeds it by one job in five. In the 1970s the television, computer, and aerospace industries had replaced the auto industry as far as impact on lifestyle and social prestige were concerned. Flink believes that before the end of the century we are likely to see a radical change in our social and economic structure. The death knell of the car culture has sounded:

The automobile culture and the values that sustained it are no longer tenable. . . . The ending of the age of automobility undoubtedly marks a significant turning point in American historical development. . . . The question for the future is whether the new era of American history that is dawning will continue to develop as the age of the superstate serving the supercorporation, with self-interest, greed, and waste being its cardinal, and ultimately self-destructive, values. An alternative future characterized by true community and expanded democracy, free from the privatism, materialism, escapism, and exploitation that the automobile culture encouraged, is also within our grasp. Achieving it requires only our will, intelligence, and collective effort.[20]

Such an inspired vision of a brave new world of balanced transportation and closer-knit communities is certainly appealing. The question remains, however, Is it really coming? How accurate is the diagnosis of the fatal weakness of the car culture? Is this not a case of the auto's critics predicting something they passionately desire in the hope that perhaps their predictions will help history along in the right direction?

Books alone will not bring down General Motors and the car culture. But the critics did perform an important historical and cultural function. They helped to bring about what amounts to a transvaluation of values in public opinion. Where once we saw progress and growth, now we can also see pollution and disruption.[21] The critics were correct in pointing out that the market alone is not an adequate mechanism for regulating the auto's relationship to society. The market emphasizes the auto's advantages, most of which are enjoyed privately, but disguises its disadvantages, most of which are experienced publicly. The agitation of the critics, coupled with the continued deterioration of the quality of life as automobility reaches ever higher levels, has changed perceptions of the auto. Public opinion is now aware of the disadvantages of the auto, and it supports government action to deal with them. The question is whether this government action will be merely superficial action which helps smooth some of the rough spots for the car culture, or whether a dynamic process has been started that will eventually bring about a serious weakening of the auto's position. To answer both, we must first examine how public authority has been used to cope with some of the principal disadvantages of the car: traffic fatalities, pollution, and excess energy consumption.

SAFETY AND POLLUTION PROBLEMS

Let us begin by translating the critics' arguments into the language of analysis we have been using in this book, the market versus authority paradigm. Essentially what the critics charged was that the automobile imposed costs on society not covered by the market transactions of making, selling, and operating automobiles. Neither the manufacturer nor the motorist paid anything toward cleaning up the air the automobile polluted. Neither motor vehicle taxes nor insurance premiums paid the full costs of operating the complex police-rescue-hospital-court system that tried to cope with auto accidents. In these and other areas the externalization of a major portion of the total true costs of the automobile system enabled people to buy and operate cars more cheaply and hence enabled car makers to sell more cars and reap more profits than if they had to pay 100 percent of the true costs in a market transaction. The motorist and the motor industry were being subsidized by their ability to impose their unpaid costs on the general public.

In the United States automobile safety issues brought on the first clash between the national government and the car makers. In the early 1960s there began a growing public concern over what editorial writers liked to call the carnage on our highways. Rising auto ownership and use levels, higher speeds from more powerful cars, more young drivers from the baby boom generation combined to produce an upsurge in traffic deaths (see table 8.1). In 1966 the traffic death toll reached 50,000, and some million people were injured.[22] Dramatic publicity by the National Safety Council (in which running tabulations of holiday weekend auto deaths were widely broadcast and drivers were constantly reminded that "The life you save may be your own") served not so much to reduce accidents as to stimulate a demand among the attentive public that the government do something to reduce these grizzly figures.

Safety engineers know that the accident rate is a product of three main variables: highway design, human behavior, and vehicle characteristics.[23] Improving auto safety would entail changes in some or all of these variables. Which ones would receive most attention? Re-engineering the nation's highways would be expensive and time consuming, and the desired payoff of a drop in the accident rate would not be realized for many years. The more feasible plan seemed to be to incorporate the latest safety features into new construction and concentrate on the other two areas. Modifying driver behavior promised quicker payoffs but also presented more political difficulties. The states enforce the drunk driving laws and the speed limits. Some state officials, most notably Governor Abraham Ribbicoff of Connecticut, had scored great success in public opinion with crackdowns on speeders in the late 1950s.[24] Other states had no crackdowns. However, there was no inclination on the part of the states to yield their authority to the federal government. That left vehicle characteristics as the one area in which political action could be taken nationally without great new public expenditures and with the promise of a reasonably rapid result.

Table 8.1 Motor vehicle deaths in the United States (selected years)

Year	Total motor vehicle deaths
1924	18,400
1937	37,819
1960	36,399
1963	41,723
1965	47,089
1966	50,894
1973	54,052
1974	45,196
1975	44,525
1977	47,671[a]

Source: U.S., Department of Transportation, National Highway Traffic Safety Administration, *Motor Vehicle Safety 1977* (Washington, D.C.: Government Printing Office, 1978), pp. 6–7, A–B.
[a]Preliminary statistics.

In this manner the internal nature of the safety problem combined with the dynamics of the American political-economic system to produce a unique political struggle over auto safety. The elements were classic: rising public concern over highway fatalities and politicians who were eager to respond to this rising concern because they had seen the political benefits of the safety issue at the state level (Abraham Ribbicoff, in 1965 a U.S. senator, was chairing the subcommittee that would consider safety legislation). Since the federal government's authority could not extend to the regulation of driver behavior, the focus of federal safety efforts turned to the safety characteristics of the vehicles themselves. This put the government into a novel and dramatic confrontation with one of the most powerful economic interests in the country, the car-manufacturing industry and its legions of supporters.

The drama of the attempt of the public authorities to induce the auto makers to get moving on safety was heightened by the spectacular confrontation between the General Motors Corporation and Ralph Nader. Nader has since gone on to become the best-known consumer advocate in the country. But in 1965 he was a virtual nobody, a young lawyer working as a consultant on auto safety for the Senate commerce committee. In this capacity he produced a report (which became the nucleus of his book, *Unsafe at Any Speed*)[26] highly critical of the auto industry in general and General Motors in particular. When GM learned of the tone of this report, it hired private investigators to look into Nader's background and personal life for information that could discredit his testimony. Nader found out about these rather clumsy attempts to "dig up some dirt" on him and counterattacked masterfully. He put GM on the defensive and forced the president of the company, James Roche, to apologize publicly for its actions. The uproar created by this David-versus-Goliath battle stirred public and congressional support for two bills that became the foundation for the entire edifice of federal policy on auto safety, the National Traffic and Motor Vehicle Safety Act of 1966 and the Highway Safety Act of the same year.

The first of these acts was what Detroit objected to most. It empowered what became the National Highway Traffic Safety Administration (NHTSA) to develop and promulgate safety standards for all automobiles sold in the United States. Failure to comply with these standards could result in a fine of up to $10,000 a car. Between 1967 and 1976 some fifty standards were imposed by the NHTSA, including regulations governing such areas as seat belts, steering column, head restraints, school bus safety, and motor cycle helmet protection.[27] Also included in NHTSA standards were new crash-resistant bumpers and antitheft devices as well as other nonsafety related consumer protection items such as the odometer disclosure requirements. As if this were not displeasing enough to Detroit, the legislation also gave NHTSA the authority to issue recall orders on vehicles found to have safety-related manufacturing defects. In the years 1966 to 1975 some 52.4 million vehicles were recalled under such orders. This represents 43 percent of the total production of the period.[28]

Measuring the impact of safety standards in terms of the number of lives saved would appear to be a difficult and controversial task. It is surprising, therefore, to note that both the federal government and one of the leading critics of federal auto safety policy agree that the standards probably save about 3,500 lives per year, or a total of 28,000 lives between the end of 1966 and 1974.[29] While acknowledging that the standards have saved lives, Bruce-Briggs believes that the cost has been too high. He estimates it at some $2 billion per year or approximately $6 million per life saved. This amounts to $240 per car, however.[30] As the safety law's proponents point out, car buyers spend an average of five times as much as that for luxury and convenience options on their cars.[31] This is perhaps the key point to be made about auto safety policy in the United States. Car buyers were so affluent, the unit cost of motor vehicle safety standards so low, the auto companies so tempting a target for a little harmless show of public power, that everyone could ease their consciences by allowing Congress to tell them to buy more safety equipment. It really did not hurt Detroit, despite the car makers' complaints, nor keep people from buying cars or car makers from making profits. Detroit simply passed the added cost on to the consumer, with a few dollars of profit added on for good measure.

When federal officials attempted to act in the other two areas, highway design and human behavior, they met with much less political support and hence much less success. The Highway Safety Act of 1966 authorized the secretary of transportation to withhold up to 10 percent of a state's federal aid highway funds if it failed to meet federal design standards in its highways. However, in 1975, when the Department of Transportation finally lost patience with states that had been in noncompliance for years and decided to withhold the funds, Congress quickly intervened to prevent such an action.[32] Even more significant was the failure to achieve a system to require the use of seat belts in cars. Seat belts are the single most effective life-saving device that can be installed in autos. Buckling up before driving is a minor inconvenience, however, and so only a minority of American drivers (approximately 20 percent) bother to use them.[33] Federal safety officials hoped to encourage greater seat belt usage by requiring manufacturers to install lights and buzzers that signaled when the belts were not buckled. The most effective device of this sort would have been an ignition interlock system which would prevent the car from starting until the driver and, if appropriate, the passenger seat belts were buckled. Public resistance to such a device was so strong that Congress prohibited safety officials from requiring it. Needless to say there is no chance that Congress would pass a law requiring the states to enforce the wearing of seat belts, and no state presently has such a law of its own.

The one area in which Congress has acted to modify driver behavior is the 55 mph speed limit. The original motivation for the limit was energy conservation, not safety. But after the first year of the limit the highway death toll dropped so steeply that safety policy makers proposed keeping the limit even though the gas shortage had eased considerably. The number of highway fatalities dropped from 54,052 in 1973 to 45,196 in 1974. Not all of this decline can be attributed to the speed limit, of course. The severe recession that began in 1974 resulted in a drop in the total miles driven and hence in total fatalities. Government safety officials believe that the speed limit was responsible for about one-half of the decline, but opponents of the speed limit dispute even this estimate.[34] One thing is undisputable. Since 1975 there has been a noticeable relaxation in the enforcement of the 55 mph speed limit by the states. Since total miles driven are also again increasing along with average speed, highway deaths are rising back toward their pre-1973 levels.

The issue of automotive air pollution followed closely behind safety as a topic on the federal policy agenda. Haagen-Smit's experiments on the origins of photochemical smog in the early 1950s confirmed that automobile exhaust contributes significantly to air pollution.[35] Unlike auto accidents, however, the damage done to health and property by automotive air pollution is slow, subtle, and hard to measure in precise terms. It is difficult for scientists to link air pollution in general and auto emissions in particular to any specific level of damage to the public health. Thus it is hardly possible to define what constitutes a safe level of air pollution or to know exactly what health benefits would flow from any given reduction in air pollution levels.[36] These problems, along with widespread public apathy, inhibited governmental action in the area for many years. The auto companies had no incentive to do anything about emissions levels either. In fact in the 1950s they signed a cross licensing agreement, ensuring that all domestic car manufacturers would have access, on a royalty-free basis, to any air pollution control devices invented.[37] This removed the profit incentive for a company to push development of such devices. No car maker could produce a relatively pollution-free auto and then lobby Congress or the state legislatures for standards that only vehicles equipped with its device could meet. If "Safety doesn't sell," was Detroit's dictum on market incentives and safer cars, "Pollution control doesn't pay," was its judgment on the auto and the environment. The industry was not going to deal with the problem on its own initiative. As in the safety area there were several distinct approaches or strategies that the public authorities could use in dealing with the problem of automotive air pollution.[38] One option was simply to limit the amount of driving that could be done in cities and congested areas, thus limiting the amount of pollution that could be produced. There was actually an attempt to give the Environmental Protection Agency (EPA) the authority to require strict transportation control plans in the country's Air Quality Control Regions (AQCR). To be effective in controlling pollution, such transportation controls would have to be so draconian that they would cause severe disruption to the citizens affected by the plan, and Congress quickly postponed the EPA's projects that would have forbidden people to drive their cars to town.[39] A second option, a favorite with economists, was to enact an emissions tax whereby the owner of a highly polluting automobile pays a fee or tax roughly equal to the marginal social cost of the pollution his vehicle creates. Whatever the difficulties of calculating such a cost, it is clear that in such a scheme the tax would have to be sufficiently high to discourage a significant number of drivers from buying such vehicles. However, such a tax could not be favored by the automobile companies. Many environmentalists tended to look suspiciously on such plans as proposing a license to pollute. The general public is never enthusiastic about a new tax of any kind. Hence emission charges applied to automobiles never had a chance to be put into operation. In other words, much the same political dynamic was involved in the air pollution issue as on the safety issue. Policies that would involve a significant amount of disruption or inconvenience to the public were ruled out, as were policies that would threaten to hurt auto sales. Instead a pattern of policies and politics that was very similar to that established on safety questions emerged. This involved governmental mandating of desired vehicle characteristics (levels of exhaust emissions). It also involved periodic, well-publicized confrontations between congressional committees and auto company executives, the setting of deadlines and the granting of extensions, the threat of high levels of fines that were never applied, and so forth.

The key dates in the federal auto emissions control field are 1967 and 1970. Prior to 1967 Congress had acted very cautiously, and some state governments, especially California, showed signs of preparing vigorous auto emissions standards of their own. Fifty, or even a dozen different standards, were too many for Detroit to contemplate. It acquiesced in the Air Quality Act of 1967 by which Congress preempted the states (except for California) from establishing their own standards. The environmental movement gained support in public opinion and in Congress during the next several years and finally resulted in the Clean Air Act of 1970, which set the basic federal emissions standards and deadlines that Detroit would have to meet. This act was portrayed as a very stern challenge to the car manufacturers. Indeed the standards were high, and the five-year deadline short. The legislators could claim to be holding the industry's feet to the fire, forcing it to come up with whatever new technology was necessary to clean up the air. One political scientist who has studied the 1970 legislation notes that the car industry did not resist the act nearly as much as it might have been expected to.[40] He believes that this was because the very shortness of the allotted time period meant that the industry would have to be content with adapting the internal combustion engine it strongly preferred. Moreover the deadline schedule was such that it would appear reasonable to ask for delays if the standards could not be met—especially since failure to grant delays would mean a fine of $10,000 per vehicle produced which would effectively shut down the industry if applied.

In 1972 the auto companies requested the first in a series of delays in meeting the federal standards. Between then and 1977, although there was steady improvement in the exhaust levels of the prototype vehicles tested by the EPA, the full application of the standards was delayed four times.[41] With each successive delay environmentalists and critics of the car became more aware of the basic political-economic reality of the situation: Congress and the American people were not going to insist upon any seriously disruptive changes in Detroit's methods of making and marketing automobiles. Substantial improvements in emissions levels could be brought about with little hardship and the expense passed on to the buyers of cars. Much of the public could be comforted by the sight of the federal government acting to force the auto makers to comply with its standards. That portion not comforted would simply have to remain unhappy.

What has federal action on auto emissions standards accomplished? Has it begun to fulfill its promise to clean up the air? There is limited evidence that over the past several years the concentration of carbon monoxide and photo-chemical oxidants in the air has declined somewhat, along with concentrations of hydrocarbons and oxides of nitrogen.[42] The question then arises as to whether this improvement in air quality is worth the cost of achieving it. Several major studies conducted for the federal government in the early and mid-1970s concluded on strict cost-benefit calculations that the emissions standards were not worth it. A study by the National Academy of Sciences, for example, estimated the annual benefits that would be achieved by reducing auto emissions to the levels demanded by the 1970 standards (which have not yet been met) would total about $5 billion per year. The costs were estimated at $8 billion.[43] Whatever the precise cost-benefit ratio, it seems clear that the existing program of federal emissions standards is relatively expensive in terms of its total social costs.[44] This repeats the pattern from safety policy. In both areas there are many arguments and a good deal of evidence that other strategies could have achieved the same goals (or better) at less cost. Mandatory seat belt laws could have lowered the death rate far more than any of the existing NHTSA safety standards. Transportation control plans could do a better job than adding more and more antipollution equipment to more and more cars. Such proposals run up against serious political obstacles from the general public. Such objections are harder to bypass than complaints from the auto industry about overregulation. The United States auto industry was so strong, demand for cars so great, and buyers so affluent that the United States could afford the luxury of squabbling over safety and pollution problems and even choosing relatively expensive, convenient solutions.

In Europe there was no dramatic confrontation between governments and car manufacturers over safety and pollution issues. This is not to say that there was no concern for these problems in policy-making circles. Rather the problems were dealt with in a very different style. Observers who have compared the way in which environmental issues are handled in the United States and Europe agree that the American style is quite distinctive. Cynthia Enloe notes that United States environmental groups have had much greater success at mobilizing large numbers of supporters. They have forced environmental issues out into the open, subjected them to public debate and court tests, whereas in Europe such questions are usually handled out of sight in a system of closed politics where the major actors are bureaucrats.[45] On most environmental questions (except the nuclear power issue) there is an excitement and vitality in America that is lacking in Europe. There always seems to be a new issue, a new fight, a new policy response. But, as Solesbury points out,

the final outcome in terms of adequate response and issue resolution is less than satisfactory. New policies and programs and institutions frequently do not build upon the foundations of their predecessors; they simply overlay them and leave them to wither. Good intentions are often dashed on the rocks of implementation. . . . It might be said that the Americans are good at innovation but poor at implementation, while the British are good at implementation but poor at innovation.[46]

These general patterns were doubly true in the case of the automobile sector. In a very real sense the Europeans could not afford the luxury of confrontation politics over cars. The domestic market for automobiles is far smaller in all European countries than in the United States. Governments are aware of the fact that their manufacturers are dependent on exports for a high percentage of their sales and earnings (see table 8.2). They hesitate to impose costly safety or pollution requirements that might make their car companies less competitive in the international market. In addition European car makers that export to the United States must meet American safety and pollution standards, and European governments do not wish to impose any additional burdens.

This awareness of mutual dependence has contributed to the growth of a very different style of relations between automobile industry and government. In some countries the government itself is in the car business through public ownership of an auto firm. British Leyland, Renault, and Volkswagen are the leading examples of such firms. But even where the car makers are private concerns, as most of them still are, the government is not anxious to provoke a confrontation. Plowden's description of

Table 8.2 Automobile production and exports in Europe and the United States (1973)

Country	Total auto production (thousands)	Total auto exports (thousands)	Exports as percent of production
West Germany	3,643	2,204	60.5
France	3,202	1,340	41.8
Italy	1,823	643	35.3
Great Britain	1,747	598	34.2
Netherlands	114	88	77.2
Belgium and Luxembourg	959	839	87.5
Sweden	341	183	53.6
United States	9,667	509	5.3

Source: Statistical Office of the European Communities, *The Motor Vehicle in the Member States of the European Communities and in the World* (Brussels: European Community Information Service, 1977).
Note: Includes vans that may be used as either passenger or commercial vehicles.

the British situation is more or less typical of the general European pattern:

The manufacturers are always consulted about changes in the law affecting the construction of vehicles; voluntary action . . . has sometimes made legislation unnecessary. . . . The close relationship between the industry and the Ministry of Transport has made it possible for many questions to be settled in private negotiations, without the need for public discussion in Parliament or elsewhere. . . . This relationship has helped to prevent the development of the kind of gap between private practice and public requirements which in the United States led to recriminations.[47]

The Common Market authorities in Brussels take a dim view of any country that would unilaterally impose harsh standards because it could be interpreted as a nontariff barrier to intra-European trade. Within the European Economic Community there is of course a procedure for developing a set of standards for industrial products, including automobiles. But these procedures are very complex and very slow. Moreover they work on the lowest common denominator basis, with national governments having a veto power over anything that might seriously disrupt a national industry.[48] European pollution control policies as applied to the auto are not technology forcing but rather technology negotiating, as governments and car makers discuss what is desirable, what is feasible, and what the costs to the car companies and the public will be.

On the other hand, some European governments seem to be more willing to use authority to regulate directly how and where their citizens drive their cars. In the area of automotive air pollution several European governments have experimented with traffic restraint plans as a means of reducing pollution levels in the most densely populated and heavily traveled quarters of their cities. When Vienna established a traffic-free zone in the center of the city in 1971, researchers found that daytime levels of carbon monoxide declined over 60 percent.[49] European authorities and traffic planners have found that public acceptance of pedestrian zones is generally high. Banning or otherwise restricting traffic is not only an effective measure against spot concentrations of automotive air pollutants but works against other nuisances such as excessive noise as well. Over one hundred European cities have established pedestrian districts in portions of their downtown areas.[50]

This same willingness to regulate citizen behavior is also seen on safety questions. At the end of 1976 ten western European countries had some form of mandatory seat belt law.[51] Most of these were to be found among those law-abiding northern countries where citizen compliance is almost taken for granted (Sweden, Finland, Norway, the Netherlands, Switzerland, and West Germany). Norway's law does not provide for a penalty in the event of noncompliance; nevertheless, seat belt usage in Norway is significantly higher than in the United States. In Sweden a driver can be fined up to the equivalent of $100 for not wearing his seat belt. Studies show that the Swedish law, which went into effect on January 1, 1975, raised the proportion of drivers wearing seat belts from 36 to 79 percent.[52] It is estimated that less than 20 percent of American drivers wear their seat belts. Sweden has also traditionally had very strong and strictly enforced laws against drunken driving. In Sweden, if the alcohol count in a driver's blood is found to have exceeded a specified amount, the driver is automatically imprisoned. Accident studies in Sweden indicate that the incidence of intoxication of fatally injured drivers is approximately 30 percent, compared to 50 percent in America.[53]

THE IMPACT OF THE ENERGY CRISIS

Another negative side effect, or externality, associated with the car culture is the threat to the United States international political and economic position raised by the ever-increasing reliance on Middle East oil. Today the United States imports about 50 percent of its petroleum at a cost of over $42 billion per year.[54] This contributes greatly to the balance of payments deficit and the decline of the dollar. If present trends continue, the year 2000 could see the United States dependent on imports for 70 percent of its oil and paying out at least $142 billion (in 1975 dollars) for the privilege.[55] But in this scenario we may not even make it to the year 2000:

By 1985 or 1986 or 1987 . . . we'll be staring at an energy crisis far worse than the one we went through in the early 70s. . . . Prices will double or triple, in real terms, within a short time. The standard of living of every American will nosedive. The international monetary system will shudder and shake. Industrial nations will be pitted against each other in a bruising scramble for oil. The Western alliance could be shattered. In a number of countries, democracy itself might not be able to survive.[56]

This gloomy prospect, which is taken quite seriously by many governmental and academic policy forecasters, puts the American automobile squarely in the middle of the energy crisis. American cars and trucks use one-seventh of all the oil and gasoline used in the world every day.[57] The United States imports nearly a quarter of all the oil in world trade, and since 1970 American imports have risen by more than 100 percent. Western European and Japanese imports have risen only 11 percent in the same period.[58] Obviously the voracious demands of America's car culture are a key factor in creating the demand that has permitted the OPEC countries to raise their prices to present levels. Critics of the car culture who secretly despaired of ever making real progress when the stakes were only lives, lungs, and lifestyles have taken heart at the sight of long gas lines and skyrocketing oil prices.[59] The forces of world politics, however, have succeeded where the car's critics could not, and the production cutbacks in the Persian Gulf oil in 1979 forced the United States government to begin to impose the kind of energy-efficient transport policies these critics have been calling for all along. At the very least the United States must move toward the type of balanced, resource-efficient transport systems that exist in Europe.

What are the prospects for this really coming about? To answer, we must first examine the differences between the European and American transport systems in terms of energy consumption and then look at the policy factors that brought about the energy efficiency of European cars.

A study for Resources for the Future, *How Industrial Societies Use Energy*, describes in detail the differences between United States and western Europe energy consumption patterns.[60] The data in table 8.3

Table 8.3 Energy consumption by sector (1972)[a]

Sector	United States	France	West Germany	Sweden	Great Britain
Transformation losses	100	56.0	68.0	106.8	101.6
Energy	100	42.2	54.8	24.4	60.0
Transport	100	35.8	40.4	37.0	44.3
Industry	100	70.9	96.8	89.0	102.9
Household-commercial	100	59.6	80.2	93.3	72.5
Nonenergy use[b]	100	44.2	64.0	20.9	61.6
Total energy consumption	100	53.7	78.0	71.8	75.7

Source: Joel Darmstadter, Joy Dunkerley, and Jack Alterman, *How Industrial Societies Use Energy: A Comparative Analysis* (Baltimore: Johns Hopkins University Press, 1977), p. 26.
[a]Index for the United States = 100.
[b]Energy raw materials used for petrochemical industry.

show that the United States was roughly as energy efficient as other Western nations in the industrial sector, somewhat less efficient in the household, commercial, and other sectors, but far less efficient in the transport sector. In fact the authors of the Resources for the Future study calculated that the transportation sector alone was responsible for nearly 50 percent of the total difference in United States and European energy consumption levels.[61] These data obviously support the need for United States energy conservation measures in transport. The specific opportunities for such conservation measures are clear when the data in tables 8.4 and 8.5 are considered. These show that in 1973 per capita national energy consumption in the United States was approximately double that of European countries. American consumption of gasoline

Table 8.4 Energy consumption, auto ownership, and fuel consumption (1973)

Country	Per capita energy consumption in 1973[a]	Number of motor vehicles per 1,000 population in 1973	Consumption of road motor fuels per 1,000 population in 1973[b]
France	3.54	319	41.5
West Germany	4.75	296	41.6
Sweden	4.75	327	47.7
Great Britain	4.35	287	39.9
United States	9.06	575	138.0

Sources: *The OECD Observer* 74 (March–April 1975); Alexander French and Lyle D. Wylie, Highway Transport and Energy Problems in Europe, *1975 World Survey of Current Research and Development on Roads and Road Transport* (Washington, D.C.: International Road Federation, 1975), pp. 579–582.
[a]Tons of oil equivalent.
[b]Metric tons.

Table 8.5 Passenger mileage, modal split, and miles per gallon (1972)

Country	Total per capita passenger miles all modes	Percent of public transport	Average annual mileage per car	Estimated miles per gallon all cars
France	3,975	20.4	7,146	20.1
West Germany	5,874	17.6	9,942	23.9
Sweden	6,282	15.0	8,669	18.5
Great Britain	4,989	19.9	8,823	28.0
United States	11,288	2.9	9,942	11.5

Sources: Joel Darmstadter, Joy Dunkerley, and Jack Alterman, *How Industrial Societies Use Energy: A Comparative Analysis* (Baltimore: Johns Hopkins University Press, 1977), pp. 75, 87; Alexander French and Lyle Wylie, Highway Transport and Energy Problems in Europe, pp. 583–584.

and diesel fuel in the road transportation sector was more than triple the European per capita consumption. Very little of the extra margin of fuel consumption can be accounted for by the higher average miles driven by car. About half the difference is due to the higher per capita ownership of cars, and the resultant higher total passenger miles of auto travel in the United States. The rest is due to the greater fuel consumption of United States automobiles (fewer miles to the gallon) and to the fact that so few of the total trips in the United States are taken on energy-efficient mass transit. Darmstadter and his colleagues in the Resources for the Future study have attempted to apportion precisely the relative contribution of bigger cars and less reliance on public transit to the fuel consumption deficit of America. They calculate that intensity factors—the greater weight and fuel consumption of United States vehicles—were responsible for some 39 percent of the United States and Europe differences in fuel consumption. The modal mix effect—the proportion using mass transit versus the private car—accounted for only 18 percent of the difference.[62] In other words, the fact that Europeans rely more on public transit is only about half as significant as the fact that American autos are less energy efficient than European autos. Darmstadter and his fellow authors acknowledge that a shift toward more travel by public transit in the United States would undoubtedly save some energy. But they fear that the cost in public subsidies might be too high. They believe that the greatest opportunity for energy savings in transportation lies in improving the energy efficiency of the U.S. automobile.

European public policies toward the automobile, based on the assumption that the private motor car and its fuel are luxuries a nation cannot afford to overindulge in, have tended to keep the cost of owning and operating an auto significantly above U.S. levels. One study showed that in terms of the share of personal consumption expenditure, the cost of buying a car was 32 percent higher in France, 51 percent higher in West Germany, and 87 percent higher in Britain than in the United States. Gasoline expenditures ranged from 92 percent higher in Britain to 247 percent higher in Italy.[63] Such costs obviously would tend to hold down the growth of per capita auto ownership and the number of miles traveled by auto. The same study showed that the price of public transportation in Europe averaged 30 percent below the U.S. level. In addition to these considerations the structure of European motor vehicle taxes is designed to encourage the purchase and production of smaller, more fuel-efficient cars. The Europeans have had their version of the gas guzzler tax for decades. In West Germany, for example, the annual motor vehicle tax (KFZ-Steuer) is based on the engine displacement. The annual tax on a 1,000 cubic centimeter (61 cubic inch) engine, such as might be found in an old Volkswagen Beetle, was 144 DM (about $72) in 1974. But the annual vehicle tax on a large U.S. sized 5,700 cubic centimeter (5.7 liter) or 350 cubic inch V-8 engine was 917 DM or about $456.[64] Thus, if one owned an American *Strassenkreuzer* ("street cruiser") in Germany, over a period of five years one would pay some $2,280 in annual motor vehicle taxes for the privilege. However, few people are able or willing to pay that much for the privilege. Some affluent Germans do own big American cars. Even more own cars such as the Mercedes-Benz, which is large by German standards but has a relatively small engine. In this way a certain amount of freedom of choice (at least for the rich) is preserved while at the same time the auto industry and the public is encouraged to concentrate on smaller, energy-efficient cars.

Ironically, because their long-term policies had been so successful in encouraging fuel efficiency in the automobile sector, European policy makers did not have as much maneuvering room as their American counterparts during the energy crisis of 1973 to 1974. There was less energy fat to be trimmed away before the bone and muscle of the transportation system was reached. Two small nations, the Netherlands and Sweden, instituted gasoline rationing programs. Most other European nations responded with Sunday driving bans, lowered speed limits, and some increases in the gasoline tax. Often transport ministries used the opportunity to win parliamentary approval for new rail and urban public transportation projects. By the late spring of 1974 the crisis had eased and most of the emergency measures were lifted.[65] Oil consumption remained low for a period because of the severe recession of 1974 to 1975. But as prosperity returned, so did increased consumption of motor fuels. By 1979 there were 22 percent more cars on the roads in France than in 1973, and gasoline consumption was up 21 percent. Motor fuel use was up 16 percent in West Germany and 10 percent in Britain, despite gasoline prices equivalent to $2.45 per gallon in Bonn and $2.32 in London.[66]

The European experience tends to suggest that high fuel prices alone may not be as effective in conserving gasoline as some economists estimate. An official of the French Ministry of Industry stated, "We've concluded that price isn't effective in conservation. It might stun people momentarily, but the effect doesn't last." If the vehicle fleet is already quite fuel efficient people prefer to absorb higher fuel costs rather than sacrifice mobility. A recent poll found that French drivers declared that gasoline would have to cost from six to ten francs per liter ($5.25 to $8.70 per gallon) before they would substantially change their driving habits.[67] No European government is prepared to bring about such increases through taxation.

The fact that there has been less political sound and fury over various energy plans in Europe does not mean that policy makers do not take the problem seriously. European governments prefer to work quietly with their auto industries to encourage the development of vehicles that are even more fuel efficient. In Britain car makers have voluntarily agreed to raise the fuel economy of their fleets by 10 percent between 1979 and 1985. West German auto manufacturers have agreed to similar fuel efficiency improvements and are being aided by government help for research and development.[68]

American policy makers have been very skittish about levying any sort of tax increases designed to promote fuel efficiency. Consumers are also voters. In the wake of the Arab oil embargo of 1973 to 1974 there was a good deal of talk about a gas guzzler tax of some kind. But U.S. auto sales were down sharply, and the administration did not wish to push the economy further into recession. In the spring of 1975 the Democratic members of the House Ways and Means Committee produced a comprehensive energy plan that included a stiff excise tax on fuel-inefficient new cars beginning with the 1980 model year. The plan would have imposed a one-time tax of $75 for cars getting less than 20 miles per gallon (mpg), rising to $500 for cars getting less than 15 mpg. This was coupled with a tax rebate to purchasers of energy-efficient cars getting more than 24 mpg.[69] But in June the full House turned down this tax-based plan and substituted a schedule of fuel efficiency standards for new cars that would be enforced by civil fines on manufacturers. The mileage standards finally approved in the Energy Policy and Conservation Act of 1975 (EPCA) can be seen in table 8.6.

The fines to be levied against manufacturers failing to comply with these standards were set at $5 for each one-tenth of a mile per gallon that a new car fell below the standard, multiplied by the total number of cars built or imported by a manufacturer. An interesting aspect to this choice

Table 8.6 Fuel economy standards mandated by the energy policy and conservation act

Model year	Sales-weighted new car fleet average mpg[a]
1978	18[b]
1979	19[b]
1980	20[b]
1981	22[c]
1982	24[c]
1983	26[c]
1984	27[c]
1985	27.5

Source: U.S., Congress, Office of Technology Assessment, *Changes in the Future Use and Characteristics of the Automobile Transportation System* (Washington, D.C.: Government Printing Office, 1979), p. 113.
[a]The mpg units are those achieved on EPA prototype vehicle dynamometer tests. Fuel consumption in actual in-use vehicles will be 10 to 20 percent less.
[b]Mandated by EPCA of 1975.
[c]Administratively determined by secretary of transportation.

of fines, as opposed to taxes, is that both the auto companies and the United Auto Workers union lobbied hard against the tax and actually seemed to prefer the system based on fines.[70] Perhaps this was because they believed that such fines would never actually be levied against them. Indeed it is difficult to conceive of the Congress standing by and watching such fines put American Motors or Chrysler out of business. The experience with the air pollution standards suggests that the mileage standards can and will be revised downward if the auto manufacturers plead a good faith inability to meet them.

President Jimmy Carter took up the idea of a gas guzzler tax as part of the comprehensive energy package that he presented to Congress in April 1977. He called for a gradually rising excise tax on fuel-inefficient new cars. By 1985 he proposed a maximum tax of $2,488 on gas guzzlers and a rebate of $493 on gas misers. Carter's plan also called for a 5 cent per gallon hike in the federal gasoline tax in years in which gas consumption exceeded the previous year's level. The tax could rise a maximum of 50 cents per gallon in ten years. Congress flatly rejected the gasoline tax hike and diluted the administration's gas guzzler proposal quite a bit. The rationale for such action was clearly laid out in a report commissioned by the Senate Finance Committee. The report stated that, if the president's proposed gas guzzler tax and fuel efficiency rebate were enacted, "manufacturers located in the United States would make fewer sales of new passenger automobiles." It predicted that consumers would switch to imports and 32,000 jobs would be lost in the auto industry by 1985. It also concluded that, in light of the fuel economy standards already mandated by Congress, such taxes and rebates "would not contribute meaningfully to the domestic industry's ability to meet the fuel economy standards required by present law."[71] Congress finally decided to drop the fuel efficiency incentive plan altogether and to pass an excise tax ranging from $550 for cars getting less than 13 mpg to $200 for cars getting 14 but less than 15 mpg in the 1980 model year. Taxes would rise each year until 1986, when cars getting less than 12.5 mpg will be taxed $3,850.[72] By 1986 it is doubtful if any manufacturer will be producing cars that get less than 12.5 mpg on the EPA dynamometers. Moreover these taxes do not apply to light trucks and vans which make up a rapidly growing portion of the motor vehicle market and get lower gas mileage than passenger cars. Thus the sharpest teeth of the gas guzzler tax are reserved for nonexistent vehicles, while Congress is counting on Detroit to be able to meet its mileage standards so that the pattern of exempting the industry from the standards will not have to be repeated again. There is little doubt that, if Detroit can prove that meeting mileage standards would work economic hardship, another exemption would be forthcoming.

Secretary of Transportation Brock Adams attempted to keep up the pressure on the industry to comply with the standards. In the spring of

1979 he called on the industry to reinvent the car and to join, not fight, governmental efforts to achieve dramatic improvements in automobile fuel efficiency, instead of always trying to get federal standards lowered. He indicated that the federal government intends to proceed with research in this field, and if it develops a prototype vehicle that can get 50 or 100 mpg, it will turn it over to Detroit to mass produce.[73] Another indication as to how policy makers may view the future of government and auto industry relations in the context of the energy crisis is found in the Office of Technology Assessment (OTA) study of the automobile transportation system. This report notes that government will have to develop programs to help ease the transition to more fuel-efficient vehicles. As the study pointedly notes, "the preservation of automobility is the underlying reason for promoting a transition program."[74] Fuel shortages are likely to occur even with a successful switch to fuel-efficient cars by 1985. Rising world demand for oil casts doubt on the ability of the OPEC countries to produce enough oil to meet demand. Even before physical shortages are encountered, the price will have risen so high that there will have to be a massive shift to coal and nuclear power. Most of the oil produced will be reserved for use in transportation and petrochemical feedstocks. "The implications of this potential shortage are profound and pose a serious threat to our continued reliance on the automobile as the predominant mode of personal transportation," the study states.[75] In view of this threat it will be necessary sooner or later to shift from petroleum to alternative sources of energy for the automobile. A strong federal program of financial support may be needed to smooth the transition. The report notes that federal regulations have imposed extra costs on the industry. The smaller firms of Chrysler and American Motors may not be able to raise the funds needed to make the transition to the new technology. The implication is that in the future the federal government may well have to find ways to become partners in the industry's transition efforts. Certainly President Carter's July 1979 call for an $88 billion synthetic fuels program fits into the OTA scenario perfectly.

The OTA analysts do not believe that public transportation will be able to make a major contribution to America's mobility requirements. Even with increased federal subsidies (rising from $1.6 billion in 1975 to $4.4 billion in 1985 and $7.2 billion in 2000 in constant dollars) the report forecasts that total transit ridership will rise only about 25 percent (from 5.4 billion riders in 1975 to 6.8 billion in 2000). They conclude that "the potential of public transportation, ride sharing, and transportation system management is small—in most cases resulting in less than a 5 percent reduction in VMT [vehicle miles traveled] nationally."[76]

While the report does not foresee a great spending increase on public transportation between now and the turn of the century, it does acknowledge that both government and industry will have to spend hundreds of billions in developing new sources of fuel and new fuel-efficient cars to keep the automobile transportation system operating. In other words, the OTA analysts do not foresee a need or an effective political demand to attempt to switch back to a reliance on less resource-intensive public transportation. The transition to be planned and directed by an emerging government-industry partnership will be from a resource-intensive auto system which is too dependent on scarce petroleum to an even more resource-intensive auto system in which other resources—capital, research, new technology, alternative energy sources—have been substituted for petroleum.

The long-run implications of the energy crisis are far more serious than either the safety or pollution problems. They will require major adjustments by both business and government. In its immediate response to the energy problems posed by the automobile the political system followed the pattern established in the two other areas. It mandated product standards for the industry, while leaving consumers/drivers generally untouched by direct government power. In instances where zealous bureaucratic enforcement of congressional policy threatens harm to the auto companies or auto workers, Congress retains the option of stepping in with exemptions and postponements. Thus, though the energy problem's impact has been great, it has not yet led policy makers to adopt the radical solutions envisioned by the critics of the car culture.

THE FUTURE OF THE CAR CULTURE

What are the prospects for the automobile-centered socioeconomic complex we have called the car culture? Will the critics' hopes be borne out? Or will things continue much as they have in the recent past, with much controversy but little basic change in the car's role in transportation and society? Predicting the future is difficult at best, and doubly so when the future depends on the interaction of technology, market forces, and public policy.[77] It seems clear that the car culture can never again be as autonomous and independent of the political system as it once seemed to be. No longer are the crucial decisions simply those made by consumers and corporate management. Instead the complexities of middle eastern politics, international trade, the strength of the dollar, the role of multinational corporations, legislative and regulatory pressures, and many other factors now play major parts in the political and social processes that will determine the expansion or contraction of the car culture.

Business and government feel they cannot afford to be caught unprepared by any developments that might bring about major shifts in the automobile system. Thus there have been quite a number of studies in recent years that seek to establish where the auto complex is going. We will briefly review some of these efforts, make some crucial distinctions, raise some problems that often are overlooked, and try to link the concerns of the critics with the economic and political realities that are portrayed in conventional projections of the car's future.

There are at least two dimensions to the car culture that need to be considered in this exercise. The first and most often studied dimension is the state of the automobile industry itself, its production, sales, employment, and profits. This dimension is so important to the overall economic prosperity of the nation that the U.S. Department of Commerce issues separate figures on the Gross Auto Product as a bellwether of the GNP. The second dimension of the car culture consists of its ability over the past thirty-five years to shape the metropolitan area cityscape, the patterns of where people live and work, take their recreation, do their shopping, relate to their neighbors, and so forth. It is at least conceivable that the strong link between a growing, prosperous auto industry and the sprawl development of the metro area could be weakened or broken so that the auto's power to shape metropolitan development could be reduced without at the same time severely damaging the economic situation of the motor industry and the general economy.

Each dimension will be affected differently by the two major factors we have been using in our analysis: markets and authority. Table 8.7 shows how these two dimensions interrelate with the two political-economic allocation modes to create conflicts or dilemmas whose resolution will have significant impact on the future of the car culture. The particular conflicts illustrated are the ones most likely to have a decisive influence on the automobile's future impact on our society.

Consider the first conflict, the need to protect the prosperity of the auto industry versus the need to regulate the safety, environmental, and energy impacts of its products. In the past fifteen years the policies of the U.S. federal government shifted from uncritical support of the auto's expansion to a more nuanced position that attempted to reduce some of the

Table 8.7 Dilemmas in the future of the car culture

	Public policy	Market forces
Automobile industry	Protection of jobs and profits versus Regulation of safety, emissions and energy	Need for rising sales versus Cost of cars and gasoline
Metro area cityscape	Planning metro area growth versus Institutional and ideological difficulties	Momentum of sprawl versus Costs and changing lifestyles

undesirable side effects of mass automobility. Even at the height of the activist regulatory period, however, the underlying thrust of government policies was supportive of the auto. Recall that the analysts at the OTA recommended capital assistance to the industry, that President Carter recommended an $88 billion synfuels program that would benefit the auto industry substantially, and that President Nixon removed the federal excise tax from retail auto sales in order to stimulate the economy. Further the OTA has projected future growth not decline of the automobile industry and automotive system under presently prevailing policies and conditions. These projections to the year 2000 are found in table 8.8. Within broad limits policy changes that may come about are as likely to favor the auto as to limit it.

The political system's reaction to the sales slump in the U.S. auto industry in 1979 to 1980 is a lesson in how fast adversary politics can be suspended when serious trouble appears. Between June 1979 and June 1980 sales of domestically made cars dropped 29 percent.[78] The larger, more profitable models were especially hard hit. Company profits plunged at a time when auto makers had to raise an estimated $80 billion to resize their fleets for 1985.[79] The slump hurt GM and Ford, but it pushed Chrysler to the brink of bankrupcy. Chrysler, the weakest of the so-called Big Three in America, lost $1.1 billion in 1979. It could not sell its large cars to a suddenly fuel economy conscious public, but it did succeed in selling Congress on the idea that it was too big and too important to be allowed to go under. Chrysler was joined in its lobbying campaign by the United Auto Workers, hundreds of its banks and creditors, its suppliers, its nationwide dealer network, and the White House,

Table 8.8 Trends in the automobile transportation system, projections to the year 2000 under present policies and programs

	1975	1985	2000
Population (millions)	214	233	250
GNP (trillions of dollars)	1.52	2.22	3.72
Consumer price index	161.2	261.7	471.3
Automobiles in operation (millions)	95	118	148
Annual new car sales (millions)	8.6	13.1	16.4
Automobile vehicle miles (trillions)	1.03	1.43	1.80
Annual fleet fuel consumption (billions of gallons)	76.0	73.9	73.3
Annual highway expenditures (billions of 1975 dollars)	28.2	28.2	28.2

Source: U.S., Congress, Office of Technology Assessment, *Changes in the Future Use and Characteristics of the Automobile Transportation System,* vol. 2 (Washington, D.C.: Government Printing Office, 1979), chap. 3.

where chief domestic policy advisor Stuart Eizenstat was quoted as saying, "The nation's 10th largest industrial corporation is not going to go bankrupt during the Carter administration."[80]

The result of the lobbying effort was the Chrysler Loan Guarantee in which the federal government agreed to back $1.5 billion in loans to the corporation in what Treasury Secretary G. William Miller called "the most complex financing operation in U.S. history."[81] In return for the government's help in bringing the desperately needed infusion of cash, the corporation had to accept far-reaching government supervision over its policies and operations.[82] If, as many observers fear, this initial installment of aid is not enough to turn Chrysler around, then the government may find itself facing the prospect of, in effect, going into the car business by acquiring control of Chrysler.[83]

The other important effect of the automotive recession has been to create a more favorable environment for industry attempts to dilute or eliminate many of the regulatory standards imposed during the activist years.[84] The industry contends that federal regulations have been hamstringing its efforts to meet the challenge of foreign competition and imposing serious economic hardships, especially on the smaller firms. There is no doubt that many auto executives, long accustomed to complete laissez faire in the design and marketing of their products, are sincerely troubled by the increasing intrusion of public policy requirements into their business. The political process is not as easy to master as the marketing of automobiles. Yet it is not at all clear that the industry's call for regulatory rollback is any better thought through than the regulators' plea for even stricter standards. General Motors sent a white paper, or wish book, to the White House and Congress in June 1980 that called for 14 changes in EPA regulations already in force, elimination or postponement of 10 scheduled new regulations, 7 changes in existing safety standards, 14 changes in pending NHTSA requirements, and large rollbacks of other federal regulations, including OSHA workplace safety rules.[85]

While the controversy over federal regulation is now tending to find the side favoring less regulation winning more support, it is by no means certain that federal standards have done serious harm to the industry.[86] In fact it is possible to point to at least one set of standards that can be said to have greatly helped the nation's car manufacturers, namely, the fuel efficiency standards imposed by EPCA.[87] Without the early start required by the scheduled fuel economy improvements between 1978 and 1985, Detroit might have been even more vulnerable to foreign imports. As it stands, with the prospect of substantial improvements in the fuel efficiency of American made vehicles, Detroit's competitive position should improve. Between 1963 and 1979 foreign imports increased their share of the U.S. auto market from 5 to 22 percent. In the first four months of 1980 imports had captured 26.7 percent of total sales.[88] This represents a loss of approximately $10 billion in annual revenues for

Detroit.[89] Thanks to Congress' passage of EPCA in 1975, the American industry will soon be in a better position to win back some of this money.

The world market also beckons as a source of possible new profits for U.S. auto companies. With the dollar cheap, and a fuel efficient world car to sell, American producers can be expected to improve their positions in foreign markets. Of course GM and Ford are already well established in Europe. In the past their European products were quite different from their North American line. With the advent of the smaller American cars European automakers are concerned that the U.S. giants will be able to organize production of many of their models on a world level. They fear that by taking advantage of the economies of scale the Americans might be able to win a larger share of the markets in Europe and third world countries. Components will be mass-produced in different countries (engines in Mexico, transmissions in Germany, bodies in America) and shipped to still other countries for final assembly (usually a political requirement of auto sales in countries like Brazil and Nigeria).[90]

Competition on a world scale will pose many difficult problems for corporate strategy and public policy. In the short run there are likely to be increased pressures from both companies and unions for tariff barriers or quotas against foreign, namely, Japanese, competition. In the longer term, however, the companies and the unions may split, as multinational auto firms resort more and more to offshore sourcing (production in low wage countries) to meet international competition, which may well be coming from Korea or Brazil by the year 2000. As automotive technology becomes more widely diffused around the world, many nations can be expected to encourage automobile production for export as well as for domestic consumption.[91] The amount of world resources that would be consumed in a massive drive to motorize the populations of the third world to anything near U.S. or European levels have caused many observers to wonder if it will ever be possible. Yet, can the affluent nations continue to consume a disproportionate share of world resources, particularly petroleum, to support a car culture that is out of reach of the majority of the world's people?[92] European governments are acutely aware of the coming struggles in the world car market and are actively seeking ways to enable the generally smaller European auto companies to compete effectively with both the Americans and the Japanese.[93] Transnational mergers and other forms of cooperation across national boundaries appear to be inevitable, as does the creation of a common set of standards and policies for the European auto industry.[94] It will be an effort for some traditional auto-producing nations (such as Britain) to remain a power on the world auto scene. European policy makers are not going to do anything to damage the prospects of their auto industries. But the desire to protect the employment and foreign exchange earnings that a strong auto industry provides does not mean that European policy makers faced with the dilemma of planning metropolitan growth are prepared to permit the automobile to determine completely the future development of their cities and metropolitan areas. Certainly one major factor is their concern to preserve the esthetic and historical values of their central cities. A second objective, somewhat unevenly pursued in different countries, is to channel suburban growth into patterns compatible with public transportation and the preservation of the countryside.

It is probably safe to say that the western European city will never be adapted to the automobile in the same way that most American cities have been. In the chaotic period of explosive auto growth of the 1950s and 1960s expressways were built dangerously near the centers of some historic European capitals and even more in less well-known provincial towns. Freeway revolts similar to the motorway box rebellion in London stopped some of these expressways. Others fell victim to a disenchantment with massive road projects at high policy levels, as when French President Valery Giscard d'Estaing canceled the proposed expressway on the left bank of the Seine alongside the cathedral of Notre Dame.

In the 1970s the tide in Europe turned against massive highway projects in favor of traffic restraint, pedestrian zones, bicycle lanes, and reliance on public transportation for center city mobility.[95] Hundreds of small- and medium-sized towns have introduced car-free areas in which flowers, trees, benches, fountains, vendors, and artists have filled the space vacated by the car. Even large cities have made substantial progress in pedestrianization. Munich's central pedestrian area covers more than a third of a square mile. The Greater London Council is preparing a plan to link over 200 pedestrian streets into a unified system.[96]

The European concept of winning back city streets for people often does not entail the complete banishment of the car. In the Netherlands planners have developed the *woonerf,* or neighborhood courtyard, in which the architecture and appearance of a residential street is changed from that of a traffic artery into a paved public garden. Traffic is slowed down by putting in sharp turns, speed bumps, and obstacles such as trees, benches, and bike racks. The curbs are eliminated and pedestrians, bicyclists, and children are encouraged to use the entire width of the street for walking, playing, meeting with friends, and the whole variety of activities that one might do on the public green of an old village. The German state of North Rhine-Westphalia has instituted a substantial effort inspired by the Dutch experience which is aimed at taming traffic in residential areas (*Verkehrsberuhigung in Wohngebieten*). The German experiment, in addition to improving urban amenity, brought about a substantial reduction in the number of accidents and injuries reported on streets where traffic had been tamed and on tangential streets as well.[97]

There is growing interest in such schemes among U.S. city planners. Another type of traffic and transportation practice that may have even more relevance to the North American environment is the manner in which some European governments are trying to prevent the growth of unplanned suburban sprawl. Sweden has the highest per capita car ownership in Europe and an important national automobile industry (Volvo, Saab). The Swedes have refused to cede control over the growth of their cityscapes to the automobile. Rather Swedish policy has been to develop new communities around subway (*Tunnelbana*) and rail stations. Each planned community consists of several neighborhood areas, sharing a shopping center and a community center. The community centers are planned as car free zones, and, with the neighborhoods designed around a *Tunnelbana* station, walking distances are kept to a minimum.[98] Although the Swedish experience is perhaps the best-known one, other European countries are also trying to preserve their countryside from auto-dependent suburban sprawl. In the Netherlands the town of Bijlmermeer is being built as a satellite town to concentrate a significant portion of the suburban growth of Amsterdam. It is planned that the new town will have a population of 110,000, four-fifths of whom will live within 500 meters of metro stations.[99] In Germany Hamburg's development plan calls for growth to be concentrated along seven transport corridors leading to major suburban centers. In France, where planners have long struggled with the somewhat different problem of how to deconcentrate population and industry from Paris, they are attempting to channel new growth in the Paris region into five new towns (Cergy-Pontoise, St. Quentin-en-Yvelines, Marne-la-Vallée, Evry, and Melun) linked to central Paris by public transport (the new regional express metro, or new SNCF rail lines) and by highways. Each new town will contain enough jobs, housing, shopping, and community facilities so that the need for daily commuting to central Paris will be discouraged.[100]

These examples have been cited not because they could be easily imitated in the United States. There are many political and administrative obstacles to this kind of planning in the United States that do not exist in Europe. But the European attempts to channel suburban growth into areas that do not generate the need for greatly increased auto travel and make provision for public transportation show that it is possible to make distinction between policies supporting the future of the national automobile industry and policies aiming at reducing the impact of the automobile on the cityscape. When American critics of the car say they foresee the decline or downfall of the car culture, they are in effect expressing the possibility of reducing the impact of the car on the environment, as witnessed by the European examples. Perhaps through a series of public policy decisions the car's role as a decisive shaper of lifestyles can be reduced. Rothschild's thesis on the decline of the auto industrial age is more insightful on the psycho-cultural level than on the political-economic level. The automobile has done just about as much as it could do to shape the U.S. urban and suburban environment. Time has proved that fears that the downtowns of our great cities would eventually be ghost towns because of the auto were exaggerated. Political authorities stepped in to prevent the definitive abandonment of the city for suburbia and exurbia. The political forces that protected the cities also brought about some improvements in mass transit. But they have neither the will nor the power to challenge the auto's dominance directly.

Most transportation analysts agree that the automobile will remain the predominant mode of passenger transport in the United States at least until the end of the twentieth century.[101] While some of its characteristics will change (it will be smaller, more fuel-efficient, safer, probably run on diesel or synthetic fuel, be more expensive, and so forth), the car itself will continue to dominate passenger travel until a situation is created that either prevents people from relying on the car or reduces the need for it. In an energy emergency transit systems would be utterly swamped if they tried to handle all or even a major portion of the travel demand that cars now handle. During the 1973 and 1979 crises many people were forced to rely on the more cost-efficient use of car pooling, which along with gasoline rationing seems to be the most feasible means of assuring the minimum mobility needed to keep the economy operating. As far as creating a situation in which people will no longer need to use automobiles very much is concerned, this is a long-term option that would be applied primarily to planning the new growth of yet undeveloped regions of American cities and suburbs. Its impact on the total transportation system would be felt only very gradually in population shifts. It will, however, require a major change in the way we view the role of transportation and personal mobility in our society. It will necessitate a rather fundamental reformulation of our paradigm of public choice in transportation.

9
CONCLUSIONS

TRANSATLANTIC CONTRASTS IN
TRANSPORTATION POLICY

The material presented in the preceding chapters is by no means exhaustive. Rather it offers sufficient evidence from which we may begin to draw conclusions concerning the major policy contrasts in the U.S. and European modes covered, especially contrasts in how markets and authority are used in making decisions. These contrasts in turn may help to suggest ways in which the American policy paradigm might be modified to achieve new social goals in transportation policy or old goals in a more effective manner. The differences in the European and American views of their transportation policy paradigms have three crucial aspects to them: the nature of the priorities given to certain transportation modes, the scope accorded to market processes in the transportation sector, and the ends and means of the authority exercised in that sector.

Europeans tend to have a different image of the ultimate social meaning of transportation than Americans. While they recognize the need for efficient methods of moving people and goods from one location to another, they are in general not as enraptured by the very process of motion as Americans. They tend to give greater weight to the societal costs of transportation and be somewhat more skeptical of the benefits of additional increments of transportation capacity above what seems adequate to the task. Perhaps this stems from the smaller geographical size of these nations and the denser, older, more rooted pattern of settlement. This appears to produce a more emotional attachment to localities, a greater sense of the value and fragility of a specific valley, village, or neighborhood. Public officials of this tradition thus permit society to invest its wealth in purchasing no more transportation capacity and services than are necessary by conservative estimate. The French government took the lead in designing the *étoile* radial rail network that eliminated duplication of facilities by the private companies that were to build and operate it, and British cabinets saw little need for haste or expense in responding to the annoying clamor of the motorists for better roads.

By contrast Americans tended to see transportation as a positive good, something desired not only as a means but also as virtually an end in itself. Mobility of people and goods was a vital means in opening up the vast hinterland of the continent and knitting its far-flung settlements together into a proud and mighty nation. But it was an end in itself as well: it provided jobs and profits; Americans preferred these to the ambiance of any particular place. They expressed this preference by using a higher percentage of their total social product to consume transportation than Europeans did.

The notion of the market did not have the emotional and ideological significance in European transportation policy paradigms that it did in the United States. Adam Smith was British and laissez faire French, but whole-hearted acceptance of the doctrines of classical liberalism was, as Louis Hartz reminded us, uniquely American.[1] The traditions of royalism, mercantilism, and statism were too strong in Europe ever to be banished completely from the policy paradigm in so important an area as transportation. Private property in a free market was often useful and desirable, but it was never patriotically essential, as so often seemed to be the case in American policy debates. If in France today the concept of *le marché des transports* is at the center of the policy debate, it is as a tool in the hands of the same class of technocrats that relied heavily on *dirigismé* in the past. Their goal remains the same: a strong French state ruling a strong, prosperous France. In the United States the market was and continues to be the quintessentially legitimate mode of social choice. Only in the case of market failure (monopoly) or where no market existed (police protection, roads) was the government justified in intervening in the economy to provide goods and services. In some cases government intervention tended to fixate on protecting the private ownership component of the system at the expense of supply and demand interaction cues which are equally as important. Thus in the case of ICC railroad regulation private property was preserved but hedged about with so many regulations of both a restrictive and protective nature that the signals needed to adapt to a changing economy were not reliably transmitted. The goal of regulation itself was not a particular set of transport policy outcomes, just procedural fairness to the interests of the directly affected parties.

The authority exercised and obeyed in transportation policy in Europe was not due to socialist ideology or the strength of socialist parties but to a legacy of historical traditions. Bismarck's nationalization of the Prussian railroads put that government in the urban transportation business via commuter railroads as early as the 1880s. Conservative French governments took over rail networks in the nineteenth and early twentieth century in exercises of authority for the public good that did not become feasible in America until the 1970s. In addition European publics have tended to be more willing to accept higher tax burdens and more government restrictions on their personal transportation activities than Americans. High motor vehicle taxes, parking and traffic restraint, mandatory seat belt laws, and national government drunk driving programs have been accepted on a scale that remains impossible in America to this day. In America public authority's role in the transportation system was limited to promoting transportation modes and providing for increases in capacity. When public authority had to be used directly to regulate a transportation sector, it was viewed as the lesser of two evils. It assumed the role of an umpire (the ICC refereeing conflicts between railroads, shippers, truckers) rather than that of leader or planner. The posture was reactive rather than projective, responding to pressures from its transportation constituents rather than leading demand and production in directions determined to be in the public interest.

The point to be derived from these contrasts is not that European policy makers were more foresighted than Americans or that their policy paradigms were wiser. Rather Europeans have responded to a different set of historical, geographical, and economic circumstances which necessarily shaped different policy paradigms than those developed in America. Nineteenth-century French governments would have been derelict in their duty to defend *la patrie* if they had permitted private rail companies to concentrate their investments in competing lines between Paris and Lille while neglecting the vital supply routes to the Vosges and Sedan. The British lag in providing for automobility growth is more logical for a country concerned about growing dependence on imported oil from overseas and a declining currency, as Britain was from 1914 onward, than for a rising continental power that was self sufficient in oil and most other raw materials, as the United States largely was until the 1970s. Timely aid for urban transit is more easily provided when an institutional framework of public ownership has long been in place and ridership is rising as in West Germany, than when the ownership pattern is rapidly changing and ridership is declining as in the United States.

The lesson is not that Europeans were smarter, and so we should learn from their wisdom; it is that their policy paradigm was a logical response to their objective situation. Insofar as conditions in the United States are changing and coming to resemble European conditions, it is useful to consider if a European style paradigm might not be a more satisfactory response to the situation than the traditional American paradigm. Many European observers are convinced that Americans will sooner or later be obliged to make major changes in the way they define and deal with the new problems confronting the nation. The observers also believe that Americans will have serious political difficulties in doing so, however. A cartoon on the cover of *Der Spiegel* illustrated this view. It showed a glum Jimmy Carter on an empty oil barrel crossing out the "un" on what the Germans consider the U.S. national slogan: *USA: Land der unbegrenzten Möglichkeiten* ("Land of Unlimited Opportunity").[2]

Some Americans might prefer to ignore the lessons implicit in the contrast with Europe. They would stress the uniqueness of the United States and maintain that the European experience is largely irrelevant to American policy choices. Europe's different geography, history, and traditions cannot be reproduced on American soil and thus really have little to teach us. They would argue that we must find our own solutions to our own problems. The American way is not that of authority and austerity. It relies instead on technology and freedom of choice. American expertise, if allowed to proceed unhampered, will produce the innovations that will enable us to preserve the American style of transportation with little fundamental change or disruption.

Obviously the arguments of this book are based on a different set of assumptions. While not disparaging the possibility of future technological progress that may make American style automobility less resource intensive, it assumes that such progress is not likely to free transportation from resource contraints altogether. It is the ever-tightening grip of such constraints on the options available to policy makers that makes the U.S. transportation policy arena increasingly resemble the European. But technology and authority need not be either/or choices. Both will be important in the complex policy paradigm that will emerge in the future.

TOWARD A REFORMULATION OF THE POLICY PARADIGM

These are times that try, if not men's souls, certainly their patience. The public is alternately angry, confused, and frightened by official efforts to cope with the dilemmas of modern society. Policy analysts are experiencing the joys and agonies of intellectual ferment as past principles are challenged and new paradigms posited. Nowhere is this more true than in transportation policy. The old verities about the automobile are seen as dangerous, and the new verities about mass transit as disappointing. Policy analysis has been called "a form of collective puzzlement on society's behalf."[3] Puzzlement is an apt term indeed for the process that takes place when a prevailing paradigm performs poorly. Donald Schon suggests that a successful response to such a situation resembles the following scenario: When disruptive events, crises, or prolonged policy failures exist, they produce a demand for new ideas, new ways of meeting the challenges confronting society. These new ideas may already be present in society among marginal groups and roles, or they may be imported from other more successful societies. The new ideas are mediated by vanguard roles of intellectuals, muckrakers, and social critics who gradually force them to the attention of the general public as well as the policy-making elite. The new ideas may become powerful as centers of policy debate and political conflict. Interests and organizations grow up around them and push them still closer to the center of policy making. Eventually some of them gain widespread acceptance through the efforts of those who "push or ride them through the fields of force created by the interplay of interests and commitments." These ideas, appropriately modified and adjusted, become a part of the revised paradigm of public choice.[4]

If indeed new resource constraints are moving America toward a more European-like need for parsimony in transportation policy, then the lessons of the European experiences may become valuable components in the revised American paradigm. Of course comparative studies of other nations' policy experiences are only one element among many in the debate. Not all the lessons thus derived may prove applicable to the American context. Some changes may not be acceptable for specific geographical or sociological reasons. For example, the very size of the United States and the distances between major cities may mean that a national rail passenger system will never have the relative success it has had in Europe, although within certain regions such as the northeast corridor it may well have great potential. Downtown pedestrian malls in U.S. cities may not be as successful as in Europe because of the greater fear of crime here. Nevertheless, while the process of paradigm revision and the specifics of the programs will necessarily be complex, the general thrust of what the European experience can contribute to the American policy debate is simple. It can be summarized in three main directives: (1) use authority authoritatively, (2) use markets creatively, and (3) use transportation sparingly.

To use authority authoritatively means to use it frankly and unequivocally to achieve an important public purpose. It means to recognize that all authority carries with it an inevitable threat of coercion. Americans, perhaps more than most other peoples, do not like the coercive implications of the use of authority. They are inclined to put more emphasis on their rights vis-à-vis public authority than on their publicly enforceable obligations to the community. This feeling about authority may be a good argument for restricting its use to very important public problems, but it is not a reason for attenuating its impact to the point where it undercuts authority's capacity to achieve its goals. The classic American example of the nonauthoritative use of authority is the attempt to regulate the railroads by means of the ICC. The impact of authority was so muffled by the complex legalistic procedures prescribed by law and developed by precedent that the system became virtually a publicly sanctioned private cartel.

A large segment of the U.S. policy-making elite, especially comprising advisors to the president, is now in the same frame of mind as the British elite of the 1920s, when Churchill fulminated against allowing motorists claims on road tax revenues to cripple the fleet. Presidential administrations worry that motorists' demands for imported petroleum may cripple the balance of payments and destroy much of America's economic and political influence abroad. One of President Carter's principal public stances was to preach long-term national interests over short-run private interests. Unfortunately for him, he did not have the same institutional authority that Churchill used in his raids on the road fund. Policy makers in both the executive and legislative branches apparently believed that it was too risky, even in the face of a potential international energy and financial crisis, to raise the cost of motoring directly through higher taxes. Instead they preferred to let impersonal market forces take the blame. Thus costs were raised by the decontrol of domestic oil prices instead of by wellhead or retail taxes.

To use markets creatively means to take advantage of the fact that the decentralized decision-making processes of markets are often better mechanisms for achieving publicly desired outcomes than the application (and especially the misapplication) of authority. It also means recognizing that there is no such thing as an absolutely pure free market, uninfluenced by public laws, policies, and expenditures. Charles L. Schultze's recent book, entitled *The Public Use of Private Interest,* makes this point very well. He recommends the use of marketlike incentives instead of highly bureaucratic regulatory agencies to achieve important public goals.[5] There are many problems in transportation policy that might better be attacked by a coordination of the market impact of public incentives and disincentives than by formal exercise of authority. For example, it is doubtful if a federal bureaucratic program to slow down the growth of energy-wasting sprawl development would have the same kind of success that coordinated transportation and land use planning has had in Sweden. There are too many opportunities for subverting the intent of the program in our fragmented federal system. But, as was suggested in chapter 7, a policy that coordinates federal incentives (FHA, VA, HUD mortgage policies, capital grants for highways, mass transit, sewers, water systems, and the like) with emerging market trends might have a significant impact.

Finally, to use transportation sparingly entails potentially the most significant change of all. It is the general goal toward which efforts under the first two points should be directed. In the past Americans could logically seek solutions to a variety of socioeconomic problems by substituting transportation solutions for sociopolitical ones. Cheap land, cheap fuel, and cheap transportation (first trolleys, then buses, then cars) allowed individuals to increase their transportation expenditures somewhat and move to a suburb rather than organize collective efforts to rehabilitate existing dwellings in urban neighborhoods and improve schools and whatever else. There were many gradually rising social costs associated with this ever more intensive mobility pattern. Only with the prospect of a severe energy problem have these costs become serious enough to alarm large segments of the national policy-making elite, however. The elite's first response, naturally enough, tends to be to try to preserve the pattern by finding alternate sources of fuel. This runs into contradictions that seem inherent in the traditional assumption of more is better. What answer does the traditional paradigm offer to multiple dilemmas created when a freeway revolt and an energy crisis lead to a demand for more public transportation just at a time when transit deficits are skyrocketing and a mood of tax revolt is spreading across the nation? Or when business decries a capital shortage and government proposes to divert hundreds of billions to a synthetic fuels program?

An illustration of the implications of this third point can be seen by way of analogy to the policy prescriptions recently put forward by Amory B. Lovins in the area of energy.[6] Lovins, a gadfly scientist, is a critic of the world's increasing reliance on nuclear power. Along with his criticisms, however, he offers an intriguing alternative: hard energy technologies represented by giant, centralized power stations (both nuclear and conventional) based on dangerous or depletable resources should be replaced by soft technologies based on decentralized production from renewable energy sources. Such soft technologies use energy more appropriately, more in tune with the second law of thermodynamics. Using a nuclear power plant with temperatures of 10,000 degrees to produce electricity to heat homes to 72 degrees is ridiculously inappropriate. Using a solar collector, a windmill, or the biomass in garbage is appropriate. Moreover adopting such soft energy paths will have beneficial social effects. They do not require huge concentrated capital investments that perpetuate economic inequality and social dependence. Soft energy investments can be highly decentralized and made in smaller increments. Individuals and small groups can make such decisions on their own, and they can cooperate with others to make their investments even more effective. The success of soft energy paths depends not on a massive federal crash program and billions of dollars in subsidies but on thousands or millions of individual actions responding to market and marketlike incentives selected and coordinated by public policy.

The notion of hard and soft technologies has clear application to transportation. For example, both superhighways and rail transit systems are hard transportation technologies. They require massive amounts of capital and land; they are environmentally intrusive; they tend to create bureaucratic or interest group constituencies with vested interests in protecting their funding and hence in policy inflexibility. Obviously there must be an important role for such technologies in urban transportation policy. But policies that continue to rely on expansion of hard transportation paths to expand mobility in our already mobility-intensive society are as inappropriate as policies that rely on atomic power to increase energy in an already energy-intensive economy. Individuals should not have to drive a 4,000 lb automobile several miles for a pack of cigarettes as many suburbanites now have to do. Cities and towns should not be obliged to buy expensive rail rapid transit systems to offer their citizens an alternative to the automobile. Public officials should not feel constrained to plan for future growth only in the context of travel-inducing sprawl on the metropolitan fringe. Innovatively old-fashioned methods of community design and transportation organization that minimize the need for long trips by hard transportation modes and substitute shorter trips by softer modes is what the third principle suggests.

It is not within the scope of these concluding remarks to examine such methods in detail. Suffice it to say that there is evidence of rising interest among policy makers in the whole gamut of soft transportation technologies and the experience gained with such methods in this country and abroad. From express bus lanes on existing streets and highways,[7] to ride-sharing programs,[8] to community planning to permit more trips to be made by pedestrians and bicycles,[9] one sees an upsurge not only of studies but of practical steps by both public and private actors.

In the past the pattern of change in transportation has been for one system of technology and land settlement to be superseded by a newer more resource-intensive technology which greatly expanded the total amount of mobility produced by the system. The canal barge was overshadowed by the railroad which was in turn surpassed by the automobile, truck, and airplane. Remnants—often important ones—of older systems remained, however (barges still move a lot of freight). Thus even if the newer softer technologies should succeed beyond the expectations of their most ardent proponents, they will never banish the older technologies completely. The automobile in particular, according to most knowledgeable observers, will continue to play the dominant role in the transportation until we are well into the twenty-first century.[10] But the auto's social and intellectual dominance will be less overwhelming than in the past. It will no longer be at the cutting edge of social change. As the costs of the car (to both individuals and communities) continue to rise, there will be new and powerful incentives to explore and adopt alternatives to exclusive reliance on automobility. The car culture will not suddenly collapse, but it will begin to crumble at the edges.

NOTES

CHAPTER 1

1. The 1974 figure was $115.3 billion. See U.S., Department of Commerce, Bureau of the Census, *Statistical Abstract of the United States 1976* (Washington, D.C.: Government Printing Office, 1976), p. 396.

2. To cite only a few examples from among the many critical studies of the hypertrophy of the transportation system in the United States, see Ivan Illich, *Energy and Equity* (New York: Harper and Row, 1974), Tabor R. Stone, *Beyond the Automobile: Reshaping the Transportation Environment* (Englewood Cliffs, N.J.: Prentice-Hall, 1971), and K. H. Schaeffer and Elliot Sclar, *Access for all: Transportation and Urban Growth* (Baltimore: Penguin, 1975).

3. Charles W. Anderson, Public Policy and the Complex Organization: The Problem of Governance and the Further Evolution of Advanced Industrial Society, in *Politics and the Future of Industrial Society,* edited by Leon M. Lindberg (New York: David McKay, 1976), p. 195.

4. See Charles E. Lindblom, *Politics and Markets: The World's Political-Economic Systems* (New York: Basic Books, 1977), pp. 247–260, and Aaron Wildavsky, *Speaking Truth to Power: The Art and Craft of Policy Analysis* (Boston: Little, Brown, 1979), pp. 109–141, for their more detailed explications of the two models.

5. Eliot J. Feldman, Comparative Public Policy: Field or Method? *Comparative Politics* 11 (January 1978), p. 299.

6. Theodore J. Lowi, What Political Scientists Don't Need to Ask about Policy Analysis, *Policy Studies Journal* 2 (autumn 1973), p. 66.

INTRODUCTION TO PART I

1. U.S., Department of Transportation, Office of the Secretary of Transportation, *Innovation versus Nationalization: Proposals for Change in the Nation's Rail System* (Washington, D.C.: Department of Transportation, 1979).

2. U.S., Congress, Senate, Committee on Commerce, Surface Transportation Subcommittee, *Northeastern Railroad Transportation Crisis; Hearings on S.1031,* 93rd Congress, 1st session, serial no. 93-8, part 2, p. 562.

3. On the significance of the different paths to public ownership see James A. Dunn, Jr., Railroad Policies in Europe and the United States: The Impact of Ideology, Institutions, and Social Conditions, *Public Policy* 25 (spring 1977), pp. 205–240.

CHAPTER 2

1. The standard work in English on the development of the French railroads from their beginnings until the outbreak of World War II is the excellent study by Kimon A. Doukas, *The French Railroad and the State* (New York: Columbia University Press, 1945). See also Louis Armand et al., *Histoire des chemins de fer en France* (Paris: Presses Modernes, 1963), F. Legueu, *La SNCF: de la diligence à la B.B.* (Paris: Plon, 1962).

2. Charles P. Kindleberger, Technical Education and the French Entrepreneur, in *Enterprise and Entrepreneurs in Nineteenth-Century France,* edited by Edward C. Carter II, Robert Forster, and Joseph N. Moody (Baltimore: Johns Hopkins University Press, 1976), pp. 6–7. For further details on the background of this most technical of technocratic corps, see Jean-Claude Thoenig, *L'Ère des technocrats* (Paris: Editions de l'Organisation, 1973). See also, F. Ridley and J. Blondel, *Public Administration in France* (New York: Barnes and Noble, 1965).

3. Doukas, *French Railroads,* p. 21.

4. Ibid., p. 56.

5. The growth of the trucking industry and its regulatory framework is described in Albert Boyer, *Les Transports routiers* (Paris: Presses Universitaires de France, 1973).

6. Doukas, *French Railroads,* p. 180.

7. Ibid., p. 210.

8. A recent scholarly reconsideration of the Popular Front and its historical meaning is Paul Warwick, *The French Popular Front* (Chicago: The University of Chicago Press, 1977), especially pp. 1–46, 139–164. For a vivid portrait of the period and the personalities see William L. Shirer, *The Collapse of the Third Republic: An Inquiry into the Fall of France in 1940* (New York: Simon and Schuster, 1969), pp. 285–325.

9. Doukas, *French Railroads,* gives details on the organization of the SNCF in 1937. For information on the way in which the new mixed enterprise company fit into the French legal and administrative framework see Jean-Marie Auby and Robert Ducos-Ader, *Grands Services publics et entreprises nationales,* vol. 2: *Transports-energie* (Paris: Presses Universitaires de France, 1973), pp. 9–59.

10. Doukas, *French Railroads,* pp. 257–263.

11. Charles de Gaulle, *Mémoires de guerre,* vol. 3, *Le Salut 1944–1946* (Paris: Plon, 1959), pp. 5–6.

12. Compare this ease of communication among technocrats with the difficulty in establishing a dialogue between technocrats and elected politicians. Suleiman quotes a French *haut fonctionnaire* as saying he could not talk to deputies of the national assembly "because we simply do not speak the same language . . . a deputy understands nothing of what I deal with. He simply does not have the necessary knowledge. Ezra Suleiman, *Power and Bureaucracy in France: The Administrative Elite* (Princeton: Princeton University Press, 1974), p. 299.

13. For a concise and positive assessment of the record of French indicative planning see John Ardagh, *The New French Revolution,* pp. 12–45. See also Stephen S. Cohen, *Modern Capitalist Planning: The French Experience* (Cambridge, Mass.: Harvard University Press, 1969), and Jack Hayward and Michael Watson, eds. *Planning, Politics and Public Policy: The British, French and Italian Experience* (Cambridge, England: Cambridge University Press, 1975).

14. René Parès, *Le Chemin de fer en France* (Paris: La Documentation Française, Notes et études documentaires 4121–4122, 1974), pp. 37–38, 75–77.

15. Ardagh, *The New French Revolution,* p. 47.

16. U.S. rail passenger mile figures taken from Association of American Railroads, *Comparative Transportation Statistics* (Washington, D.C.: Association of American Railroads, 1966), p. 6, and U.S., Department of Transportation, *National Transportation Statistics: Summary Report* (Washington, D.C.: Department of Transportation, 1971), p. 43.

17. Société Nationale des Chemins de Fer Français, Assemblée Générale des Actionnaires, *Rapports: exercice 1975* (Paris: SNCF, 1976), pp. 64–65.

18. Maurice Parodi, *L'Économie et la société française de 1945 à 1970* (Paris: Armand Colin, 1971), p. 188.

19. Ibid., p. 192.

20. Institut National de la Statistique et des Études Économiques, *Les Transports en France 1971–1972* (Paris: Les Collections de l'INSEE, 1974), p. 13.

21. Groupe de Travail du Comité Interministériel des Entreprises Publiques, *Rapport sur les entreprises publiques* (Paris: La Documentation Française, 1967).

22. The verbal distinction between laissez faire and *faire faire* was suggested by Jean Noël Chapulut, Jean Frébault, and Jacques Pellegrin, *Le Marché des transports* (Paris: Éditions du Seuil, 1970), p. 123.

23. The management's version of the reform of the SNCF, which goes so far as to suggest that they initiated the whole thrust of the move toward the *contrat de programme,* contractual basis of state railway relations, is given in the special issue of the *Revue générale des chemins de fer,* entitled La Réforme de la SNCF, (April 1972), especially in the articles by Roger Guibert, André Ségalat, and Jules Antonini, all top officials of the SNCF. This special issue provides an excellent overview of the administrative, political, and economic issues reform.

24. For further details on the policy principles guiding the reform see Chapulut, Frébault, and Pellegrin, *Le Marché des transports,* pp. 33–128; M. Jacquit, La Réforme de la SNCF et l'apparition d'une notion nouvelle de l'entreprise publique, *Droit social* (July–August 1970); La Documentation Française, Nouveaux rapports de l'état et des entreprises publiques: les contrats de programme, *Les Cahiers français* (September–October 1971).

25. Organization for Economic Cooperation and Development, *Statistics of Energy 1959–1973* (Paris: OECD, 1974), pp. 295–314.

26. Parès, *Le Chemin de fer en France,* p. 75.

27. Le Plan gouvernemental: les mesures concernant les transports, *Le Monde* (March 8, 1974), p. 4. See also, Les Consequences de la crise de l'énergie, *Le Monde* (July 20, 1974), p. 21.

28. See, for example, the three-part story, La SNCF au péril de la route, *Le Monde* (April 16–18, 1973).

29. Parès, *Le Chemin de fer en France,* p. 76.

30. Jean Meilhaud, Le Programme de développement de la SNCF et les données nouvelles du dossier du rail, *Problèmes Économiques* (November 27, 1974), pp. 11–16.

31. Ibid., p. 12.

32. James M. Caparaso, *The Structure and Function of European Integration* (Pacific Palisades, Calif.: Goodyear, 1974), pp. 87–109.

33. The first major agreement was reached on June 22, 1965, and was aimed at creating a common transport market within the community, harmonizing competition between modes and organizing the market. This accord was not implemented until the issuance of five EEC regulations in July 1969. The next major accord did not come until the end of 1973. See Chapulut, Frébault, and Pellegrin, *Le Marché des transports,* pp. 125–127. See also Commission des Communautés Européennes, *Politique Commune des transports: objectifs et programme* (Brussels: EEC Commission, 1974).

34. l'Union Internationale des Chemins de Fer, *Plan directeur du chemin de fer européen de l'avenir* (Paris, 1973).

35. Ibid. See also I. B. F. Kormos, Les Liaisons et les transports terrestres dans la communauté européenne, *Documentation européen* (1974), pp. 1–4.

36. For the text of the Guillaumat report see Commission d'Étude sur l'Avenir des Transports Terrestres, *Orientations pour les transports terrestres* (Paris: La Documentation Française, 1978). The SNCF's critical response to the report is summarized in SNCF, *Note d'information* (October 1978). See also La SNCF et les routiers doivent évoluer dan un climat de concurrence demande la commision Guillaumat, *Le Monde* (July 12, 1978), p. 28.

37. SNCF, *Le Contrat d'entreprise entre l'état et la SNCF* (Paris: Service de l'Information et de Relations Publiques de la SNCF, 1979). See also Antoine Silber, La SNCF: ce que la liberté va changer, *Le Point* 332 (January 29, 1979), pp. 48–49.

38. François Dupuy and Jean-Claude Thoenig, Public Transportation Policy Making in France as an Implementation Problem, *Policy Sciences* 11 (August 1979), p. 18.

39. "Le Programme d'équipement de la SNCF le chemin de fer sur la bonne voie, *Le Monde* (November 29, 1978), pp. 38–39.

CHAPTER 3

1. For an overview of the early years of rail development in the United States see John F. Stover, *The Life and Decline of the American Railroad* (New York: Oxford University Press, 1970).

2. The rail industry's position is that in the long run the railroads repaid the U.S. government for the land grants by the lower rates for federal property and mail. There is no doubt that the rate reductions amounted to more than the unimproved land was worth in the nineteenth century. Some rail companies still own the land today, and its value is many times what it was a century ago. See Paul W. Gates, The Railroad Land Grant Legend, *Journal of Economic History* (spring 1954), pp. 143–146.

3. For a recent balanced summary of the creation and development of the ICC see Ari and Olive Hoogenboom, *A History of the ICC: From Panacea to Palliative* (New York: Norton, 1976).

4. Gabriel Kolko, *Railroads and Regulation 1877–1916* (Princeton: Princeton University Press, 1965).

5. Albro Martin, *Enterprise Denied: The Origins of the Decline of American Railroads 1897–1917* (New York: Columbia University Press, 1971).

6. Susan Armitage, *The Politics of Decontrol of Industry, Britain and the United States* (London: Weidenfeld and Nicholson, 1969), p. 98.

7. Ibid., pp. 98–99.

8. See, for example, George W. Hilton, *The Northeast Railroad Problem* (Washington, D. C.: American Enterprise Institute for Public Policy Research, 1975), pp. 7–10.

9. Peter Lyon, *To Hell in a Day Coach: An Exasperated Look at American Railroads* (Philadelphia and New York: Lippincott, 1968), p. 170.

10. Eastman's fruitless efforts to achieve coordination are detailed in Earl Latham, *The Politics of Railroad Coordination 1933–1936* (Cambridge, Mass.: Harvard University Press, 1959).

11. U.S., Department of Transportation, *Northeast Railroad Problem: A Report to the Congress* (Washington, D. C.: Department of Transportation, 1973), p. 17.

12. U.S. Railway Association, *Preliminary System Plan,* vol. 1 (Washington, D.C., 1975), pp. 1–2.

13. U.S., Department of Transportation, *A Prospectus for Change in the Freight Railroad Industry* (Washington, D.C.: Department of Transportation, 1978), p. 40.

14. Transportation Association of American, *Transportation Facts and Trends* 13th ed. (Washington, D. C., 1977), p. 10.

15. American Trucking Associations, Inc., *American Trucking Trends, 1976 Statistical Supplement* (Washington, D.C., 1977), p. 17.

16. U.S., Department of Transportation, *A Prospectus for Change,* p. 48.

17. American Trucking Associations, Inc., *Truck Taxes by States,* 25th ed. (Washington, D.C., 1977), p. 3.

18. A study commissioned by the Department of Transportation concluded that a single heavy truck causes approximately 2,500 times more damage to the road surface than a passenger car. See Charles River Associates, *Competition Between Rail and Truck in Intercity Freight Transportation* (Springfield, Va.: Clearinghouse for Federal Scientific and Technical Information, 1969), p. 59.

19. Association of American Railroads, *Government and Private Expenditures for Highway, Waterway, Railroad and Air Rights-of-Way* (Washington, D.C., 1977), table 5.

20. The Federal Highway Administration agreed with the railroads on this issue. It calculated that in 1969 a five-axle diesel powered 60,000 lb gross weight tractor trailer paid $1,294 in federal user taxes but imposed an annual federally funded cost on the highway system of $2,011. See U.S., Department of Transportation, Federal Highway Administration, *Allocation of Highway Cost Responsibility and Tax Payments* (Washington, D.C.: Department of Transportation, 1969), p. 17.

21. The critical literature is abundant. It ranges from muckraking studies by a Ralph Nader group, Robert C. Fellmeth, ed., *The Interstate Commerce Omission: The Public Interest and the ICC* (New York: Grossman Publishers, 1970), to scholarly studies such as Ann F. Friedlander, *The Dilemma of Freight Transport Regulation* (Washington, D.C.: The Brookings Institute, 1969).

22. U.S., Congress, House, Committee on Interstate and Foreign Commerce, *USRA Final System Plan: Hearings before the Subcommittee on Transportation and Commerce,* 94th Congress, 1st session, 1975, serial no. 94-44, p. 706.

23. Ibid.

24. U.S., Department of Transportation, *A Prospectus for Change,* p. 117.

25. This critique of the problems of interrailroad cooperation was made in *Improving Railroad Productivity,* Final Report of the Task Force on Railroad Productivity, a report to the National Commission on Productivity and the Council of Economic Advisers (Washington, D.C., 1973), pp. 1–50. See also George W. Hilton, *The Northeast Railroad Problem,* pp. 3–22.

26. The three districts were defined many years ago by the ICC. The eastern includes the eastern half of Illinois and all states to the east and north of Kentucky and North Carolina. The southern encompasses everything south of the eastern and east of the Mississippi, including a part of eastern Louisiana. The western includes Wisconsin, western Illinois, and all states to the west of the Mississippi.

27. Hilton, *The Northeast Railroad Problem,* p. 33.

28. U.S., Department of Transportation, *A Prospectus for Change,* p. 21.

29. As Stephen Ailes of the Association of American railroads told Congress "when you take the industry as a whole, you have four or five different segments which have totally different interests in this thing (the northeast rail problem) . . . there is not any way that there is going to be one voice in the industry." U.S., Congress, House, *Final System Plan,* p. 709.

30. The essence of the rail industry's new political strategy is summarized in a report prepared by the consulting firm of Temple, Barker and Sloane, Inc., *New Perspectives on the Railroad Problem* (Wellesley, Mass., 1970). The report was originally presented to the executive board of the Association of American Railroads in October 1970; it served as the centerpiece of a New York symposium, The Railroad Industry: A Crisis of Confidence, which was attended by representatives of government, the railroads, and the business community.

31. U.S., Congress, House, Committee on Interstate and Foreign Commerce, *Supplemental Hearings before the Subcommittee on Transportation and Aeronautics on HR 17849 (Rail Passenger Service Act of 1970),* 91st Congress, 2nd session, 1970, p. 67.

32. Ironically, although the U.S. government owns no stock in Amtrak, the Canadian government does. One of the four railroads that chose the stock option was the Grand Trunk Western, a wholly owned subsidiary of Canadian National Railways.

33. Irwin B. Arieff, Congress Bars Cutbacks in Amtrak Service Before 1979, *Congressional Quarterly Weekly Reports* (August 19, 1978), p. 2199.

34. Amtrak gets the bad news: a 43% route cut *Railway Age* (February 12, 1979), p. 11.

35. The 40 pages of fine print of the 3R act are summarized in Nixon Signs Unprecedented Rail Reorganization Plan, *Congressional Quarterly Weekly Report* 29 (January 5, 1974), pp. 13–18. The act is analyzed by Robert W. Harbeson, Some Policy Implications of Northeastern Railroad Problems, *Transportation Journal* 14 (fall 1974), pp. 5–12. A critical evaluation is offered in George W. Hilton, *The Northeast Railroad Problem,* pp. 45–52.

36. U.S., Congress, House, *Final System Plan* pp. 707–708.

37. Information on the changes in USRA and Conrail legislation is from U.S., Congress, House, *Railroad Revitalization and Regulatory Reform.* Report of the Conference Committee on S 2718. HR report no. 94-781 (January 23, 1976). See also U.S., Department of Transportation, *A Prospectus for Change,* pp. 140–141.

38. Ibid.

39. The intellectual background to the regulatory reform sections of the 4R act may be found in the papers collected in Paul Mac Avoy and John W. Snow, eds., *Railroad Revitalization and Regulatory Reform* (Washington, D.C.: American Enterprise Institute for Public Policy Research, 1977).

40. The extent and the impact of the specific regulatory changes in the 4R act, as well as the desirability of extending them even further are discussed in U.S., Department of Transportation, *A Prospectus for Change,* pp. 113–134.

41. See Conrail Subsidy Increased, *Congressional Quarterly Weekly Report* (August 5, 1978), p. 2056, and Rough Ride for Conrail, *Time* (October 23, 1978), p. 87.

42. U.S., Department of Transportation, *A Prospectus for Change,* p. 11.

43. Irwin B. Arieff, Carter Plans Deregulation Drive in 1979, *Congressional Quarterly Weekly Report* (December 9, 1978), p. 3422.

44. See in particular the chapter entitled "The Privileged Position of Business" in Lindblom, *Politics and Markets,* pp. 170–188.

45. Ibid., p. 179.

46. Even the staff of the Securities and Exchange Commission concluded that the Penn-Central merger was impeded by "personality conflicts and by the significant difference in philosophy and approach of the two roads." It believed that too much emphasis was put on "who would hold what management positions in the new company, as various parties maneuvered for good jobs for themselves and their associates." See Securities and Exchange Commission, *The Financial Collapse of the Penn-Central Company,* staff report to the Special Subcommittee on Investigations (Washington, D.C.: Government Printing Office, 1972), p. 15.

47. The Department of Transportation charged that the ICC has been too interested "in protecting specific shippers, communities, or carriers. . . . [and that] the effect of many of these changes [under the 4R act] . . . was minimized by the ICC." See U.S., Department of Transportation, *A Prospectus for Change,* p. 113.

48. Ibid., p. 3.

49. Ibid., pp. 79–99.

INTRODUCTION TO PART II

1. See, for example, Hans J. Stueck, Urban Transit Model, *Saturday Review* (December 5, 1970), pp. 62–63; Charles B. Barnard, Commuter's Dream City: Hamburg, Germany—One Place in the World Where Its a Pleasure to Ride on Public Transportation, *Lamp* (N.Y.: Standard Oil Co., winter 1971), pp. 24–29; Wolfgang S. Homburger and Vukan R. Vuchic, Federation of Traffic Agencies as a Solution for Service Integration, *Traffic Quarterly* 24 (July 1970), pp. 373–392; and, Edward C. Burks, Europe's Answer to Traffic Jams: Mass Transit Boom, *New York Times* (May 12, 1975), p. 53.

2. The best explications for a market paradigm applied to urban transit are found in transport economics texts, preferably those published a decade or more ago. See, for example, Hugh S. Norton, *Modern Transportation Economics* (Columbus, Ohio: Merrill, 1963).

3. The case for the social subsidy paradigm is often found in critical studies and monographs that plead for policy innovation. See, for example, K. H. Shaeffer and Elliot Sclar, *Access for All: Transportation and Urban Growth* (Baltimore: Penguin, 1975) and Independent Commission on Transport, *Changing Directions* (London: Coronet, 1974).

4. U.S., Secretary of Transportation, William T. Coleman, Jr., *A Statement of National Transportation Policy* (Washington, D.C.: Government Printing Office, 1975), p. 8.

CHAPTER 4

1. On the historical development of the urban public transit industry in Germany see Fritz Voigt, *Verkehr,* vol. 2 (Berlin: Dunker and Humblot, 1965), pp. 650–780, and John P. Mc Kay, *Tramways and Trolleys: The Rise of Urban Mass Transit in Europe* (Princeton: Princeton University Press, 1976).

2. Frederic Howe, *European Cities at Work* (New York: Charles Scribner, 1913), p. 345.

3. Manfred Zachcial, *Unternehmensgrössenprobleme im Verkehrssektor* (Göttingen: Verlag Otto Schwarz, 1976), p. 117.

4. Ibid., p. 123.

5. Bundesverband des deutschen Personenverkehrsgewerbes, *Verkehrszahlen des privaten Strassen-Personenverkehrsgewerbes* (Bonn, 1973), p. 27.

6. Bundesminister für Verkehr, *Zielsetzungen des Bundesministers fur Verkehr für die Unternehmungspolitik der deutschen Bundesbahn und für den öffentlichen Personennahverkehr* (Bonn, 1975), p. 16.

7. Hans-Georg Lange, Finanzierungsprobleme des öffentlichen Personennahverkehrs, *Zeitschrift für Verkehrswissenschaft* 46 (1975), p. 227.

8. Bundesminister für Verkehr, *Zielsetzungen,* p. 15.

9. See, for example, Vukan R. Vuchic, The Role of Public Transportation in Hamburg, Germany, *Traffic Quarterly* 18 (January 1964), pp. 118–140; F. Pampel, "The Hamburg Transport Community: An Example of Coordination and Integration in Public Transport" (paper presented to the 38th Congress of the International Union of Public Transport, London, 1969); Wolfgang S. Homburger and Vukan R. Vuchic, Federation of Transit Agencies as a Solution for Service Integration, *Traffic Quarterly* 24 (July 1970), pp. 373–392.

10. Homburger and Vuchic, Federation of Transit Agencies, p. 381.

11. Ibid.

12. Hamburger Verkehrsverbund, *Organisation, Arbeitsweise, Ergebnisse, Perspektiven* (Hamburg: HVV, n.d.); Hamburger Verkehrsverbund, *Bericht* (Hamburg: HVV, annually from 1967 to 1975).

13. Hamburger Verkehrsverbund, *Bericht 1975,* p. 19.

14. For information on the creation of transit federations in other West German cities and the different types of organization structures being developed, see Ernst Brockhoff, *Kooperation im öffentlichen Personennahverkehr: Tarifgemeinschaft, Verkehrsgemeinschaft, Verkehrsverbund* (Dusseldorf: Alba Buchverlag, 1973), and A. Caprasse, Verkehrsverbund—Kooperation in der Verkehrsbedienung, *Stadtetag* 25 (no. 7, 1972), pp. 399–402.

15. An overview of the evolution of the West German federal government's policy toward urban public transit to the early 1970s is given in Bundesminister für Verkehr, *Konzept zur Verbesserung des öffentlichen Personennahverkehrs* (Bonn, 1971), pp. 3–25.

16. Ibid., p. 21.

17. Ibid., p. 22.

18. Ibid.

19. Bundesminister für Verkehr, *Bericht über die Verwendung der Finanzhilfen des Bundes zur Verbesserung der Verkehrsverhältnisse der Gemeinden für das Jahr 1976* (Bonn, 1978), p. 12.

20. Data on transit aid by federal, state and local governments in the United States is from U.S., Department of Transportation, *National Transportation Trends and Choices* (Washington, D.C.: Government Printing Office, 1977), p. 316.

21. Bundesminister für Verkehr, *Verkehrspolitik '76: Grundsatzprobleme und Schwerpunkte* (Bonn: 1976), p. 11.

22. Spiegel gespräch: Verkehrsminister Kurt Gescheidle über sein Konzept für Schiene und Strasse, *Der Spiegel* (March 21, 1977), pp. 100, 102.

23. Bundesminister für Verkehr, *Vorschläge für eine Neuordnung des organisatorischen Rahmens für den öffentlichen Personennahverkehr* (Bonn, 1977), p. 7.

24. See Stellungnahme der Länder zum Neuordnungskonzept des Bundes, in ibid., pp. 9–13.

25. See, for example, Hans Erb, *Auto, Auto über Alles* (Hamburg, 1966); and Hans Dollinger, *Die totale Autogesellschaft* (Munich: Carl Hanser, 1972).

26. *Der Spiegel*, p. 104.

27. Bundesminister für Verkehr, *Verkehrspolitik '76*, p. 5.

28. Ibid., pp. 20–24.

29. Statistisches Bundesamt, *Statistisches Jahrbuch 1975 für die Bundesrepublik Deutschland* (Wiesbaden, 1975), pp. 51–57; U.S. Department of Commerce, Bureau of the Census, *Statistical Abstract of the United States 1976* (Washington, D.C., 1976), p. 11.

30. *Der Nahverkehr—Probleme und Lösungssätze* (Essen: Girardet, 1976), p. 11.

31. U.S., Department of Commerce, Bureau of the Census, Population of Urbanized Areas Established Since the 1970 Census, for the United States: 1970, *1970 Census of Population; Supplementary Report* PC(S7-106) (October 1976), p. 10.

32. Reinhold Koch, Wanderungen und Rezession, *Information zur Raumentwicklung* (no. 12, 1977), p. 882.

33. Joachim Balderman and Georg Heckling, Wanderungsmotive und Stadtstruktur, *Schriftenreihe des Städtebaulichen Instituts der Universität Stuttgart*, vol. 6 (Stuttgart, 1976), table 3.1/1.

34. Ulrich Pfeiffer, Market Forces and Urban Change in Germany, *The Management of Urban Change in Britain and Germany*, edited by Richard Rose (London and Beverly Hills, Calif.: SAGE, 1974), pp. 46–47.

35. The 1975 and 1960 West German auto and population figures are taken from the United Nations, *Statistical Yearbook* (New York: United Nations, annual), for the appropriate years. The 1975 U.S. auto and population figures are from the same source. The 1921 U.S. auto ownership figures are from U.S., Department of Transportation, *Highway Statistics: Summary to 1965* (Washington, D.C.: Government Printing Office, 1967), p. 23.

36. Conrad J. Weiler, Jr., Metropolitan Reorganization in West Germany, *Publis, the Journal of Federalism* 2 (spring 1972), p. 28.

37. George M. Smerk, *Urban Mass Transportation*, p. 141.

38. U.S., Department of Transportation, *Economic Characteristics of the Urban Public Transportation Industry* (Washington, D.C.: Government Printing Office, 1972), pp. 2–3.

39. Zwei Fragen-Zwei Antworten: Was steckt in einem 86,0-Pfennig Tankstellenpreis? Was macht der Bund mit jeder vom Kraftfahrer an der Tankstelle kassierten D-Mark? *Strasse und Wirtschaft* (April 1977), p. 5.

CHAPTER 5

1. There is no comprehensive history of the growth of the urban public transportation industry as a whole, or of its treatment by public policy, but there are some good short works on the early period. See, for example, George M. Smerk, The Streetcar: Shaper of American Cities, *Traffic Quarterly* 21 (October 1967), pp. 569–584, and the same author's The Development of Public Transportation and the City, in *Public Transportation: Planning, Operations and Management* edited by George E. Gray and Lester A. Hoel (Englewood Cliffs, N.J.: Prentice-Hall, 1979), pp. 4–21.

2. Smerk, Public Transportation and the City, p. 19.

3. See Arthur Salzman, The Decline of Transit in *Public Transportation*, Gray and Hoel, eds., pp. 22–39.

4. Bradford C. Snell, *American Ground Transportation: A Proposal for Restructuring the Automobile, Truck, Bus and Rail Industries*, printed for the use of the Subcommittee on Antitrust and Monopoly of the Committee on the Judiciary, U.S., Senate, *Industrial Reorganization Act Hearings* 93rd Congress, 2nd session (Washington, D.C.: Government Printing Office, 1974), appendix to part 4, pp. A-1–A-103.

5. William L. Mc Corkle, Area Transit History: Gold Mine to Millstone, *Kansas City Star* (March 10, 1976), p. 1B.

6. U.S., Department of Transportation, *Economic Characteristics of the Urban Public Transportation Industry* (Washington, D.C.: Department of Transportation, 1972), pp. 2–3.

7. George M. Smerk, *Urban Mass Transportation: A Dozen Years of Federal Policy* (Bloomington: Indiana University Press, 1974), p. 141.

8. Frank C. Colcord, Public Transit and Institutional Change, in *Public Transportation,* Gray and Hoel, eds., p. 586.

9. The way in which local officials perceived and responded to urban transit problems is also discussed in Wilfred Owen, *The Metropolitan Transportation Problem* (Washington, D.C.: The Brookings Institution, 1966), and John R. Meyer, John F. Kain, and Martin Wohl, *The Urban Transportation Problem* (Cambridge, Mass.: Harvard University Press, 1965).

10. Information about early state transit aid efforts can be found in U.S., Department of Transportation, *Feasibility of Federal Assistance for Urban Mass Transportation Operating Costs* (Washington, D.C.: Department of Transportation, 1971), chapter 3.

11. R. L. Carstens, C. R. Mercier, and E. J. Kannel, Current Status of State-Level Support for Transit, *Urban Transportation Finance* (Washington, D.C.: Transportation Research Board, Transportation Research Record 589, 1976), p. 14.

12. Calculated from data given in ibid. and in U.S., Department of Transportation, *Urban Mass Transportation Administration: Statistical Summary* (Washington, D.C.: Department of Transportation, n.d.).

13. Ibid.

14. U.S., Department of Transportation, Urban Mass Transportation Administration *Statistical Summary* (Washington, D.C.: Department of Transportation, n.d.), p. 1.

15. For details on the growth of federal transit legislation and programs see U.S., Department of Transportation, *Federal Assistance for Urban Mobility* (Washington, D.C.: Department of Transportation, n.d.). See also George M. Smerk, *Urban Mass Transportation,* pp. 40–89, and George W. Hilton, *Federal Transit Subsidies: The Urban Mass Transportation Assistance Program* (Washington: American Enterprise Institute for Public Policy Research, 1974), pp. 1–12.

16. Lyle C. Fitch, ed., *Urban Transportation and Public Policy* (San Francisco: Chandler Publishing Company, 1964).

17. Smerk, *Urban Mass Transportation,* p. 56.

18. Hilton, *Federal Transit Subsidies,* p. 11.

19. Ibid.

20. Section 121 (e) (2) of the Federal Aid Highway Act of 1973 states: "Notwithstanding section 209 (f) (1) of the Highway Revenue Act of 1956, the Highway

Trust Fund shall be available for making expenditures to meet obligations resulting from projects authorized by subsection (a) (2) of this section." The projects thus authorized include, beginning in fiscal 1975 "the purchase of buses, and beginning with the fiscal year ending June 30, 1976, . . . the construction, reconstruction, and improvement of fixed rail facilities, including the purchase of rolling stock . . ." PL 93-87 (87 stat. 250). The act also allowed cities that choose not to build a segment of the interstate highway system to exchange money authorized for highway construction for an equal amount of general fund money to be applied to mass transit programs. For a layman's description of the act's provisions see, Highway Act: Compromise on Mass Transit Funds, *1973 C Q Almanac* (Washington, D.C.: Congressional Quarterly, 1974), pp. 435–440. See also Smerk, *Urban Mass Transportation,* pp. 82–84.

21. Alan A. Altshuler, Changing Patterns of Policy, The Decision Making Environment of Urban Transportation, *Public Policy* 25 (spring 1977), p. 184. See also Alan Altshuler with James P. Womack and John R. Pucher, *The Urban Transportation System: Politics and Policy Innovation* (Cambridge, Mass.: The MIT Press, 1979), pp. 19–84.

22. Altshuler, Changing Patterns of Policy, p. 187.

23. Ibid., p. 193.

24. Ibid., pp. 187–189.

25. Ibid., p. 192.

26. Altshuler, *The Urban Transportation System,* p. 43.

27. In addition to Hilton's *Federal Transit Subsidies* see also his The Urban Mass Transit Assistance Program, in *Perspective on Federal Transportation Policy,* edited by James C. Miller III (Washington, D.C.: American Enterprise Institute for Public Policy Research, 1975), pp. 131–144.

28. Charles A. Lave, Transportation and Energy: Some Current Myths, *Policy Analysis* 4 (summer 1978), pp. 297–316.

29. Altshuler, *Urban Transportation System,* pp. 165–166.

30. Denis J. Dingemans, Rapid Transit and Suburban Residential Land Use, *Traffic Quarterly* 32 (April 1978), p. 289.

31. Andrew M. Hammer, *The Selling of Rail Rapid Transit* (Lexington, Mass.: Lexington Books, 1976), p. 21.

32. Dingemans, Rapid Transit, p. 306.

33. Altshuler, *Urban Transportation System,* p. 406.

34. Mathew J. Betz, Land-Use Density, Pattern, and Scale as Factors in Urban Transportation, *Traffic Quarterly* 32 (April 1978), pp. 263–272.

35. Boris Pushkarev and Jeffrey M. Zupan, *Public Transportation and Land Use Policy* (Bloomington, Ind.: Indiana University Press, 1977), pp. 184–193.

36. Real Estate Research Corporation, *The Costs of Sprawl* (Washington, D.C.: Government Printing Office, 1974), 2 vols.

37. See Altshuler, *Urban Transportation System,* pp. 379–391, for a detailed critique of *The Costs of Sprawl.* Altshuler concludes that the savings to be achieved by planned communities would be substantially lower than the estimates of the Real Estate Research Board.

38. U.S., Congress, Office of Technology Assessment, *Energy, the Economy, and Mass Transit: Summary Report,* printed for the Transportation Subcommittee, Senate Committee on Appropriations (Washington, D.C., June 1975), p. 68.

39. Pushkarev and Zupan, *Public Transportation and Land Use Policy*, p. 199, citing John Pastier, Redoing L. A. via Rapid Transit, *Los Angeles Times* (August 25, 1975).

40. Altshuler, Changing Patterns of Policy, p. 201.

41. Aaron Wildavsky, *Speaking Truth to Power: The Art and Craft of Policy Analysis* (Boston: Little, Brown, 1979), p. 23.

42. James Cornehls, The Automobile Society: Urban Design and Environment, *Traffic Quarterly* 31 (October 1977), p. 588.

CHAPTER 6

1. Great Britain, Parliament, *Parliamentary Debates*, 4th series (April 18, 1907) col. 1197, cited in William Plowden, *The Motor Car and Politics in Britain* (Harmondsworth, England: Penguin, 1971), p. 73.

2. *The Automobile*, 14 (January 11, 1906), p. 107, cited in John B. Rae, *The Road and the Car in American Life* (Cambridge, Mass.: The MIT Press, 1971), p. 55.

3. R. E. Gallman, Gross National Product in the United States, 1834–1909, *Studies in Income and Wealth*, vol. 30, National Bureau of Economic Research (New York: Columbia University Press, 1966).

4. D. G. Rhys, *The Motor Industry: An Economic Survey* (London: Butterworths, 1972), pp. 7–8.

5. Ibid., p. 9.

6. Plowden, *The Motor Car*, p. 267.

7. *Economist* (July 14, 1928), p. 12.

8. British Road Federation, *Basic Road Statistics 1973* (London: British Road Federation, 1973), p. 2.

9. Plowden, *The Motor Car*, p. 338.

10. G. E. Cherry, Town Planning and the Motor Car in Twentieth Century Britain, *High Speed Ground Transportation Journal* 4 (January 1970), p. 70.

11. Beatrice and Sidney Webb, *The Story of the King's Highway* (London: Frank Cass & Co., 1963), p. 238.

12. This was the first year national motor vehicle statistics were collected. See *Basic Road Statistics 1973*, p. 2.

13. Royal Commission on Motor Cars, *Minutes of Evidence, Appendices and Index* (Cd. 3081). Published as vol. 48 of *British Parliamentary Papers* (1906), cited in Plowden, *The Motor Car*, p. 61.

14. Great Britain, Parliament, *Parliamentary Debates*, 5th series, vol. 4 (1909), p. 601, cited in Plowden, *The Motor Car*, p. 85.

15. Royal Commission on Motor Cars, *Minutes.*

16. Plowden, *The Motor Car*, p. 85.

17. Ibid., p. 84.

18. Ibid., pp. 100–101.

19. Gilmore Jenkins, *The Ministry of Transport and Civil Aviation* (London: George Allen and Unwin, 1959).

20. Great Britain, Public Records Office, *Treasury Series* T. 170/250-51, cited in Plowden, *The Motor Car*, p. 198.

21. Plowden, *The Motor Car,* pp. 209–212.

22. Great Britain, Parliament, *Report of the National Expenditure Committee* (London: HMSO; Cmd 3920, 1931), p. 296.

23. Great Britain, Parliament, *Parliamentary Debates,* 5th series (April 21, 1936), col. 55.

24. *Basic Road Statistics,* 1973, p. 24.

25. K. M. Gwilliam, *Transport and Public Policy* (London: George Allen and Unwin, 1964), p. 149.

26. The first Trunk Roads Act was passed in December 1936, and it transferred some 4,505 miles of main roads in England, Scotland, and Wales to the Ministry of Transport. The ministry assumed all financial responsibility for these roads, although it did permit local authorities to carry out work on the roads as its agents. A further 3,685 miles of roads were designated as trunk roads and transferred to the Ministry of Transport by the second Trunk Roads Act of 1946. The Special Roads Act of 1949 was the enabling legislation for a system of national motorways. Again the Ministry of Transport was to have complete financial liability for these motorways. For the remaining roads the Minister of Transport announced in 1946 that for class I, or principal roads, the central government would pay for 75 percent of the cost of approved maintenance and improvement. But all remaining expenditure would have to be paid by local government, as would the expenditure on class II and III (other) roads. However, the central government would give rate support grants to local authorities covering part of their expenditure on these roads. See *Basic Road Statistics 1973,* pp. 24, 27.

27. Derek Alcroft, *British Transport Since 1914: An Economic History* (London: David and Charles, 1975), p. 262.

28. *Basic Road Statistics,* p. 2.

29. Aldcroft, *British Transport,* p. 260.

30. John W. Shepherd, London: Metropolitan Evolution and Planning Response, *World Capitals: Toward Guided Urbanization,* edited by H. Wentworth Eldredge (Garden City, N.Y.: Anchor Press/Doubleday, 1975), p. 108.

31. Great Britain, Ministry of Transport, *Traffic in Towns: A Study of the Long-term Problems of Traffic in Urban Areas* (London: HMSO, 1963).

32. Colin Buchanan, *Mixed Blessing* (London: Leonard Hill, 1958).

33. Shepherd, London, pp. 116–117.

34. For details on the political struggle over London government reform see F. Smallwood, *Greater London: The Politics of Metropolitan Reform* (New York: Bobbs-Merrill, 1965), and G. Rhodes, *The Government of London: the Struggle for Reform* (London: Weidenfeld and Nicolson, 1971). For a study of the impact of the reorganization on the transport policy machinery of the city see M. E. Collins and T. M. Pharoah, *Transport Organization in a Great City: The Case of London* (London: George Allen and Unwin, 1974).

35. The story of the motorway box rebellion is told in Simon Jenkins, The Politics of London Motorways, *The Political Quarterly* 44 (July–September 1973), pp. 257–270.

36. Shepherd, London, p. 117.

37. S. K. Brooks and J. J. Richardson, The Environmental Lobby in Britain, *Parliamentary Affairs* 28 (summer 1975), pp. 317.

38. Jenkins summarizes the arguments of the antimotorway groups and assesses their impact on public opinion. See The Politics of London Motorways, pp. 260–266. The official reaction to their arguments is found in the so-called Layfield Report: *Greater London Development Plan—Report of the Panel of Inquiry* (London: HMSO, 1973).

39. Greater London Council, *Transport Policies and Programme 1975–1980* (London: Greater London Council, 1974).

40. Ibid., p. 9.

41. Ibid., p. 11.

42. Ibid., p. 10.

43. Ibid., p. 40.

44. Jenkins, The Politics of London Motorways, pp. 257–258.

45. Stephen Plowden, *Towns against Traffic* (London: Andre Deutsch, 1972).

46. The Independent Commission on Transport, *Changing Directions* (London: Coronet Books, Hodder Paperbacks Ltd., 1974).

47. Motorist groups were among the most active supporters of the Tory campaign to win back control of the Greater London Council in the 1977 elections. They conducted an extensive propaganda campaign against the Labor transport planners, accusing them of "planning against the car, not for it." See Roads Group Accuses GLC of Attacking Motorists, *The Times* (March 26, 1977), p. 3. The campaign was effective, for the Conservatives won the elections. While the Tories intend to abolish some of the more stringent traffic restraint measures imposed by the Laborites, "there will be no return to large road building, and the ill-famed motorway box will not be revived . . . (because) there was neither the money available nor the public acceptability for a big road programme." See Michael Baily, GLC Road Plan Aimed at Attracting Industry, *The Times* (July 8, 1977), p. 2.

CHAPTER 7

1. Rae paints a vivid portrait of the state of American roads in the early twentieth century. He also discusses the bicyclist origins of the good roads movement. See John B. Rae, *The Road and the Car in American Life* (Cambridge, Mass.: The MIT Press, 1971), pp. 23–39.

2. A historical sketch of the beginnings of state programs is found in U.S., Department of Transportation, Federal Highway Administration, Bureau of Public Roads, *Highway Statistics: Summary to 1965* (Washington, D.C.: Government Printing Office, 1967), p. 56.

3. Data on the growth of automobile registrations and the length of paved road are from ibid., pp. 23, 119.

4. Ibid. See also John Chynoweth Burnham, The Gasoline Tax and the Automobile Revolution, *The Mississippi Valley Historical Review* 68 (December 1961), pp. 435–459.

5. U.S., Department of Transportation, *Highway Statistics: Summary to 1965,* p. 87.

6. For a discussion of the difficulties involved in breaking state highway trust funds see Drew Salaman, Towards Balanced Urban Transportation: Reform of the State Highway Trust Funds, *Urban Lawyer* 4 (winter 1972), pp. 77–87.

7. U.S., Department of Transportation, 1974 *National Transportation Report: Current Performance and Future Prospects* (Washington, D.C.: Government Printing Office, 1975), p. 470.

8. 48 Stat. 993.

9. Charles L. Dearing, *American Highway Policy* (Washington, D.C.: The Brookings Institution, 1941), pp. 178–179.

10. See Rae, *The Road and the Car,* for details on the evolution of federal aid highway legislation. Federal highway aid figures and data on the federal gasoline tax are from U.S., Department of Transportation, *Highway Statistics: Summary to 1965,* pp. 168–169.

11. 58 Stat. 838.

12. Rae, *The Road and the Car,* pp. 173–183.

13. U.S., Department of Transportation, *Highway Statistics: Summary to 1965,* p. 23.

14. Rae, *The Road and the Car,* pp. 173–183.

15. Wilfred Owen and Charles L. Dearing, *Toll Roads and the Problems of Highway Modernization* (Washington, D.C.: The Brookings Institution, 1951).

16. A detailed discussion of the politics of creating the Federal Highway Trust Fund and accelerating construction of the interstate highway system can be found in the long and very useful article by Gary T. Schwartz, Urban Freeways and the Interstate System, *Southern California Law Review* 49 (March 1976), pp. 406–513. See also Richard O. Davies, *The Age of Asphalt: The Automobile, the Freeway, and the Condition of Metropolitan America* (Philadelphia: Lippincott, 1975), pp. 16–27, and Mark H. Rose, *Express Highway Politics* (Ph.D. dissertation, Ohio State University, 1973).

17. Eisenhower was unable to attend the conference because of a death in the family; Nixon spoke from notes prepared by the president's office. Schwartz, Urban Freeways, p. 427n.

18. For the Clay committee report see President's Advisory Committee on a National Highway Program, *A 10-Year National Highway Program,* HR doc. no. 93, 84th Congress, 1st session (1955).

19. On Byrd's crusade against highway-funding indebtedness see Daniel J. Hanson, Sr., The Highway Trust Fund Is Needed, *Public Works* (February 1976), p. 74.

20. Schwartz, Urban Freeways, p. 434.

21. Ibid., p. 435.

22. 70 Stat. 374 and 387.

23. Why did Eisenhower, a cautious, balanced-budget president, initiate what has been called "the largest public works project in history" and became quite controversial in the 1960s and 1970s? Schwartz cites evidence that it was Francis du Pont, Eisenhower's Bureau of Public Roads Commissioner, who convinced him to take up the superhighway, which had been a sort of Du Pont family hobby since they built their own five-mile stretch on private land in Delaware in the 1920s. Schwartz also maintains that Ike misunderstood the whole interstate program. "The truth is that in 1956 Eisenhower was operating under the incorrect assumption that the interstate program had adopted the policy of bypassing urban areas. Ignorant of the fact that the urban interstates would intrude into inner cities, he was quite disturbed when his ignorance was finally dispelled . . . [in] 1959, when he chanced to query urban planners who were showing him the freeway network planned for the District of Columbia." Schwartz, Urban Freeways, pp. 427–428n, 444–445.

24. Davies, *Age of Asphalt,* p. 22.

25. Figures on the distribution of the highway trust fund revenue are from U.S.,

Department of Transportation, *Highway Statistics: Summary to 1965*, p. 169, and from U.S., Department of Transportation, *1974 National Transportation Report*, p. 293.

26. See A. Q. Mowbray, *Road to Ruin* (Philadelphia: Lippincott, 1969), pp. 7–21.

27. Congressional Quarterly, Impoundment Suits, *C. Q. Almanac 1973* (Washington, D.C.: Congressional Quarterly, Inc., 1974), p. 253.

28. Jack Linville, Troubled Urban Interstates, *Nation's Cities* 8 (December 1970), p. 10.

29. Helen Leavitt, *Superhighway—Superhoax* (Garden City, N.Y.: Doubleday, 1970), p. 201. For more details on the San Francisco Freeway Revolt see W. H. Lathrop, San Francisco Freeway Revolt, *Transportation Engineering Journal* 97 (February 1971), and Ben Kelley, *The Pavers and the Paved* (New York: Donald W. Brown, 1971), pp. 94–97.

30. Alan Lupo, Frank Colcord, and Edmund P. Fowler, *Rites of Way: The Politics of Transportation in Boston and the U.S. City* (Boston: Little, Brown, 1971), p. 41. This is an excellent account of Boston's freeway revolt. Other descriptions of the process may be found in Allan K. Sloan, *Citizen Participation in Transportation Planning: The Boston Experience* (Cambridge, Mass.: Ballinger, 1974), and Ralph Gakenheimer, *Transportation Planning as Response to Controversy:* The Boston Case (Cambridge, Mass.: The MIT Press, 1976).

31. Details on the pro-transit coalition may be found in William Lilley III, Urban Report: Urban Interests Win Transit Bill with "Letter Perfect Lobbying," *National Journal* (September 19, 1970), pp. 2021–2029, and in Congressional Quarterly, Movement Began in Late 1960s to Modify Trust Fund, *C. Q. Almanac 1975* (Washington, D.C.: Congressional Quarterly, Inc., 1976), p. 736.

32. For a discussion of the politics of breaking the federal highway trust fund and the details of the complicated arrangements that allow some of the trust fund money to be used for transit see George M. Smerk, *Urban Mass Transportation: A Dozen Years of Federal Policy* (Bloomington: Indiana University Press, 1974), pp. 72–89.

33. Congressional Quarterly, Highway Extension Sent to Conference, *C.Q. Almanac* 1975 (Washington, D.C.: Congressional Quarterly, Inc., 1976), p. 735.

34. Congressional Quarterly, Highways Have Dominated U.S. Transportation Policy, *Congressional Quarterly Weekly Report* (August 26, 1978), p. 2241.

35. Irvin B. Arieff and Bob Livernash, Senate Acts on Highway Bill, But Transportation Package Faces Logjam in Congress, *Congressional Quarterly Weekly Report* (August 26, 1978), p. 2240.

36. Irvin B. Arieff, Carter Signs $54 Billion Highway Bill, *Congressional Quarterly Weekly Report* (November 11, 1978), pp. 3273–3277.

37. Investigate Road Costs, *Philadelphia Inquirer* (December 2, 1978), p. 3.

38. Peter D. Hart Research Associates, Inc., *A Survey of American Attitudes toward Transportation* (Springfield, Va.: National Technical Information Service, 1978), pp. 44–45.

39. Gail Gregg and Dale Tate, "Carter Seeks Balanced Budget in New Plan to Fight Inflation," *Congressional Quarterly Weekly Report* (March 15, 1980), pp. 707–709.

40. Richard D. Lyons, "Judge Rules Carter Cannot Impose Fee on Gasoline Sales," *New York Times* (May 14, 1980), p. A1.

41. Martin Tolchin, "House and Senate Vote Down Oil Fee by Large Margins,"

New York Times (June 5, 1980), p. A1; "Oil Import Fee Dies as Senate Overrides Carter by 68 to 10," *New York Times* (June 7, 1980), p. 1.

42. The need for more revenues to pay for highway maintenance was indeed the line being stressed by transportation officials in the aftermath of the ten cent per gallon import fee defeat. See "U.S. Highway Chief to Urge Tax Boost on Gasoline in '81, *Wall Street Journal* (June 19, 1980), p. 14.

INTRODUCTION TO PART IV

1. This advertisement, which appeared in U.S. weekly news magazines in the spring of 1979, went on to say, "Don't take your wheels for granted. There are people in government, and others, whose *only* answer to our environmental and energy problems is to restrict the use of the automobile." It called on readers to "Help us protect your freedom to drive."

2. John B. Rae, *The Road and the Car in American Life* (Cambridge, Mass.: The MIT Press, 1971), p. 359.

3. Garrett Hardin, The Tragedy of the Commons, *Science* 162 (December 13, 1968), pp. 1243–1248. See also the article by Martin Wachs, Transportation Policy in the Eighties, *Transportation* 6 (1977), pp. 103–120.

CHAPTER 8

1. James J. Flink, Three States of American Automobile Consciousness, *American Quarterly* (1972), pp. 451–473.

2. Ibid., p. 472.

3. John Allpass, Urban Centers and Changes in the Center Structure, in *Urban Core and Inner City,* edited by the University of Amsterdam Sociographical Department (Leiden: Brill, 1967), p. 105.

4. From among Mumford's many works, see, for example, the title essay in Lewis Mumford, *The Highway and the City* (New York: Harcourt, Brace and World, 1963); Jane Jacobs's best-known work is *The Death and Life of Great American Cities* (New York: Random House, 1961).

5. John Keats, *The Insolent Chariots* (Philadelphia: Lippincott, 1958).

6. A. Q. Mowbray, *Road to Ruin* (Philadelphia: Lippincott, 1969).

7. Helen Leavitt, *Superhighway—Superhoax* (Garden City, N.Y.: Doubleday, 1970).

8. Kenneth R. Schneider, *Autokind vs. Mankind* (New York: Norton, 1971).

9. Ben Kelley, *The Pavers and the Paved* (New York: Donald W. Brown, 1971).

10. John Burby, *The Great American Motion Sickness* (Boston: Little, Brown, 1971).

11. Tabor R. Stone, *Beyond the Automobile* (Englewood Cliffs, N.J.: Prentice-Hall, 1971).

12. K. H. Schaeffer and Elliot Sclar, *Access for All* (Baltimore: Penguin, 1975).

13. W. Valderpoort, *The Selfish Auto* (Amsterdam: Amsterdam Press, 1953).

14. Alfred Sauvy, *Les Quatre Roues de la fortune: essai sur l'automobile* (Paris: Flammarion, 1968).

15. Hans Erb, *Auto, Auto über Alles* (Hamburg, 1966).

16. Hans Dollinger, *Die totale Autogesellschaft* (Munich: Carl Hanser, 1972).

17. Emma Rothschild, *Paradise Lost: The Decline of the Auto-Industrial Age* (New York: Random House, 1973).

18. James J. Flink, *The Car Culture* (Cambridge, Mass.: The MIT Press, 1975).

19. Flink, *The Car Culture*, p. 231.

20. Flink, *The Car Culture*, p. 233.

21. Of course this perceptual shift took place over a far greater range of issues than just the automobile. The whole concept of modern economic growth was called into question by such works as E. F. Schumacher's *Small Is Beautiful* (New York: Harper and Row, 1973) and the Club of Rome's *The Limits of Growth* (New York: New American Library, 1972). Nevertheless the automobile was one of the most salient manifestations of this shift.

22. U.S., Department of Transportation, National Highway Traffic Safety Administration, *Motor Vehicle Safety 1977* (Washington, D.C.: Government Printing Office, 1978), pp. A-13, A-14.

23. U.S., Department of Health, Education, and Welfare, *Report of the Secretary's Advisory Committee on Traffic Safety* (Washington, D.C.: Government Printing Office, 1968).

24. For a provocative analysis of the safety results of Ribbicoff's campaign see D. T. Campbell and H. L. Ross, The Connecticut Crackdown on Speeding: Time-Series Data in Quasi-Experimental Analysis, *Law and Society Review* 3 (1968), pp. 33–53.

25. Ralph Nader, *Unsafe at Any Speed* (New York: Grossman, 1965).

26. A detailed description of Nader's clash with GM can be found in Robert F. Buckhorn, *Nader: The People's Lawyer* (Englewood Cliffs, N.J.: Prentice-Hall, 1972).

27. U.S., Department of Transportation, National Highway Traffic Safety Administration, *Traffic Safety '76* (Washington, D.C.: Government Printing Office, 1976).

28. U.S., Congress, Office of Technology Assessment, *Changes in the Future Use and Characteristics of the Automobile Transportation System* vol. 2 (Washington, D.C.: Government Printing Office, 1979), p. 196.

29. For the government estimates see General Accounting Office, *Effectiveness, Benefits, and Costs of Federal Safety Standards for Protection of Passenger Car Occupants,* Report to the Committee on Commerce, U.S., Senate (Washington, D.C.: Government Printing Office, 1976); for the estimates of one of the leading pro-car writers see B. Bruce-Briggs, *The War against the Automobile* (New York: Dutton, 1977), p. 140.

30. Ibid.

31. U.S., Congress, OTA, *Automobile Transportation System*, p. 214.

32. Ibid., pp. 198–199.

33. Ibid., p. 215.

34. Ibid., p. 218.

35. See Lester B. Lave and Eugene P. Seskin, *Air Pollution and Human Health* (Baltimore: Johns Hopkins University Press, 1977). See also M. M. Fox and A. J. Haagen-Smit, Automobile Exhaust and Ozone Formation, *Vehicle Emissions— Part I* (New York: Society of Automotive Engineers, 1964), pp. 1–16.

36. A study by the National Academy of Sciences and the National Academy of Engineering in 1973 concluded that auto emissions "may account for as much as one-quarter of one percent of the total urban health hazard representing as many

as 4,000 deaths." See U.S., Congress, Senate, Committee on Public Works, *Air Quality and Automobile Emission Control,* vol. 1, summary report. 93rd Congress, 2nd session, September 1974, p. 13. This figure is a maximum estimate, however. Pro-car spokesmen charge that the lack of hard scientific knowledge in the area is evidence that environmentalists have jumped to conclusions on auto emissions. B. Bruce Briggs, for example, summarizes his position in this manner: "Most air pollution is not caused by automobiles. We do not know the effects of automobile emissions on public health; what little evidence is available suggests that the effects are at most trivial." *The War against the Automobile,* p. 101.

37. The cross licensing agreement was eventually challenged by the Department of Justice in an antitrust suit filed in 1969. The suit was settled by a consent decree, without admission of guilt by the auto companies. See Eugene P. Seskin, Automobile Air Pollution Policy in *Current Issues in U.S. Environmental Policy,* edited by Paul R. Portney (Baltimore: Johns Hopkins University Press, 1978), pp. 84–85.

38. For an overview of air pollution control strategies see Frank P. Grad et al., *The Automobile and the Regulation of Its Impact on the Environment* (Norman: University of Oklahoma Press, 1975), especially chapter 1, "Defining the Strategy Options," and chapter 7, "Future Emission Control Technology." See also Donald N. Dewees, *Economics and Public Policy: The Automobile Pollution Case* (Cambridge, Mass.: The MIT Press, 1974).

39. The EPA had set mid-1977 as the deadline for promulgation of transport control plans by the states. The Clean Air Act Amendments of 1977 (PL 95-95) extended the deadline to the end of 1982 and, if necessary, to 1987, and governors were allowed to suspend offending portions of existing transport control plans. See Major Clean Air Act Amendments Enacted, *Congressional Quarterly Almanac* 33 (1977), pp. 627–628.

40. H. Margolis, The Politics of Auto Emissions, *The Public Interest* (fall 1977), pp. 3–21.

41. See Seskin, Automobile Air Pollution Policy, pp. 74–75.

42. For the evidence on improvement of air quality see Council on Environmental Quality, *Environmental Quality—1976: The Seventh Annual Report of the Council on Environmental Quality* (Washington, D.C.: Government Printing Office, 1976). See also Seskin, Automobile Air Pollution Policy, pp. 71–73.

43. U.S., Congress, *Air Quality and Automobile Emission Control,* p. 115.

44. Margolis calls this the problem of political externalities. In the policy debate between government and industry there was no one to argue the case minimizing the total costs to society. See The Politics of Auto Emissions, pp. 19–21.

45. Cynthia H. Enloe, *The Politics of Pollution in a Comparative Perspective* (New York: David McKay, 1975), pp. 188, 281–283. For a study by a European that describes the bureaucratic nature of environmental politics in West Germany see Renate Mayntz, Environmental Policy Conflicts: The Case of the German Federal Republic, *Policy Analysis* 2 (fall 1976), pp. 577–588.

46. William Solesbury, Issues and Innovations in Environmental Policy in Britain, West Germany, and California, *Policy Analysis* 2 (winter 1976), pp. 35–36. See also S. K. Brookes and J. J. Richardson, The Environmental Lobby in Britain, *Parliamentary Affairs* 28 (summer 1975), pp. 213–328.

47. William Plowden, *The Motor Car and Politics in Britain* (Harmondsworth, England: Penguin, 1971), pp. 398–399.

48. For details on the manner in which the European Economic Community authorities bring about the approximation of the laws of the member states in the

matter of air pollution and other areas see W. E. Burhenne, ed., *Environmental Law of the European Communities* (Berlin: Erich Schmidt, 1976).

49. R. Baumann, K. Irlweck, and J. Schedling, Fussgängerzonenexperiment—Wien 1971, *Umweltschutz* 9 (1972), p. 127.

50. See C. K. Orski, *Vehicle—Free Zones in City Centres* (Paris: OECD, 1971), p. 19. See also J. Michael Thomson, Methods of Traffic Limitation in Urban Areas, in *The Automobile and the Environment: An International Perspective*, edited by Ralph Gakenheimer (Cambridge, Mass.: The MIT Press, 1978), pp. 131–228.

51. U.S., Congress, OTA, *The Automobile Transportation System*, p. 216.

52. Ibid.

53. Ibid., p. 219.

54. Ibid., p. 107.

55. Ibid.

56. Daniel Yergin, The Real Meaning of the Energy Crunch, *New York Times Magazine* (June 4, 1978), p. 32.

57. Ibid.

58. John C. Sawhill, Keichi Oshima, and Hans W. Maull, *Energy: Managing the Transition* (New York, Tokyo, and Paris: The Trilateral Commission, 1978), p. 75.

59. See, for example, many of Tom Wicker's columns in the *New York Times*.

60. Joel Darmstadter, Joy Dunkerley, and Jack Alterman, *How Industrial Societies Use Energy: A Comparative Analysis* (Baltimore: Johns Hopkins University Press, 1977).

61. Ibid., p. 27.

62. Ibid., p. 82.

63. Irving B. Kravis et al., *A System of International Comparisons of Gross Product and Purchasing Power* (Baltimore: Johns Hopkins University Press, 1975), cited in Joel Darmstadter, *Industrial Societies*, p. 84.

64. Alexander French and Lyle D. Wylie, Highway Transport and Energy Problems in Europe, in *World Road Statistics 1969–1973* (Washington, D.C.: International Road Federation, 1974), p. 602.

65. For a description of the short-term European reaction to the energy crisis of 1973 to 1974 see Alan E. Pisarski and Niels De Terra, American and European Transportation Responses to the 1973–74 Oil Embargo, *Transportation* 4 (1975): 291–312. Background on the oil regimes and policy development in the two largest European economies can be found in Horst Mendershausen, *Coping with the Oil Crisis: French and German Experiences* (Baltimore: Johns Hopkins University Press, 1976). An overall view of the energy policies of Europe on a country by country basis is given in International Energy Agency, *Energy Policies and Programmes of the IEA Countries 1977 Review* (Paris: OECD, 1978).

66. June Kronholz, Europe's Drivers Don't Reduce Gasoline Use Despite Soaring Prices, *Wall Street Journal* (May 12, 1980), p. 1.

67. Ibid.

68. Car Companies Drive at Energy Savings Targets, *New Scientist* (July 12, 1979), p. 107; John M. Geddes, German Car Makers Get Fuel Cut, *New York Times* (July 5, 1979), p. iv, 5.

69. Energy Tax Bill Stalls in Senate, *C. Q. Almanac 1975* (Washington, D.C.: Congressional Quarterly, Inc., 1976), pp. 207–219.

70. Ibid. See also Ford Ends Stalemate, Signs Energy Bill, *C. Q. Almanac 1975* (Washington, D.C.: Congressional Quarterly, Inc., 1976), pp. 220–245.

71. U.S., International Trade Commission, *The Fuel Efficiency Incentive Tax Proposal: Its Impact upon the Future of the U.S. Passenger Automobile Industry*, a report to the Committee on Finance of the United States Senate (Washington: Government Printing Office, 1977), p. 6.

72. Energy Bill: The End of an Odyssey, *C. Q. Almanac 1978* (Washington, D.C.: Congressional Quarterly, Inc., 1979), pp. 639–667.

73. *The New York Times* (March 25, 1979), p. 27. See also Jack Germond and Jules Witcover, Automakers Are Warned to Think Small, *Philadelphia Inquirer* (December 31, 1978), p. 7-D.

74. U.S., Congress, OTA, *The Automobile Transportation System*, p. 137.

75. Ibid.

76. Ibid., vol 1, p. 13.

77. Let us hope our present-day prognosticators are better than those of the recent past. A study of predictions of future technological change and its social effects made by Americans between 1890 and 1940—a period of rapid change—found that less than half were correct. Even technical expertise did not significantly increase the accuracy record. See George Wise, The Accuracy of Technological Forecasts, 1890–1940, *Futures* (October 1976), pp. 411–418.

78. U.S. Car Production, *Automotive News* (June 2, 1980), p. 55.

79. The $80 billion figure is the industry's own estimate. See Robert W. Irvin, Unprecedented Change Seen in Next Decade, *Automotive News* (January 7, 1980), p. E1.

80. Judith Miller, Chrysler: The Anatomy of a Loan, *New York Times* (June 29, 1980), p. F1.

81. Ibid.

82. Judith Miller, U.S. Is Assuming Supervisory Role over Chrysler Management Policy, *New York Times* (May 27, 1980), pp. A1, D3.

83. Andy Pasztor, U. S. Clears Chrysler Aid But Warns Slump Has Eroded Firm's Chances of Surviving, *Wall Street Journal* (June 25, 1980), p. 2.

84. By the early summer of 1980 the climate in Washington, particularly in the White House and Congress, was more favorable to the auto industry than it had been in years. See for example Albert R. Karr and Christopher Conte, Rescuing Detroit. U.S. Now Plans to Aid Ailing Auto Industry, Strive for Cooperation: Government Likely to Ease Safety, Pollution Rules, Help Tool for Small Cars, *Wall Street Journal* (June 27, 1980), p. 1.

85. Helen Kahn, GM White Paper Proposes Easier Auto Regulations, *Automotive News* (June 23, 1980), p. 1.

86. To defend itself against increasingly strident industry complaints the National Highway Traffic Safety Administration issued a report on *The Contributions of Automobile Regulation* (Washington, D.C.: NHTSA, 1978).

87. Even the case of the fuel economy standards remained the subject of controversy. A Boston consulting firm did a study that purported to show that the fuel economy standards were not cost effective. See Harbridge House, *Energy Conservation and the Passenger Car: An Assessment of Public Policy* (Boston: Harbridge House, 1979). Critics immediately disputed the study's assumptions (that gasoline prices would remain $1 per gallon) and the motives of the firm (that it solicited business from auto companies in the same area). See David Rogers,

193   Notes to Pp. 155–160

Congress Probes Boston Firm: Harbridge House Contracts with U.S., Industry in Conflict, *Boston Globe* (June 18, 1980), p. 6.

88. U.S., Congress, House, Committee on Ways and Means, Subcommittee on Trade, *Auto Situation: 1980,* 96th Congress, 2nd Session, Committee Print 96-61 (Washington, D.C.: Government Printing Office, 1980), p. 4.

89. In 1978 the value of assembled imported passenger cars (exclusive of cars made in Canada) was just under $10 billion. Total imports of all automotive products from all nations were valued at $26 billion in 1978. Motor Vehicle Manufacturers Association, *MVMA Motor Vehicle Facts and Figures '79* (Detroit: MVMA, 1979), p. 83.

90. For a somewhat alarmist European view of the future world auto market competition see Jean Gloaguen, Automobile: la lutte pour la vie, *L'Express* (March 31, 1979), pp. 42–48. For the corresponding U.S. view see Gerald R. Rosen and Jean Ross-Skinner, The Auto Clash Goes Global, *Dun's Review* (April 1978), pp. 48–53.

91. For two views on the way in which the "product cycle" (the tendency for production of a commodity to shift from high wage to lower wage countries) see Louis T. Wells, Jr., The International Product Life Cycle and United States Regulation of the Automobile Industry, in *Government, Technology and the Future of the Automobile,* edited by Douglas H. Ginsburg and William J. Abernathy (New York: McGraw-Hill, 1980), pp. 270–292; and William J. Abernathy, The Competitive Status of the U.S. Automotive Industry: Import Implications, Statement to the Subcommittee on Economic Stabilization of the Senate Committee on Banking, Housing, and Urban Affairs (April 3, 1980).

92. The moral dimension of the policy dilemmas posed by the auto is portrayed in Lester R. Brown, Christopher Flavin, and Colin Norman, *Running on Empty: The Future of the Automobile in an Oil Short World* (New York: Norton, 1979).

93. For an excellent presentation of the French government's thinking on the dilemma of how to protect the national auto industry while also protecting society from the worst side effects of the auto see *L'Avenir de l'automobile: rapport du groupe interministériel de reflexion sur l'avenir de l'automobile* (Paris: La Documentation Française, 1976). For the results of a dialogue between the French government and French auto industry leaders stimulated by this report see *Tables rondes sur l'avenir de l'automobile* (Paris: La Documentation Française, 1976).

94. Terry Dodsworth, Driving towards an EEC Policy on Cars, *Financial Times* (March 6, 1978), p. 25. See also Reginald A. Stuart, Car Makers Forging New Alliances, *New York Times* (February 3, 1980), p. F3, and Jan P. Norbye, World Outlook—Growth, Shifting Alliances, *Automotive News* (January 7, 1980), p. E3.

95. For a detailed overview and evaluation of projects in these areas see Organization for Economic Cooperation and Development, *Urban Transport and the Environment* (Paris: OECD, 1979), especially volumes 1 and 2.

96. Howard J. Simkowitz, Innovations in Urban Transportation in Europe and Their Transferability to the United States, paper presented at the 59th Annual Meeting of the Transportation Research Board, Washington, D.C., January 21–25, 1980, p. 8.

97. Der Minister für Wirtschaft, Mittelstand und Verkehr des Landes Nordrhein-Westfalen, *Grossversuch "Verkehrsberuhigung in Wohngebieten"* (Bonn: Kirschbaum Verlag, 1979), pp. 36–38.

98. J. Michael Thomson, *Great Cities and Their Traffic* (London: Victor Gollancz), p. 199.

99. Thomson, Methods of Traffic Limitation, p. 199.

100. Prefecture de la Region Parisienne, *Plan Global des Transports* (Paris, 1972).

101. To say that the automobile will remain the dominant mode of passenger transportation is not to say it will be free of problems. The growing awareness of the many serious policy problems of national and international scope posed by the auto have given rise to a number of conferences and study projects dealing with the automobile. To cite only the most prominent, there was the Harvard Business School Symposium on Government, Technology, and the Automotive Future in October 1978, the results of which were published in the volume edited by Ginsburg and Abernathy cited in note 91. There is the four year multinational project on "The Future of the Automobile: A Comparative Perspective" being directed by Alan Altshuler and Daniel Roos of MIT which is bringing together scholars, businessmen, and policy makers from the United States, Europe, and Japan. It is likely that a major international conference on problems of automobile production and trade will be held under the auspices of the OECD as well.

CHAPTER 9

1. Louis Hartz, *The Liberal Tradition in America* (New York: Harcourt, Brace, 1955).

2. *Der Spiegel* (July 16, 1979).

3. Hugh Heclo, *Modern Social Politics in Britain and Sweden* (New Haven: Yale University Press, 1974), p. 305.

4. Donald Schon, *Beyond the Stable State* (London: Temple Smith, 1971), pp. 128–136.

5. Charles L. Schultze, *The Public Use of Private Interest* (Washington, D.C.: The Brookings Institution, 1977).

6. Amory B. Lovins, *Soft Energy Paths: Toward a Durable Peace* (Cambridge, Mass.: Ballinger, 1977). See also Amory B. Lovins, Energy Strategy: The Road Not Taken? *Foreign Affairs* 55 (October 1976), pp. 65–96.

7. See U.S., Department of Transportation, Federal Highway Administration and Urban Mass Transportation Administration, *Transportation Systems Management: State of the Art* (Washington, D.C.: Government Printing Office, 1977).

8. See Ronald F. Kirby et al., *Paratransit: Neglected Options for Urban Mobility* (Washington, D.C.: The Urban Institute, 1974), and U.S., Department of Transportation, Federal Highway Administration, *Double Up America: Car Pool Kit* (Washington, D.C.: Department of Transportation, 1975).

9. See Julie Anna Fee, European Experience in Pedestrian and Bicycle Facilities, *International Road Federation Annual Report—1974* (reprinted by the U.S., Department of Transportation, Federal Highway Administration, April 1975); and John B. Corgil and Charles F. Floyd, Toward a New Direction in Bicycle Transportation Policy, *Traffic Quarterly* 33 (April 1979), pp. 297–310.

10. For example the OTA study on the automobile projects that, "providing there is not a severe restriction of the supply of petroleum or alternate fuels, automobiles will continue to be the dominant mode of personal transportation through the year 2000." See U.S., Department of Transportation, Office of Technology Assessment, *Changes in the Future Use and Characteristics of the Automobile Transportation System,* vol. 2 (Washington, D.C.: Government Printing Office, 1979), p. 30. See also Alan Altshuler with James P. Womack and John R. Pucher, *The Urban Transportation System: Politics and Policy Innovation* (Cambridge, Mass.: The MIT Press, 1979), p. 471.

INDEX